SYLVESTER GENIN, ESQ.

SELECTIONS

FROM THE WORKS OF THE LATE

SYLVESTER GENIN, ESQ.,

IN POETRY, PROSE, AND HISTORICAL DESIGN.

With a Biographical Sketch.

NEW-YORK:
MAIGNE & HALL, STEAM BOOK AND JOB PRINTERS.
NO 11 SPRUCE STREET.
1855.

BIOGRAPHY

OF

SYLVESTER GENIN.

SYLVESTER GENIN was born on the 22d of January, 1822, at 37 Main street, in St. Clairsville, Ohio. His parents were Thomas H. Genin, and Ann Hillard. His maternal grandparents were Thurston Hillard, and Eunice Jackson. His maternal great grand parents were Isaac Hillard and Sarah White : David Jackson and Mary Sandford. His paternal grand parents were John Nicholas Genin, and Sarah Hedges. His paternal great grand parents were Nicholas Genin, and Hellena Urbin ; Thomas Hedges and Temperance Barnes. His descent, through Urbin and Hillard, reminds of Nicholas Hilliard and Raphael Urbin, whom he resembled in his fondness for the pictorial art. His father was an accurate lawyer, and author of "THE NAPOLEAD," an epic poem. His paternal grandfather, John N. Genin, was a native of Labeurville, in the Diocese of Verdun, in France. He came to America with Gen. Rochambeau, in July, 1780, at the age of twenty-five, as clerk in the Commissary's department.

If one reads a biography at all, he generally wishes to know more than is narrated. Most lives are written long after the subject has passed away, and consequently nothing is told but what is traceable in his epistolary writings, public acts, or tradition. Small incidents, though illustrative of character and mind, are beyond the biographer's reach, and are therefore unnoticed. This defect is one of necessity ; and so general, as to possibly be mistaken for a rule in such compositions, by those who do not reflect on its source. Having the knowledge of small matters, the biographer should give them a place in his narration. Some trivial circumstances concerning the subject of this notice will therefore be mentioned as such, and not as things deemed of importance.

His birth was almost without pain. The first ten months of his existence he cried and fretted so little, that his parents feared his voice would be weakened for want of exercise of the lungs. After a few months, when he wished to be fed, he would give signs of restlessness. After receiving food, he would lie for hours, look about the room, open and shut his hands, looking intently at their form and motions. The manliness of his features, particularly the prominence of his aquiline nose, gave to laced caps a slight comic effect. Once when his mother had attempted his adornment, she exclaimed, holding him on her lap, " Why he looks worse than ever, yet mother loves him as well as if he was a perfect beauty." When twenty-two months old, he talked remarkably plain, pronouncing his words with great distinctness : which continued until the latter part of his third year, when this distinctness and clearness of utterance somewhat declined, for the same reason probably that those who write well, while careful in forming their letters, gradually write worse as they write more, and relax their efforts to improve. On the street, among the children of the town, he assumed the guardianship and protection of his brother, Thurston, about two years older than himself—entering into combats in his defence. When hurt, he would cry, but still continue the battle. An instance of this occurred in his third year. His brother ran into the house, by his direction, while he attacked two offending boys ; presently all three were crying heartily, but the two offenders were in flight. He then came into the house, wiping his tears, well satisfied with his exploit: saying, " He guessed they would let Thurston alone now." In the beginning, or sometime in the first quarter of his third year, as one was teaching the alphabet to his elder brother, Sylvester came along, and was asked if he wished to learn the letters. The pointer happened then to be at O, and he was told the names of the letters from O to Z. Some weeks afterwards, he was asked, or perhaps commanded, to come and learn the letters. He was told their names from A to O; but from O to Z he named each letter correctly. On immediately repeating from A to O, he could name but one or two letters; and he was eight or ten days, reading twice or thrice a day, learning this part of the alphabet. In the first instance he volunteered, and his mind was probably concentrated on the work, unaffected by disturbing forces. On the other occasions his attention must have been divided. Near the close of his second year, his father taking him upon his lap, was surprised to see him squirm out of his arms, indignantly, saying, "I am not a little baby." His father was accustomed, when retiring, late at night, to visit the room where his boys slept, to see that they were properly covered; and he often lingered there, gazing at Sylvester's countenance, when asleep; which, during the first four or five years of his life, he thought possessed a striking dignity, that was afterwards somewhat diminished. This the father attributed to surrounding belittling influences, perhaps erroneously; for the boy never seemed to lose confidence in himself, or to think anything unattainable which had been attained by others. He ascribed, on one occasion, his want of comprehension to the frailty of childhood. Seeing that too much was expected of him, he looked up deprecatingly, and said, "I am little." The truth of this answer made its eloquence effective. In 1826, a work in French, of 30 quarto volumes, was added to his father's library. He took great interest in the event, and asked how long it would be before he could be instructed in French, so as to read those big books. Zimmerman avers that a child should be greatly esteemed who inquires if his life will be written, as it indicates worthy aspirations. In the autumn of 1824, having, with his brother, at the close of the day, come in from the street, he proceeded, as they sat by the fire, to arraign his brother for indiscretion, in trading in pins, and made a speech, which his father immediately put in writing, as a curiosity, seeing the speaker was scarce two years and nine months old. It read as follows, " Mother, do you want a pin? Thurst! where is your quill full of pins? You will not tell mother where *they* are. Marion Ellis can tell where they are.

BIOGRAPHY.

He knows who is foolish. I don't go through the street, fooling pins away, do I father? Can you, Thurst, tell what you got for your pins? Show to mother what you got for your quill full of pins."

This was spoken with rapidity, without waiting for reply to the interrogatories, and with singular energy and vivacity, contrasting surprisingly with the infantile aspect of the speaker.

He was invited in the year 1828 to take part in a school's dramatic and oratorical exhibition, at the Court House, in St. Clairsville, some three days before it was to take place. The address of Jupiter to the gods, at the commencement of the eighth book of the Iliad, was recommended as a suitable speech for him to deliver. But when he appeared on the stage, he began at the commencement of the eighth book, and recited 224 lines, with such appropriate gesticulation and modulation of voice as quite amused the audience. A gentleman who had assisted in preparing the scholars for the occasion, remarked that after all their efforts a little fellow, not belonging to the school, had carried off most of the glory of the exhibition. A few days afterwards this little fellow was observed by his mother to be unhappy. On enquiring the cause of his distress, "O," said he, "I wish I had not made that speech the other night; for all the boys have been mad at me ever since. If I had composed the speech myself I should think something of it; but to speak the words of another, with some few motions to show one feels the meaning of what he says, is a small thing. They must think a great deal of a little to be mad about that. I wish I had not made the speech." The expression of this wish inducing laughter, he left the room in dudgeon. Thus early did he feel the assaults of envy, and fail to find all the sympathy a troubled spirit required.

While at the breast it was his habit generally, when awake, to employ his hands in feeling of the nose, chin, eye-brows, and all the features of his mother's face, beginning at some point, and carefully and softly touching all its elevations and depressions. She often complained of this annoyance, but never broke him of the habit, while he slept with her.

In the fall of 1823, when he was some twenty-two months old, his father hearing him in the next room cry awhile, and then talk, alternately, inquired what was the matter. His mother replied, that he was asking her what would become of his friends; and he was only expressing his interest in their prospects. Will all the men die, and be buried? he inquired. Yes. Will father be buried? Yes. (Cries aloud a few moments.) Will mama be buried, too? Yes. (Cries.) Will Turton and Vete be put in the hole, and buried? Yes. A somewhat more intense cry followed this answer; but he soon resumed the examination; the pertinacity of a man seeming to be veiled by the weakness of a child.

In his ninth year, having just listened to the praise bestowed on the speech of a lawyer, by the people, he asked his father what languages and sciences this lawyer had acquired, apparently with the view of ascertaining the necessary accomplishments to win similar renown. As the lawyer was guiltless of much knowledge, the father referred to the school exhibition speech, in illustration of what voice and action might do for a speaker; and embraced the opportunity to explain to him the needful, the useful, and ornamental accomplishments of a lawyer.

The boy listened attentively, occasionally putting questions, leading to the belief that he was inclined to follow the legal profession. He had already, without seeming aware of being embarked in juridical studies, learned, from conversations, the personal relations; most of the definitions touching real estate; the actions, and their distinguishing features; the elementary principles of practice and pleading; the construction of contracts, and principles governing negotiable paper; and when, some years afterwards, he and his brother, on resolving to make law their chief business in life, were engaged on the books of jurisprudence, they were surprised to find they had partially gone over so much of the juridical field before.

The matters of law, among other things he had learned, had at times been reimpressed on his memory, by causing the brothers to examine each other in evenings, or when inclement weather confined them to the house.

He never went to school, except a part of two quarters, when first learning to read. His father remembering the imprisonments he had suffered in Spring and Summer in school houses at that period in life when confinement is most irksome, resolved not to mar the happiness of his children in this manner, if he could conveniently be their instructor. Other circumstances conspired to confirm this resolution, particularly the general incompetency of teachers, and the conviction that all scholars are self-made, whether studying at home, or in a college; and that even an illiterate woman can, by judicious praise of learning and learned men, in the presence of children, make better scholars than a schoolmaster, who cannot excite their ambition. If this be roused, a child can scarce be prevented from making of himself what he pleases. If he has the *will* he soon finds the *way* to learn: text books are procured, and the wise consulted.

The vulgar error that one cannot learn but at school is the cause of much ignorance. The teacher, like a finger board at the fork of a road, is useful, but not indispensable. The one and the other merely point the course. The pupil must do the labor of study or travel. Poverty is not an "unconquerable bar" and its inconveniences are more than counterbalanced by its incentives to exertion. The rich may feel the spur of ambition, but it does not propel with the force of poverty. The efficient student who feels no need of exertion for a livelihood has merit as superior as labor from choice is to labor from necessity, or acts of affection to those of interest. There are some of all classes who will not try to learn; and as they cannot be filled with knowledge as a barrel is filled with a pitcher and funnel, they remain ignorant. The wealthy may waste money on such, but the industrious and frugal middle class deserves a better fate, than to be taxed to help those, who will not help themselves.

A general respect for intellectual acquirements induces exertions in the student. This is the basis of all successful mental culture of a people. They must not exalt the ignorant, and neglect the intelligent, if they would promote education or the public interests. The people have more need of the services of the wise than the wise of the notice of the people.

Whether education be public or private, success depends on the will and exertion of the pupil. The advantages of either mode are nearly equal. If by the private there is less contammation from evil example, there is less knowledge acquired of human nature, and consequently less capacity for successful intercourse with the world. Dr. Johnson remarks of *Don Quixotte* that he was frequently outwitted, and imposed upon by Sancho Panza, though inferior in mind because Sancho possessed a meanness which the Don did not suspect existed in human nature. A knowledge of what is possible is necessary, in order to judge of what is probable.

Under the guidance of his father, the son pursued the study of the sciences and languages at home, along with his brothers, mostly at his discretion, going out to play, or work on the farm, on which he resided, near St Clairsville, when he was inclined to do so. The French, Latin, and English, were the objects of most attention among languages. He had acquired such knowledge of the Greek and German, as to ascertain the meaning of sentences, in those languages, with the aid of a grammar, and dictionary. He took great pleasure in reading books in French and in repeating the sonorous lines of Virgil, and was inclined to pay full as much attention to the dead languages as comported with the views of his father; who though he held a thorough knowledge of them useful, yet since they have ceased to be the almost exclusive repertories of knowledge, he believed time could be more advantageously employed than in their acquisition, except to a certain limited extent. To strengthen his voice he was early recommended to read aloud, and to give lectures to his brothers on what he had learned. They thus instructed one another, and re-impressed former acquisitions of knowledge by mutual examinations. Text books were not much used, but occasionally referred to; and answers were made in the language of the pupils. After going often over the same ground, they adopted at length nearly the same words and forms of expression at every examination, fragmentary specimens of which are found among their papers. As: what are elements? They are the materials of which a thing is composed. What are details? The steps taken to form a thing. What are the elements of a cross-bow? Wood, and flax. What are the details of a cross-bow? Cutting the wood, twisting the flax into cord, &c. What are the elements of epsom salts? Oxygen, sulphur, and magnesia. Oxygen combines with the radical, sulphur, forming sulphuric acid; this acid combines with magnesia, forming epsom salts or Sulphate of Magnesia. What are the elements of lime-stone? Carbon, Oxygen, and lime. Oxygen combines with the radical Carbon, forming Carbonic acid; this acid unites with lime, forming lime stone or Carbonate of lime, and so of other things in Chemistry.

What is known of nature? Very little. We are convinced that the moons revolve around the planets, as the planets around the sun; and the sun around a center in the region of the star Alcyone, in a circle so vast, that it is difficult to distinguish a great length of its orbit from a straight line. The stars in front get farther apart, while those behind get nearer together, showing the direction in which the solar system is marching. It may take eighteen millions of years to perform one revolution. Alcyone, with all his solar systems is probably revolving around some more distant center, in a circle still more vast. To day, when earth is nearest to Jupiter, a line is drawn toward the north star. Six months hence, the line seems to point at the same star though the earth has moved one hundred and ninety millions of miles, and so far that the light of Jupiter's moons is eight minutes longer in reaching the earth, showing that one hundred and ninety millions of miles is an imperceptible point compared to the distance of the north star from this planet.

What is the elementary principle of politeness? To so act as not to offend but to please others. What are the details? They would fill a dozen volumes. Common sense points them out. To look well and clean pleases more than to look ill and dirty. Graceful motions please more than awkward ones. What is common or in fashion is more agreeable than what is uncommon and odd. Respect, evinced by dress, speech, or attitude, pleases more than indifference. One should avoid all habits that make him a nuisance. Mrs A. will not invite B, Esq., to her soirees, because he engrosses all the conversation; nor G. because he casts tobacco juice on the hearth and floor; nor D.

because he smokes without caring whom he incommodes; nor E., the lawyer, because he leans back, gouging the wall with his feet on the rounds of the chair, taking off its gilding; and has even been known to put his feet against the mantle, or on a table, to the great amusement of some, and the disgust of others, who had been more fortunate in their education. These men probably have not the least suspicion that their actions certify their vulgarity and make them disagreeable.

What is the elementary principle in war? To gain a preponderance—to bring a greater force than that of your antagonist to bear on the point of action. What are the details? The drill; the movement of parts in unity; provision of supplies, &c. &c. What is the elementary principle by which one may bind another at law? Authorization by the one sought to be bound. What are the details? An express authority as to one not in a family, or business relation, or an implied authority as to wives, children, apprentices, servants, partners. Any circumstance that rebuts the presumption of authority to bind, must be noticed by the vendor; such as a wife, child, or servant, seeking to purchase things not of family need; or a partner, things not of the partnership business.

What word expresses the elementary principle of legal practice? Notice. All steps in a suit are but a succession of notices.

What are the elements of penmanship? Straight and curve lines. The details? Their combination into letters and sentences. A correct habit of writing is best acquired by making letters as large as the capacity of the hand of the writer admits.

How many Governments exist? Two: Monarchical and Republican. Monarchical is *absolute* or *limited*. The Republican is *Aristocratic* or *Democratic*. The absolute monarch rules by his *will*; the limited by the *law*. A *class* rules in an aristocracy; the *whole people* in a Democracy; but cliques rule more or less in all Governments. Where do we find despotism? It is found in *all* Governments at times, when *ill* administered. And the people are safe in *all* when *well* administered. Do the people form the Government or the Government the people? The form of Government is determined by the vice, virtue, ignorance or intelligence of the people in its first institution or birth, and afterwards strives to prolong its existence like other beings, by shaping the people to its purposes. Every people have such a Government as they deserve. If majorities infringe the rights of minorities in Democracies, force comes to curb the vicious, and creates generally an absolute monarch, for the common safety of person and property. Hence *virtue* is the preserving principle in republics and limited monarchies; and *fear* in absolute monarchies. Absolute or dictatorial power, given, or allowed to be assumed in great emergencies, is afterwards directly or gradually limited by the people. Thus republics hasten into monarchy, as rivers into the sea, and ever will as long as majorities find it so difficult to keep their hands out of their neighbors pockets. The injustice of majorities makes absolute monarchies. No people are slaves that were not first unjust. In many instances the people have fled from democratic despotism to absolute monarchy for shelter, as the least of two evils.

What is the elementary principle in political economy? Self sufficiency; independence of other nations; the retention of specie, or the vital fluid of business, within the state. What are the details? Manufacturing at home; creating a market there for the products of the ground, and providing materials for commerce. Agriculture and manufactures are two legs of a state that should be kept of equal length, or it will halt. Commerce is always at hand, if there be things for exchange. She turns up her nose at a poor state. She prefers to carry diamonds instead of sand stones, manufactured articles instead of logs. The vessel that carries a thousand dollars worth of logs, could carry ten thousand worth of goods at the same expense. A nation is but a large family and what will make a family thrive will make a nation thrive.

Why is so plain a matter disputed? Because of selfishness, or politics. What is politics? The art of effecting purposes or ends. When F got C kept at home from school, lest he might take a cold, in order that F could reach the head of the class in spelling, he enacted the politician. If one state would shape its laws by the advice of another state, it would become the slave of that state to a great extent. If Ohio would abolish all banking, she would present a fine field for the circulation of the bank paper of other states. If we send persons to make laws who have no taxable property, we shall soon have an abundance of taxation. If the cotton planter could persuade the grain-grower to dispense with a home market, and thereby compel manufacturers to be farmers, wheat would soon be cheap. Those who recommend rotation in office want apprentice-statesmen to deal with. The people are told they are wise to keep them from listening to the intelligence that is among them, taking the hint from Solomon. The Ohio canals benefitted New York more than Ohio. Statesmen of other states have been accused of fashioning our opinions for their use, and authors have been charged with publishing rules of criticism, to secure a favorable reception of their books.

The teacher's task was often performed at the table, while eating; a subject would be mentioned; some leading ideas stated, respecting it, and books referred to for further information. A few days afterwards the same subject would be mentioned, with the expectation of hearing it illustrated, and, generally the pupil was prepared for the task; taking sometimes new views, and offering reasons not contained in the books consulted. On reading a newspaper, the mention of ports, cities, and other points, presented occasions for enquiry into their geographical position, population, manners, customs, &c., and if the pupils could not readily answer, a reference to maps ensued. Some ten rules in arithmetic, including the four elementary ones, of well-known practical use, were repeatedly impressed; but no time was lost in going through any treatise on that science, spending weeks and months in attempting to solve a puzzle. The same course was observed in mathematics. In grammar, the memory was burdened as little as possible. In acquiring the languages a knowledge of the words, and construction of sentences accompanied the study of the grammar.

In his ninth year, he fell backwards into the fire, and narrowly escaped death. While confined with the burn, his father taught him the French language: every evening, reading to him a page:

first, a line, translating it literally; then a second, third, and fourth line; he repeating from the first line, on the acquisition of each new line; and at each evening repeating from the first page, for ten pages; and, as progress was made, still repeating ten pages every evening; and, weekly, reciting the whole number of pages learned. Meantime, he read over the nouns, pronouns, and verbs, getting an idea of the variations of words, in their respective declensions, and conjugations. In three months he read French very well; marking the new words, that he might recur to them, until they should be permanently impressed on his memory. He afterwards taught French in the same way to his brothers Thurston and Florian; and he studied latin by a similar process. It appears that Roger Ascham instructed the princess, afterwards Queen Elizabeth, in this manner; and that Milton and Locke have recommended it, and that the very very wise world have, with great unanimity, disregarded it. Pope, who enjoyed some advantages in the acquaintance and conversation of distinguished statesmen, avers, that this part of the human species prescribe modes of education, and objects of pursuit, so as to keep busy geniuses too much employed to look closely into affairs of state. The longer they can keep the mind in pursuit of words, the less it will accomplish in acquiring a knowledge of things. Cardinal Richlieu's institution of the French Academy, it is supposed, was intended to avert attention from his meditated hostilities against the poor remains of French liberty. He turned all heads towards the object of improving their language, while he proceeded in his sinister enterprize.

In his fourth year Sylvester was instructed in English grammar, along with his brother, near two years older than he, by way of experiment, to ascertain the capabilities of infants. By using language, that they understood, they soon learned to parse sentences of which they comprehended the meaning. No book was used: they were taught orally. In answering questions the idea was clothed in their own language. At length they adopted the language following.—We have nine classes of words.

What is a noun? It is the name of a thing—of any thing

we can see, feel, or think of—as fire, air, heat, water. What is an adjective? It is a word that tells what the noun is; as whether it is hard, soft, light, heavy, good, bad. Form a sentence of the adjective and noun only. Good boy—heavy wood. What is a verb? It is a word that tells the motion of the noun, as whether it runs, falls, stands, sits, loves, hates. Place a noun, adjective, and verb in sentence. Good boy runs. With these three classes of words, or parts of speech, we might express our ideas; but there are six other parts. What is an adverb? It is a word that tells something about the verb, adjective, and sometimes another adverb. Place the noun, adjective, verb, and adverb in connexion. Good boy runs nimbly; is very wise; runs very nimbly. Give a sentence containing a word of each class, and a noun, in each case. The yellow vine's pumpkin rolls swiftly near an orchard, and oh it vanishes. This is sufficient to give some idea of the method of instruction. In 1833, the editor of the Literary Cabinet, in St. Clairsville, hired him to make translations from Dupaty's letters; several of which were published in that paper. The first letter is given below, as a specimen of his manner at that time.

Avignon, April.

I arrived, day before yesterday, at Avignon. Despair not, at Paris, of spring,—I encountered it, at the entrance of the Earldom. My first inclinations have been for the fountain of Vaucluse. I went to see it yesterday. I know not wherefore I say yesterday; for it seems to me that I see it yet to-day. I think, even now, to see escape from the midst of a chain of mountains, as from the bottom of a vast funnel, a river, which bounds, leaps, and, all at once, arrives with an impetuosity, with a thunder, with a boiling, with a foam, with falls, that the pencil of the poet, or the painter, cannot describe—it is the fountain of Vaucluse. An instant afterwards, the river grows calm, like a happy native, whose first transports are soon moderated by good nature. It changes, then, its waves of silver into waves of azure, which subside, as it pours over a carpet of emeralds, but soon it is divided into a multitude of little streamlets that run across a charming valley. In departing from this valley these streamlets re-unite, and afterwards again separate, meandering along by an hundred different routes, under the name of Sorgue, to bedew, fertilize, and embellish the delicious earldom of Avignon.

The picture that the Abbe Delille has given of that fair residence is very exact. I have verified all the verses; they speak truth, like prose, which is not always a characteristic either of travellers or poets. Poetry however, cannot give a full and adequate idea of that place. It can only give the remembrance of it. Portraits and descriptions are alike with respect to all objects. I have not found in the verse so much tumult, nor so many murmurs as in the fountain. One sees not there those rocks so dark, which form such an admirable contrast with the snowy whiteness of the breaking waves; neither has the poet unfolded that brilliant carpet of emeralds, on which the Naiad reposes. Vaucluse offers, at once, a picture the most admirable, and a phenomenon the most singular; but I will say with the poet,—

" Those waves, that heaven, and that enchanting vale
Than Laura and Petrarch, less move my heart."

The remembrance of Petrarch and of Laura animates all the landscape, it embellishes, it enchants it. I have sought for some traces of these lovers all over the rocks. It is then here, say I, that they came to sit together; here that Petrarch so much has loved; here that he has shed so many tears; that he has breathed so many sighs, which we yet hear! I sit on the declivity of a rock, and there for hours am delighted with the noise of those waters; with the verdure of that turf; with the azure of that fair heaven; with the youth of spring, and the remembrance of Laura. There I have gathered around my heart all the objects which to it are dear. I have imagined all my children leaping upon that turf, running upon that shore, and striking, with emulation, the echoes, and my heart with a thousand cries of happiness and joy. Before departing, I have wished to ascertain whether, as the Abbe Delille assures us, 'Echo has not forgotten the sweet name of Laura,' not to displease the poet, the ingrate has forgotten the half of it.

Adieu! charming fountain of Vaucluse! Mankind scarce know the places where Alexander has gained his battles; but they will always remember the places where Laura and Petrarch have loved. The murmurs of thy wave, O Vaucluse! and the songs of the Gardens and the Months will repeat them to all ages.

In the Autumn of 1831 his father took the portraits of the three brothers, with lead pencil, to ascertain if any of them possessed the faculty of drawing. These portraits were laid away in a file of newspapers, the originals not seeming to take any particular interest in the art. Some three years afterwards, on turning over the leaves of the newspapers, as if by accident, these portraits were found, and were exhibited to show what changes time had wrought on their vizages. Sylvester, on the same day, asked for paper, on which, he said, he meant to draw all the distinguished men. The next day, he presented to his father a tolerable good likeness of Washington ; and soon after of Napoleon. Some weeks then elapsed without further attempts to draw. His father proceeded to copy the portrait of the Empress Josephine. This recalled the son's attention to the art. He formed the outline of a Josephine, without the features of the face ; and expressing some doubt, as to successfully copying the face of a woman, his father proposed to make one eye, and copy the features on one side of the face, and that the son should copy the other side of it. The joint production was not without harmony. It encouraged farther efforts ; and shortly afterwards he produced a tolerable likeness of the Empress. He soon became enamored with the art, and some half dozen miniatures, on ivory, were painted for his neighbors, at five dollars each. He then turned his attention to painting in oil, and copied a portrait of his father, which had been painted by A. D. G. Tuthill, in 1815. His likenesses were very exact; and he was told by his acquaintances, that, in his skill, he possessed an ample fortune ; but his father remarked, that the taking of portraits was rather a matter of talent, than genius, and somewhat mechanical, without affording the advantages for thrift, which are found in the trades of the carpenter, sadler, or cobler ; for these could avail themselves of the labor of apprentices and journeymen ; but the painter must necessarily, earn with his own hands, all he acquired. That if money, or wealth, were the sole end of life, there were better means of reaching that end, than the painting of portraits ; and if glory were in view, it chiefly hovered over the historical painter ; between whom, and the mere portrait painter, there was a great difference. He was observed, after this, to be quite indifferent to portraits, and, at times, to complain of the defective powers of description in most authors, except Homer, whom he stud posed must have been a practical painter. At length he was observed to be at work upon his painting of the passage of the Granicus, containing some eighty figures. Many of these were obliterated several times, and others substituted, which, not suiting his taste, were, in their turn, struck out, to give place to new conceptions of attitude and energy, showing great fertility of invention, and accuracy of delineation. A bay horse, named Fox, of remarkable power to leap fences, was often required to go through this exercise, and to ascend and descend steep declivities, that his varying positions might be noted, and spread upon the canvass. Another horse of his father's, of less strength, but of finer proportions, was accurately measured from point to point, in every direction, and from him the just proportions of horses in general were determined. The same method was pursued in reference to the human form, taking the Apollo for the model. To get a more perfect idea of this form, he often would draw its skeleton, and successively supply it with arteries, veins, and muscles; and whatever clothing was put on his figures, they were first drawn naked. He considered an accurate knowledge of anatomy essential to the limner, even when naked persons stood for models, especially if the development of the muscles was indistinct from obesity. There was difficulty in procuring well-formed persons who were willing to denude, and maintain a given posture a sufficient length of time. An Englishman, digging coal on the farm, in 1839, consented to be employed in this manner a portion of each day; but he complained of its irksomeness, and strongly recommended that the field of battle, upon which the painter was engaged, should be plentifully strewed with the dead, which, he said, " was the life of such a field;" and he felt as if he could lie down, in imitation of the fallen soldier, with much satisfaction. The placing of this man in position, with a corn stalk for a spear, requesting him to look ferocious, as if about to plunge it into the foe; the laughter which followed, contrasted with the earnest gravity of the youthful artist, intent on accomplishing the complex and grand design of the battle of the Granicus, presented an amusing scene. He could only get the Englishman's countenance to express the firm determination suited to illustrate the temper of the Macedonian cavalry. The terror and dismay of the Persians were supplied by the artist's imagination, and from observing his own face in the mirror, under affected excitement. His study of the countenance of the horse, in different states of emotion, and in various attitudes, led him to take many portraits of this animal. He often visited a neighbor's field, where some twenty or thirty colts, of various ages, pastured, to note their motions, and take sketches of their attitudes; frequently not returning until chilled and shivering with cold. He bestowed some attention on the durability of colors. Having read of the fading of Sir Joshua Reynold's paintings, and that the works of the older masters retained their hues, he inferred, that probably the materials least indebted to art, but found in a state of nature, would be most likely to supply permanent colors; for nature, he said, had by this time probably effected all the changes of which the matter is susceptible, when not in combination with oil. This was in his fifteenth year. At this time, he was thought to be somewhat more fond of the society of old men and very young children, than of those near his own age. He was often seen to lead little infants around, while temptations to play with his equals seemed very great; and he would voluntarily quit the sports, so interesting to youth, to go and converse for hours with old men: on some of whom his mother sportively accused him of having matrimonial designs, since the apparent courtship had been so long and constant. Mr. Hugh Anderson, an engraver, who executed a considerable number of the plates in the American edition of the Edinburgh Encylopedia, published in Philadelphia, settled in St. Clairsville, in 1834. Not long after his arrival, he was visited by the young artist. The gentleman, believing he was come to seek playmates among his children, directed them to be called. His visitor requested him not to take the trouble; that, understanding his connexion with the arts, he had called to ask his opinion of a miniature on ivory, which he then took from his pocket. Mr. Anderson afterwards remarked that he soon discovered he had made a mistake in judging of suitable company for his young friend; for he found him well qualified to entertain the aged. His talks from this time, with the worthy engraver, were frequent and long; often extending far into the night; embracing a great variety of topics, in art, sciences, policy, and war. He often spoke of the pleasure and instruction derived from the company of Mr. Anderson, and the Hon. Benjamin Ruggles. He painted the portraits of these gentlemen, and that of Mrs. Anderson; which constitute the whole of what he achieved in portraits in oil in his native place, except about a dozen in his own family; choosing to employ what time he snatched from other pursuits, upon historical subjects.

In his 17th year he remodelled the design of the battle of the Granicus, and painted it in oil, 48 by 30 inches. In the same year he designed and painted the battle of Arbela, with India ink, upon paper, about 12 by 18 inches, containing some 30 figures. The spirited animation and confusion of conflict, and great variety of attitude, exhibited in the Granicus, affords a striking idea of the deadly struggle of intermingled combatants. The moment of the action is that in which Cleitus, at full gallop, arrives just in time to intercept the repetition of the blow aimed at Alexander, which it was supposed, would have proved fatal. The King has already slain one Persian commander, and is charging over another with his black Thracian horse, Bucephalus, while Cleitus, commander of the life guard, with all his efforts, can scarce keep near enough to assist in the defence of his sovereign. This foremost and imperial surge of battle has a most formidable aspect, in the vizages and attitudes of both the horse and his rider. The combative fury depicted in the countenance of Bucephalus, is in admirable harmony with the fearful circumstances surrounding him, and the raging conflict in which he is engaged. Superior in dignity, a superior ardor and energy is given to this horse and his rider, as they press like a tempest-driven ship, through the hostile masses surging around them. The lines on the Resolution to attack the Persians at the Granicus appear to have been written in aid of the conception of this piece, or in its illustration. A council is called, but the ardor or quick perception of Alexander, makes the consultation very brief. Noting firm self-reliance in the faces of the veteran council, "dissipating doubts of sage Parmenio" he declares, forthwith, for fight.

> At which each vizage sudden glows with joy ;
> Enough he cries ; each from his heart assents :
> Although the sun is on his downward march,
> Bucephalus shall soon his monarch bear
> Up yonder steep : who would with him keep pace,
> By strength and valor need be greatly served.
> Haste, plunge the phalanx in the rushing waves;
> Ourself will, forthwith, lead the bounding horse.

In the battle of Arbela the principal characters, the respective heads of the Grecian and Persian nations, are conspicuous. No intervening figures obstruct a full view of their persons. It presents the action at the moment Alexander on Bucephalus, bounding over prostrate foes, with greatest vehemence, is in act to cast his spear at Darius, as he is about to quit his chariot, and mount a horse held for him by a groom. The extreme energy and impetuosity of aspect of the eager Alexander, and his fiery steed, and the hopeless dread, with which the imperial Persian beholds the swift approach of his formidable enemy, present seemingly, the highest intensity of expression of which the art is capable

It was about this period, that he executed the design of Samson pulling down the pillars of the temple ; of Samson slaying the Philistines, with the jaw bone, and of Tydides and Nestor in the storm. Of the latter he partly made an engraving on copper, and as it was his first and last attempt with the *burin*, though unfinished, it is given to the reader as he left it in his 16th year. His father did not wish him to go among artists, and connoiseurs, until he had accomplished so much on the score of design, that his genius would not be likely to be dwarfed by their affectation and pedantry. Firmly believing, that there was a reason for the rise of great painters and poets in the infancy of nations, before stupidity enacted laws for governing the motions of genius, the father was solicitous, that the son should prolong his study of painting in Ohio, in nature's school, which he held to be superior to any in the Atlantic cities, or Rome itself, until a certain confidence in his capacity, and maturity of judgement, should enable him to distinguish between the true and the false in criticism and taste : that when he should hear of impossibilities, he might consider them as merely difficulties—that when a performance should be accounted impracticable, he might recur to what he had accomplished, without suspicion, that such giants obstructed his path. It was supposed he might thus make less progress in the knowledge of details ; but the tardiness of acquisition in this line would be compensated by enlargement of views, boldness of conception, and readiness of design. Various as are the positions of the figures in the Granicus, probably twice or thrice their number, were formed, and these not suiting the taste, were obliterated, to give room to a new group, exhibiting remarkable facility in placing the form of man or horse in any desirable posture.

In the spring of 1840 he left his home, in Ohio, for the eastern cities, and did not return until February, 1841. His object was to learn what he could in relation to art and artists, to ascertain, with accuracy, the shape of ancient costumes and arms ; what colours were most permanent, and what were the prospects of artists. He was furnished with letters to persons in Philadelphia, New York, New Haven and Boston, but went no farther than New Haven. The most and best which he learned in this excursion was from a work in French, which he found in a public library in Philadelphia. From this work he copied extensively, filling many sheets, with the costumes weapons, and chariots, of many nations. He took with him several of his designs and portraits, including the battles of the Granicus and Arbela. Some of the more distinguished artists to whom he showed these designs, seemed to contemplate them with earnest attention, and, at length, broadly hinted, that there were plagiarisms contained in them from Raphael's battle of Constantine and Maxentius. No, answered the boy, they are my own designs. But these individual attitudes ; have you not seen them in some engraving ? Not at all, they are after my own fancy, founded on studies of nature, in Ohio, where my brothers, by riding up and down steep places, enabled me to sketch the varying postures of the horse and rider. A close inspection of the pictures followed this declaration. At length, without expressing any opinion of the designs, much praise was bestowed upon the portraits. His letters from the east follow.

PHILADELPHIA, June 28, 1840.

DEAR FATHER :—I arrived at this place, on Sunday the 21st, via. Pittsburgh, and Chambersburgh. I remained at the former place but two days, where I neither heard, nor saw anything of the fine arts. I am now at Mrs Crims', 108 Walnut Street, at $5 per week ; a place recommended by Titus Bennet, at whose house I was received with great hospitality. On Monday morning I visited the Artist's Fund Society, where I found the best specimens of the works of the living American artists, among whom R. Peal, Neagle, and Sully, stand preeminent. Peal's resembles Tuthill's paintings. One of Sully's male portraits, surpasses any one in the collection, both in effect and coloring ; but he not always attains such excellence. In general, Peal and Neagle are his equals. They are inferior in painting females to many other artists. I have not seen a very good female portrait by either of them, though there are several there; among which is Victoria, by no means a chef douvre : The relief is good, but it has the appearance of a wax figure, in common with the rest of Sully's female pieces. In Peal's female pictures the fault seems to consist in one's not being able to perceive the flesh through the shade. With regard to Neagle, I have not seen one bad work from his pencil His rich Blacksmith in the Academy is not beat by any in coloring and effect. The collection is composed chiefly of portraits and landscapes ; fancy sketches of Dutchmen playing cards, telling tales &c. There are one or two attempts at historical pictures, but I should not wish to exhibit such works.

On leaving this collection, I went to the Academy of the Fine Arts, and was surprised to find the execution of West's great picture far below the ideas entertained of it. The design surpassed my expectation; but the coloring and relief of the figures were not as good as Neagle's Blacksmith. The Academy, as well as the Artist's Fund Society, has some very poor pieces, and some fine designs and fancy pieces of females. The *tout en semble* is not as good as I expected to find it.

Since writing the above, I have been to see Mr. Sully. He spoke very flatteringly of my battle pieces, especially of the Arbela, and thought I could continue on in no better course than the one taken. He advised me to get permission of the President of the Academy, Judge Hopkinson, to copy the antique busts. He invited me to attend, whenever I desired, free of expense, his and Earle's Gallery of Paintings, which I have been to see, and found in it some fine paintings. One of Dominichino's—not like the pretended Italian paintings, too frequently encountered, emanations from sign painters' pencils —but a perfect beauty; rich in coloring; and having the finest features I ever saw. The shades seem to be made in the same manner as Tuthill's, in your portrait, and as mine in the fancy-piece, without mixture with white lead. There are also a couple of Sully's fancy female figures that approach it in excellence, the best I have seen from an American artist. There is also the original draft of the Queen Victoria, taken in her palace, and a large picture of an Anaconda destroying a horse and his rider, brought from London; the drawing is somewhat faulty, but the effect and color good; and the shades seem to be made without a mixture of white lead. At Mr. Bennet's, I was advised to visit a Mr. Street, a painter, who had a gallery of paintings, and was pleased to have visitors call and see them. I thither went, and he showed me several designs of his, which evince great imaginative powers, and his coloring is very good. He showed to me a piece as smooth as ivory in finish, and the effect was good a few yards distant from the picture. His method of shading, he says, is an invention of his own, and has been kept a secret. I told him my method; he said it was the same that he followed when he was young. He is as agreeable a man as I have met with in my journey. He requested me to call often, and bring the little fellow, I was traveling with, along. Hon. John Sergeant is not expected home until August. I shall go to New York about the middle of next week. I have been to see Fanny Elsler dance; and I think the newspapers should be little credited, after lavishing so much praise on such a poor subject; but men will do any thing for money—and believe any thing, if it is fashionable; thus I have heard several give their opinions concerning a distinguished artist here, saying they considered him a mediocre; but that this was their private opinion, as the declaration would make them be considered, by the public, as fools, void of understanding and taste.

I shall show my designs, hereafter, only perhaps to Mr. Trumbull.

Affectionately, yours, &c.,

S. GENIN.

NEW YORK, JULY 19, 1840.

DEAR FATHER :—I arrived in this place on the 6th inst., and intend going to New Haven, on the 23d. Before leaving

Philadelphia, I became acquainted with Mrs. Staughton, formerly Anna Peale, as also with her sister and cousin, Rembrandt Peale. Mrs. Staughton has taken the prize for miniatures, several times. She charges from eighty to one hundred dollars a piece for them. I showed my designs to her. She had much the same opinion of them as Mr. Sully, viz : that the design of the Granicus showed more of the confusion of combat ; and was, consequently, a more faithful representation of a battle, than the Arbela; that the crowded appearance of the Granicus was its greatest beauty; that the Arbela made a more pleasing prospect for the eye; and, as exhibiting a particular event of the battle, was superior to the Granicus; though, as a battle, inferior. As I became acquainted with Rembrandt Peale on the eve of my departure for this city, I did not show my designs to him. Mr. Peale has traveled over Europe, and was awhile a student of West's. He said he passed Le Brun's paintings in the Louvre without noticing them, though he had previously expected more pleasure on beholding them than any others, from the high opinion he had entertained of them from seeing the designs in engravings. But the designs were spoiled by wretched coloring ; whereas the engravings, composed merely of light and shade, showed the full beauty of the designs, freed from the incumbrance of a disgusting coloring. This is also the case with the cartoons of Raphael; but the large paintings of Raphael are as bright in their colors as when first made.

I did not go to Bordentown, as it was the opinion of Mr. Peale, that the paintings were removed to England, as Joseph Bonaparte was building a house there, with the supposed intention of making it his residence.

I arrived in New York a few hours before the National Academy of Design, consisting of the works of living American artists, closed. Thither I went, and instead of finding an Academy of Design, I found an Academy of portraits and landscapes, with one or two designs of fire-side scenes, &c. Taken as a whole, it was fifty per cent inferior to the Philadelphia Artists' Fund Collection. There were as few good pictures in the collection in New York, as there were poor ones in that of Philadelphia—from which had some half dozen been abstracted, there would not have been any very poor ones in the collection; but had all the very poor pictures been removed from the New York collection, the walls would have been left almost empty. Mr. Noah's criticisms are all very true, concerning them.

I saw here some by Powell, of Cincinnati. He has superiors,

but many inferiors. His pictures are much in the style of your portrait of Washington, by Harrison. Durand, Ingham, and Page, are the best I have seen in this city. The frames on the mass of the pictures in the Academy, are worth more than the works they enclose. Having finished my peregrinations in this Academy of Design, (they call portraits and landscapes, designs, for want of real designs, as the ancient Grecians used to raise a fictitious tomb to the shipwrecked mariner, and offer sacrifices on it, as though it were a real tomb, having given it the name). I went to see a collection of paintings, exhibited by one Clarke, all very old ; among which are some good ones. They " consist principally of the works of Leonardi da Vinci, Reubens, Vandyke, and Salvator Rosa: all original;" and it is difficult to find any dark old picture in the city, that has not the name of some great Italian painter stuck on some part of it; and, to give color to the fiction, a great price on some other part of it. Clarke has more pictures of Salvator Rosa, probably, than he ever painted. There is another collection of paintings, kept by Fraser, which private individuals have sent thither, for sale, and are generally very good. There are also some good pictures in the Barclay street collection.

I called on Mr. Brooks, who is recovering from a severe attack of the fever and ague. I was with him but a minute or two. Hon. B. F. Butler has been of considerable service to me. Through him, I was enabled to see two of the best collections in the city; one at Mr. Coleman's, a bookseller, who has an immense collection of old prints, and many paintings—one of which is the best I have seen; another at Mr. Rutlidge's, who traveled through Italy, with Mr. Butler's son-in-law, Mr. Crosby, with whom I went to Mr. Rutlidge's gallery, which is chiefly composed of Italian works; it has, also, one or two of Col. Trumbull's. It was there I first beheld Italian paintings, whose beauty equalled the fame of their reputed authors. One, by Canaletti, of the infant Jesus, sleeping, is exceedingly beautiful: and there is not one, in the whole collection, that can be called bad. Mr. Coleman's collection, to which I have alluded, is an Elysian field for me; not so much on account of the paintings, as the prints. He had sold a work, containing all of Le Brun's battles, a few days before I became acquainted with him; but he had two remaining: the battle of the Granicus, and the Arbela. The Granicus is as large as mine, and done by crayons; and the Arbela is an engraving, somewhat injured by coloring. The time of action is a few moments before that of mine. Darius is represented as sitting in his chariot, holding his bow. Alexander's body, and his horse's neck and head, only appear. The fault of the picture, is, that the principal characters are too much in the back-ground, and the attention is continually fixed on other equally conspicuous and warlike forms. It is a better battle than his Granicus, though it does not describe the particular action half as well. Mr. Coleman has nearly the whole of Napoleon's combats; but they are not designed by a Le Brun; also the principal scenes in Virgil, by Pinelli, done with great vigor; and where there are but two or three figures introduced, he succeeds better than in a crowded battle. One, describing the Volscian maid, Camilla, killing the horseman, who challenged her to dismount, and spurred his horse against her, can scarce be excelled; as also Cacus pulling the bull into his cave, by the tail, that the herdsmen could not tell in what direction he had gone.

Through J. N. Reynolds, Esq., I saw a private gallery of Mr. Ward, in which there are some good paintings, and some poor ones. I have become acquainted with several painters, and Clevenger, the sculptor: whom I accidentally met at Mr. Ward's. I showed him my Arbela, as he was anxious to see it, having, he said, heard of me, at Cincinnati.

I have been reading the original letters, in French, from your grandfather to your father—the impression, apart from their good style and handwriting, is much the same as I got from reading the translation. Our relatives are well. John N. is chief clerk in a hat store; Sidney is in a broker's office, in Wall street;—any letter you may send, he will forward to me.

Affectionately, your son,

S. GENIN.

NEW YORK, July 30, 1840.

DEAR FATHER:—Since writing letters is the "order of the day", I would like to have something of the kind going on in the West; if not letters, at least, a newspaper or two would suffice to show how the world stands in Ohio. Since I wrote last I have been out to Flatbush. It is the most beautiful place I ever saw ; excepting it, our own Belmont County exceeds any other place in rural beauty, I have seen. The Rev. Thomas Strong was travelling in the West, for the purpose of recovering his health. His father was at home, but too unwell to afford much satisfaction in conversation. Being in Clevenger's studio one day, a gentleman there informed me that Col. Trumbull was in the city. I went to his boarding house, and he had gone a few hours before to Pennsylvania. I was intending to go to New Haven the next day. He will return in two weeks. I have seen nothing very new in the painting line, and am going to the east end of Long Island to day at 4 P. M. in the Sloop Suffolk, Capt. Tuttle. I will go to Aquebogue, where sleeps one branch of my ancestors, and perhaps to East Hampton. I had a long talk with Mr. Waldo, who is considered as among the best painters in the city I enquired if he knew Tuthill, the painter. He was under the impression he was dead; both he and Spencer, who is also a good painter, objected to Tuthill, that he spent too much time in indecisive touches, with small brushes, which gave his pictures any other than a bold appearance ; however this may be, I do not think that Tuthill's portrait of you is often surpassed.

I was introduced by Mr. J. N. Reynolds to Mr. Gourley the Secretary of the Apollo Association, and also to Mr. Ridner, its President. They advised me to open a room, and as Mr. Reynolds said, roll up my sleeves and go at it in Buckeye fashion. I should like to hear your opinion on that subject. There would be some difficulties arising from such a course. After getting into business, every day might increase it, and I thus be induced to continue in a profession, which, if assiduously followed, might procure a competence ; a profession in which every cent that is made is by actual labor : in which chance seldom operates favorably, but often unfavorably. Mr. Waldo has been painting for forty years, has a good business ; Mr. Spencer has been at the same pursuit twenty years ; and by economy and continued exertion, they can live in moderate style. To get rich at it one must put on a double price, and make the mountain groan, if it produces even a mouse. Sully has had success in this way. Powell is doing well. I would not mind trying it awhile, though the law is not without its attractions. The Apollo does not open until Sept. Mr. Gourley and Ridner think I ought to finish some piece that is more gaudy and pleasing to the mass, than my fancy piece, as I could not finish my Granicus by that time. They seem to think very well of my designs. On looking at them they enquire who composed the original ; as designing any thing, seems to be among the things that have been, except as to Trumbull, Peal, and occasionally Sully, and Alston of Boston. The fancy piece is considered a pretty good picture of the old sombre style of painting in shades ; but to be in accordance with the present fashion, and pleasing to the eyes of the present race, the lights should be lighter, the shades managed so as to cover but a small space, or else, in Sully's style, to cover the greatest part, and from the deep shade to turn abrubtly into the brightest light, producing an effect resembling that which comes from the blaze of a candle ; while the dress should consist of silks, satins and tawdy ornaments, a bunch of roses bloom in the hair, a book, boquet of flowers, or musical instrument be held in the hand, and the shoulders and arms be well covered, least the delicate feelings of the very sensitive, and highly enlightened fashionables should be injuriously affected.

The facilities for painting, here, are more imaginary than real. The painters here seem to think that copying old pictures, busts, &c., is the only way to become a painter. And that is the facility so much talked of : just as if the race now in existence could not copy nature in the same manner as the authors of these old master pieces. The real facility appears to me to consist in getting good materials for the business. They have canvass here for sale, already prepared, almost as fine as ivory and paints ready ground. I have seen the steam ship British Queen and two large fires, novelties to me. The Daguerreotype is not much thought of, except for taking views of houses, copying engravings. and paintings. There is something unnatural in the likenesses, possibly the light required, may distort the muscles of the face and give unsteadiness to the eye. I saw one representing two standing figures, taken from life, in oriental costume, engaged in some play : it looked well, especially the drapery, which appears better in the daguerreotype than vizages. Likenesses are taken for five dollars, but less is done than one might expect, from the novelty of the thing, and the attention it has received. Should I meet Col. Trumbull in New York, on my return from Long Island, I shall not go to New Haven. Mr. Clevenger snd Mr. Ridner advise me to go to Boston, as it is the emporium of the arts, and will give me additional letters. Mr. Clevenger's letter will be to Washington Alston, who is considered the best original painter in the United States. Mr. Ridner's will be to a gentleman, who will show me all the private galleries there.

Affectionately, your son,

S. GENIN.

ORIENT, August 26, 1840.

DEAR FATHER :—Yours, of the 20th inst, is received. In answer to your inquiries, I have good health. I have heard but little, worth remembering, from most of the painters. Some of them were communicative, particularly Peale, Waldo, and Page ; but the time being short I had with them, their remarks were of a general nature ; though Page went considerably into details. I have learned most from a work published by

Leonardo de Vinci, which I found in the Merchant's Library, and which I shall obtain, if possible, in some of the book stores. Mr. Waldo assented, and so did Page, to the propriety of studying nature, rather than old pictures. Mr. Waldo keeps a portrait room, for exhibition. He enquired my opinion of the pictures. I pointed out those that appeared to be best. He said I had judged right, and advised me to pursue painting, as those who could detect faults, and see beauties, could, by proper effort, make a picture equal to the one he could justly criticise. When I showed him my miniature of Samuel, he said this confirmed his opinion. I took him to see some pictures Mr. Gray's son had sent to his father, from Italy, to whom I had been introduced by Mr. Ridner, and on the way, speaking of the advantages of an Europeon tour, he seemed to think it was chiefly beneficial, as an advertisement, that one was a painter, as some ostentation was necessary to success. The hook must be bated with a fly, real or unreal, to catch fish. He says there are more advantages for painters in New York, now, than there were in London, forty years ago, when he was a young man. I have got no new ideas on coloring, but have obtained all I desired in that line, my old opinion is confirmed. A little lead, mixed with the colours give them freshness and permanence. Sully's use of lead is thought to make his shades look muddy. I find that great excellence is attained by great labor and perseverance. Mrs. Staughton spends several weeks on a miniature, and seemed surprised when I told her I painted Sam's in two days.

When I left home I had three or four points to settle, viz : 1st, whether it was spending useless labor in not availing myself more of the experience of the world in past years. 2nd, whether the method I used in colouring was the most durable, and whether it was the best method of giving colors their full brilliancy. 3rd, whether the confusion of figures in my designs was a fault, or at least considered so by the best masters, whose opinions I purposed to consult in their works. I have found the method I was proceeding on in colouring, a good one, except in the use of lead, which I might use more of, to advantage. Peale, and Waldo, gave me their opinion as to what colors are the most durable. I find in Raphael's battle of Constantine the same confusion that reigns in the Granicus. The precepts you taught me, I have found to be the elements of the art ; at least, as far as I have got any knowledge of it. I have found no picture that equals nature, and none, consequently, as beneficial to copy, or study, unless it be to find out by them the above points in question ; or, if possible, the manner in which certain tints have been obtained, which vary among the greatest painters ; but not among their copyists, who, I am sorry to say, are far the greatest number. The deplorable want of originality among our painters is perhaps owing to a desire to gain the good graces of the people, by copying their favorite painters, and aiming to imitate them, and not nature ; as they, in the opinion of many, have attained the highest point of excellence. Hence, it is seldom you see a Loraine, or a Raphael. Every thing seems to be embraced in the precept : " Follow nature." A battle should have its terrors: its confusion and fury. A peaceful scene should be all harmony. The very elements should be in accordant ease and quietude. Every thing should conspire to carry out the end proposed. This is nature, and this word as far as I can at present see, includes the elements of design.

I and Sam roomed together, while in Philadelphia. Our fellow boarders were mostly southern students. A Mr. George, who was well acquainted with the St. Clairsville merchants, boarded at the same house with his family. I formed no acquaintance with any but Mr. George. The dispositions of the Southerners were as wretched as the institution of slavery in which they were nourished : the least negligence or disobedience of the servants destroyed their happiness for some time. Their infirmity of temper made me think they should be treated with indulgence.

I have no French or Latin books here. I would have bought some had I known of my stay on the Island. It occurred to me that I might as well be paid for copying the countenances of the Long Islanders by way of improving myself in painting, as to copy antique busts for its own reward ; and I have painted a miniature and two portraits in this place, and received forty eight dollars. As for my clothes they are somewhat dilapidated. The cloth has faded much, and while enquiring after permanent colors, I could not but reflect that my habiliments showed that our manufacturers as well as painters were interested in the investigation. And that my external appearance indicated wants in this respect, that might move the charitable to tell me all they knew about colors.

I had expected to pass through this Island as a stranger among the tombs of his ancestors : yet as soon as it was known who I was, I felt as if I was among old and ardent friends. On landing at the shore, I enquired for Augustus Griffin, Esq. He happened to be the man of whom the enquiry was made. On learning my name he showed an interest in me, which I scarce hoped to see any where, but at home. It was the same with his family, and some of the neighbors. Many pleasant incidents have occurred here. Captain John Brown has for some years quit the ocean. He does things in his own fashion and has something of the old Homeric sincerity of friendship. A lady in my room one fine morning exclaimed. There comes Captain Brown to the gate, in his buggy. And dressed as if for a capital occasion. What can be the matter! The good Captain had come to give the grand son (my poor self) of his friend, who had been dead thirty years, a ride; and we rode to several points, while he hit off in short pithy sentences the strong and weak points of some persons of whom I had a knowledge, and explained some particulars of the vehemence, humour, and uprightness of my paternal grand pa, who seems to have been capable of making lasting impressions. In New York, George Wilson, Esq. received me very cordially, and I spent some hours with him and his family very agreeably. They are all well. He resides in Park-row. I was several times with D. M. Cowdrey, Esq. He took me to the different courts, and to the Governors room in the City Hall. Its walls are covered with full length portraits of distinguished men. These are the best executed American paintings I have seen.

Affectionately, your son,
S. GENIN.

AQUEBOGUE, SEPT. 26, 1840.

DEAR FATHER :—I have just returned from Quoag. I went thither with Mrs. Jane Robinson and her son. On our return, the horses going very slow I got out of the carriage and walked ahead. I missed the road; taking one on the right. On travelling many miles I could not recognize the least thing that indicated I was in the road I travelled before. It was near sunset, and I had not seen a house, or clearing, for several miles. The woods were thick and dark. The sand ancle deep. I turned off at every left hand road I came to, and, just after dark, reached the shore, dripping with sweat, and covered with dust, and would not have got thither so soon, had I not adopted the expedient of trotting for the last few miles. Through the mists I saw the masts of a schooner, and heard the splash of an oar. I hallooed and asked how far I was from the port. They answered, four miles, and that they were rowing up thither. I was so warm I was afraid to get on board, and waded through the sand, onward, at a quick pace, for the mist was thick, and the air cold. I saw a marsh ahead, and climbed up the steep bank, that lines the shore from Canoe place to the landing, and for the first time walked on hard land unannoyed by the sand. After scrambling through thickets, and crossing one swamp, I came to a house, and being directed, arrived at Mr. Robinson's safe and sound with the exception of skinned toes and a pair of pumps. So much for my impatience, I have painted two more portraits, and reviewed a part of Virgil. The portraits were those of a wife and her lord. This male was a troublesome subject, and came near making a sorry figure on canvass by his teasing suggestions ; but I would not tinker his wife's to suit him, and consequently hers was the best, and he was much pleased with it. He desired me to take the likenesses of his children, but I could not do it just then ; a main objection was, that he imposed on me the tribute of reading and praising some speeches he had made in the Legislature, quite respectable, but not a whit superior to those of Demosthenes or Eschines ; so I determined to be off, as the penalty as near as I could judge, was only about half inflicted. The practice I have had here, has been of use to me in coloring. I have worked freer and bolder, and succeeded better than I probably should have done in the city, Were I to paint for nothing, I would be gainer, as l was advised by some of the artists to hire some one to sit in every possible light, while I copied. To reach the end by gaining, instead of spending, seems most desirable ; at the same time enjoying wholesome country air, and seeing different parts of the world. Besides, unless my eyes deceive me, mankind are not all alike ; complexions vary among different inidviduals, according to their occupation, blood, or climate. There are more zones than one ; more temperaments than one in the human family. Would it not be well to study these in the living subject—to copy nature in all its varieties, while studying the pictorial art ? and not confine ones self to a room in the dust and dirt of a city, copying one face over and over, like a shoe maker stitching his leather over one last continually, as though all feet were the same. Claud, of Loraine could not have confined himself to copying pictures, or one particular place, he must have gone into the fields and seen nature in all her variety ; in the stream that rushes swift, or moves slow ; in the calm of a summer eve, or the fury of a roaring tempest. It is to their neglect of nature that I attribute the monotony of features that is seen in the works of some painters.

Nov. 5th. The above was written some weeks ago. I am now at Southhold, as you have been informed by my newspapers. I have read considerable French, and some Latin, and painted nine portraits, since I came hither, averaging about three days at each. The plan I pursue is to make a good drawing, and experiment as to the coloring. In some, I have made very lucky hits. They are fine subjects for the exercise of the pencil. On some, I put the paint thick, on others thin. Here they are, ; and here will long remain ; and in a few years I can return, and note the result of my experiments. I board where I paint : and my expense is nothing. I have three more to paint, and then I will go to New York. You need make no remittance to me. I intend to keep the balance of trade, so far as I am concerned, in favor of Ohio. Direct your next letter to New York. While at Captain Hildreth's, (I have been so unused to being among relations it seems awkward to say cousin,) I designed a virgin and child, and copied your nephew's infant son, who looks out fresh and fair from the virgin's arms. He is as fine a babe as I ever beheld. My desire to take home the portrait of the child caused the design. I shall leave this Island in ten or twelve days. It was not my intention to have remained here long ; but the people are so agreeable, I have been induced to continue among them until now, and feel reluctant to leave them.

NEW HAVEN, 13th Dec., 1840.

HON. BENJ'N. RUGGLES, ESQ., &c., &c., &c.

SIR—Your favor of the 12th June was put into my hands a few days ago, by Mr. Sylvester Genin. I have seen specimens of his talents, which sufficiently show that his friends have not overrated them ; but considering the natural results of our institutions and of the national character ; both of which are opposed to the transmission of great masses of property, successsively from generation to generation, and the uncertianty of popular favor, I have advised him, (as my friends advised me.) to make the study and practice of law his great pursuit, and the art of historical painting the amusement of his hours of leisure.

Experience has taught me that my friends were right ; but I could not see with their eyes, and he perhaps will reluctantly submit to see with mine.

Wishing you health and prosperity, I am, sir,
Your obliged and faithful servant, and friend,
JOHN TRUMBULL.

The opinion of Mr. Trumbull was confirmed by the observations of the young artist. In a letter which he addressed to his friend, Hugh Anderson, just afterwards, he illustrates his opinion by reference to facts, and circumstances, and in his letter above of 19 July, he writes as if laboring under the same conviction as to the pecuniary results of artistic labors.

Mr. Hugh Anderson : New Haven, Dec. 16, 1840

Dear Sir—You must pardon my tardiness in writing to you, as the delay was occasioned not by forgetfulness of you, but a want of time ; as you are aware, everything is new to me in these parts, and the objects various which engage my attention, and absorb my time. I have seen nearly all the paintings of merit in New York, Philadelphia and New Haven. I have ascertained, sufficiently, the degree of patronage extended towards the fine arts ; and have concluded, that the profession of painter, considered in a pecuniary point of view, is not worth following. There is an apparent patronage of the arts viz : the purchasing of pictures on account of their low price ; low in appearance only, while works of merit, which have cost time and labor are neglected ; and inducements thus held out to artists to produce such works, as require little labor and time. Perhaps an instance or two may not be amiss : In the State House here, there is a copy of the signing of the Declaration, for which the State paid 500 dollars ; It is not only a disgrace to the room it is intended to adorn, but a satire on those who purchased it ; a satire rendered more pungent from the fact, that Col. Trumbull, its original designer, was still living, and would have furnished them a valuable painting, had they rewarded him sufficiently for his time and labor. The fact also that Col. Trumbull had to give his original designs to Yale College, after having vainly offered them for a long time for sale to the American people. National subjects, too. Scenes in which he had participated ; and in which he not only describes the action, but introduces the forms and features of the actors ; men and actions, which it is the interest, and, I should think, the duty of this Republic to preserve. These have been neglected ; and why ? Because the painter of them, after having travelled through England, France, and the United States, to obtain the portraits of the actors in the Revolution, could not sell them for as low a price, as less costly productions, such as copies, might be obtained for. What inducement is there, then, to follow the historical branch of the art ? When we see even national subjects disregarded, and even Legislatures defrauding the painter of the reward of his labors, by employing poor copyists to furnish a mere representation of them. Col. Trumbull told me that he studied the pictorial art chiefly for the purpose of painting the battles of the Revolution, relying on the spirit of the nation for the reward of so arduous an undertaking ; but, as he expresses it, " they care no more for the actors in the Revolution than you would for a parcel of oyster-shells after the oysters are extracted." Having thus showed the encouragement and success attendant on the labors of the historical painter, I shall proceed to show the result of my observations as to the consequences of following the profession of portrait painting as a business. If followed steadily and assiduously it might ensure a livelihood ; but to follow it with success you must descend from the rank of a copyist of nature to the subtle arts of a courtier ; flatter the vanity and conform to the bad taste of patrons ; paint many portraits of editors, and distinguished men for nothing, to appear as though you had the patronage of the great, and contrive by some means or other to keep before the public eye. By following this course assiduously, and being economical, if one of fortune's peculiar favorites you may perhaps have enough left for support, when palysing age has compelled the relinquishment of the pallet and the pencil for the staff and the crutch. In support of this opinion, I will merely advert to the condition of a few of the most successful portrait painters in this country, passing over the unknown mass whose talents have been smothered by the depressing and all absorbing cares of life. Among those who stand eminent among the fortunate artists of the day is Thos. Sully, who is believed to be pretty well off, and of whose pictures I chanced to speak to Col. Trumbull, mentioning a fault which I thought was in some of his pictures. He answered that Mr. Sully was a man of fine talents, but was compelled by the necessity of supporting his family, to work quick, and could not afford to devote much time on any particular piece ; that by unexampled success, he acquired a small amount of property ; but was not independently rich. Peale is supposed to be in tolerable circumstances ; Waldo is ditto ; but distinguished as Waldo and Jewett are, as portrait painters, I was told by the cousin of the former, that during three or four months in the summer of 1839, they had but one portrait to paint. Spencer, another painter, who is considered among the lucky, after fifteen or twenty years of labor, has had the astonishing good luck to complete the payments on a house he lives in on Canal street, and is just commencing to lay up a little cash, with constitution injured by excessive confinement. When I called, with a friend, to see him, I noticed he had more business on his hands than painters in general. He was painting a man's family for a piano, an article useless to him, but still better than nothing. Finally, I shall quote the words of Col. Trumbull, to show you his opinion concerning himself: " I would have been a beggar had I wholly relied on painting for my support." West, though apparently possessed of all possible advantages, and patronized by a great King, died poor. What temporal advantages I would ask then, has the painter ? Has he half the influence among men in general that the hoarse-voiced, mean-minded, knavish, pettifoging politician has ? If he is a talented man, he will have the respect of the intelligent ; but to the world, at large, he is an inoffensive creature, who can neither do harm or good. The conclusion I have come to, therefore, is to follow that profession which gives temporal advantages as the main business of life, while that which gratifies the mind, and the imagination, is rendered subservient and of secondary importance ; and it is my opinion, as also the opinion of Col. Trumbull, that by practising the law, I would have more leisure to paint a historical piece.

I cannot at present bear the idea of confining myself some half dozen years in a room, abandoning all historical compositions, painting one phiz after another ; this one in the style of the Florentine School, and that, after the manner of Sir T. Reynold's, Sully, &c., figuratively speaking, I cannot swallow the idea ; my feelings repel it, as the stomach repels the sickening emetic. There is, however, a pleasing delusion, an enchanting spell, hovering around the temple of art : The glory of a Raphael, an Angelo, and a Da Vinci, is an allurement which deceives the unwary ; It is a siren voice that is apt to lead astray the unsuspecting : those, I mean, who do not consider that there is a time when, and a place where, the arts may be safely and profitably followed ; and I am satisfied the place is not here, and the time is not the present, when gold purchases honors, shields crime, and decides, in a measure, the fate of elections ; to succeed in which, thousands desert the principles they believe in. When a whole nation worships gold, is it strange the arts should be neglected ? Is it strange that a soldier of the Revolution, who had given the labors of a long life to an institution in the State of Connecticut should be overlooked by that State, when a picture was wanted to adorn the walls of its capitol ? And why overlook him ? What principle were they governed by in their choice? Was it honor ? No ; that would have led them to select the man to whom they were obligated ? Was it taste ? Certainly not ; they would have selected the same had that been their guide. What was it then that governed their decision? It was gold; influenced by that, they overlooked both taste and honor, and determined their decision so as to wrest as little as possible of the dear object of their affections from their greedy hands.

The Daguerreotype is much used in these parts, and, I understand is likely to become more useful than was at first expected. Drapery, busts, pictures and buildings seem to be its best subjects. I saw in New York a picture of a man and lady walking on a heath, which was said by its possessor to have been taken from life; and there was but one thing that seemed to show that it was a copy of a picture, viz: the flow of the drapery, which could not have been supported long enough in one position to have been retained by the Daguerreotype. The portraits made by it are seldom good; the eye appears blurred, and often of a pale white. The main defect however of the Daguerreotype is that you cannot take near and distant objects at the same time: one or the other is generally blurred, owing to the focus of the lens not suiting both at once. In the sky of one piece that was taken near sun set, the pure yellow, purple-tinged color of an evening sky was almost accurately retained, which is sufficient evidence that color can be retained as well as mere shadow.

Animal magnetism, as far as I can learn, is among the things that were. I was told in Pittsburgh, that Doctor Underhill, who had wrought such miracles in Wheeling, had so expended his magnetic powers in that place that all his mysterious manipulations were of no avail in Pittsburgh. He got but one asleep, and then, as though the spirit had suddenly left him, all his subsequent efforts were of no account, though a large price was offered for one more successful attempt. It is probable, nevertheless that there is something in it; but public expectation was too much raised at first, and of course, being disappointed, they abandoned the subject entirely, without examining its merits, and are unwilling to think about it.

Among the most interesting collections of paintings I have seen, is the Trumbull Gallery. Here is a picture of the signing of the Declaration of Independence, about two feet by three, and is the only one Trumbull ever painted. It is of exquisite finish, and must have taken immense labor. The Battle of Bunker's Hill, Death of Montgomery, Battle of Princeton, and surrender of Cornwallis, in which last he has introduced his own portrait, are all near the same size as the first; and all show great care in the composition and execution. There are two or three others, viz: The Surrender of Burgoyne, and Washington resigning his Commission, which are later works, of good design, but much inferior in execution to the former, as indeed all his later works are; but the spirit of the design is as vigorous as in the former, if not more so. There are also here some original designs executed with fidelity, and as true imitations of life, are equal, if not superior to the best I have seen. One is the woman who was taken in adultery, and brought before Christ:—the confusion and disconcertedness, attendant on the response of Christ, is finely delineated on their vizages. Christ blessing the little children, is also of full size, and is well done, though rather florid in its coloring, There are also many others here of various sizes; among which, conspicuous as a vigorous design, is the figure of Joshua, attended by Death, hanging on the rear of the men of Ai. It is poorly drawn, but it is a bold and striking piece, and is among his best performances. A few portraits and miniatures in oil, complete this collection. I do not admire the coloring of his portraits: there is a redish tinge, and a sameness of complexion in all of them, which does not exist in his historical paintings. His drawing of the face is always perfect.

I have visited Col. Trumbull two or three times since I have been here: he is very frail, and has painted none for a year. He is a very agreeable man in his conversation. He has a large library, which he has collected during his long life, composed principally of French, Italian, and Spanish, works. He employs himself in reading; and is getting engravings made of drawings executed at different periods of his life, for the purpose, as I understood him, of publishing them in a history of his life. He advised me to pursue the law for a livelihood, and if I followed painting, to draw for a few weeks from the antique statues in the Academy of Arts, in New York. or Philadelphia, and as far as colors are concerned, to use only in the flesh tints, no brighter red than Indian red; no yellow, brighter than Roman ocher, burnt umber, Prussian blue, black and white.

Yours, with respect,

S. GENIN.

P.S. My health has been uniformly good. I had prepared to go to Boston; but it is doubtful whether it would be of any advantage to me to do so. It would only gratify my curiosity; though I might get some hints from W. Alston, whom all acknowledge as the head of the arts in this country. I have a letter to him. The benefit of going is uncertain, while the time and expense is certain. Col. Trumbull thinks I might as well go, as I have got this far. If I go, I shall be there two or three weeks; if not, I shall be home in four or five weeks. I arrived here on the ninth of December. New Haven is a pretty city, and more preferable as a residence than Philadelphia, or New York. The number of students gives it a lively appearance. Yale College contains at present, 574 students. You perceive I am as slow to leave off writing, as Iam to begin. Give my best respects to your family. Pardon my awkwardness in sealing this letter, so as to tear the writing. Col. Trumbull says that there is no such thing in nature as bright colors, such as carmine, vermillion; that is, in the human face; but Stuart, the best painter of heads I have seen, used vermillion. Waldo, and Jewett, also use it. Rembrandt Peale also uses vermillion, and madder lake. When I arrived in Philadelphia, I called on Mr. Parker, Senr. He was well, and also the family. He was quite busy brushing off the dust; for, as he said, business being dull, something must be done to kill time. I spent a few weeks quite pleasantly in Philadelphia, but found report always exaggerated things, making the fair more beautiful, or the ugly more horrid, especially when the report concerned pictures. I expected to see in the pictures here, mimic life, wanting only vitality, to render them perfect; but alas, I found nothing but paint, and that not always used to the best advantage. I have seen, nevertheless, some few real representations of life; some designs that are admirable; first among which, as a design merely, is West's Death on the Pale Horse. I think if you were to send some of your maps here, (the one containing both the modern and ancient names of places) you would find a ready sale. The numerous schools and institutions would consult their own interest by purchasing them. I have spoke of this map to several gentlemen, who think well of the plan, and consider it just the work that is needed.

NEW HAVEN, Dec. 19th, 1840.

DEAR FATHER :—Yours of the 29th ult., and that of 25th. July, I have taken from the post office here. I am pleasantly situated in front of the College, at Mrs. Woodworth's boarding house, at $3,50 per week. There are some eight or nine students here, with whom I have contracted but little acquaintance. I have been to see Col. Trumbull three times. He received me well. 1 shewed him my designs. He said I had grasped at too much at once; that it was a subject capable of puzzling the most expert. He said one should work at single figures some time before undertaking to manage such masses. He liked the drawing of the little miniature of yours, taken hastily by candle light the evening before I left home, and seemed to think more of the fancy portrait, my third attempt in oil, than of the Granicus. He seemed to think it impossible for one so young to compose a piece purely original. He said they might think it was so, (original), and he could not recognize any figure that he had seen before. It gratifies me much to have my works taken for performances of the old masters. Col. Trumbull merely insinuated it. Waldo, while looking at the Arbela, said, "surely you must have had access to some print or other to get these horses, they have so much the style of the old masters' though he did not recognize any of the figures as old acquaintances. After I had assured him, however, that they were all of my own conception, their style vanished, and I was wasting time and labor in attempting to do that which older artists hardly dare undertake. Indeed I should be out of all conceit of them if I had not understood the real opinion of the judges, before I gave them to understand that the paintings were not only my works, but my own designs. At last Waldo said, that he, when a young man, used to do such things for *amusement*, but found that it was waste of time, and cautioned me to that effect. 1 am confident, had I been born and bred in New York, I should never have painted a picture of much value. When I am among the connoisseurs there it requires some effort of mind to believe I have had the boldness to attempt what I have actually performed. There is in the Trumbull Gallery of paintings nearly all of his own original designs. They are finely executed, and of great richness of color. There are two of peculiar interest to me. One executed when he was eighteen years old; the other shews his method of coloring: at one end it is completely finished, diminishing by degrees in its finish, until at the other end, it becomes mere outline. His method is, first, on the white ground to draw the outline, second, slightly to tinge the drapery, flesh, hair, &c., with the color intended; deepening the whole by little and little, until the desired depth is attained. He uses considerable white lead, but not near as much as some painters, and it is of the best quality, flake white; he thinks it the most lasting substance in the picture. The subject of the half finished picture, is the battle of Princeton. There is more fury in soldiers and horses, and I think it is better than the one he finally completed; which, in comparison with this, is tame and spiritless. On my next visit to Col. Trumbull, I asked why he had altered such and such figures from the vigorous to the tame. He said he would have preferred leaving it as it was originally; but that he could not get the drawing to suit him, and that he preferred sacrificing one to obtain the other ; but it appears to me, that he sacrificed the poetic and lofty, to obtain a more flowing rhyme. Raphael, however, got both, also Le Brun, showing that this is not impossible, if perseverance is unabated, and *can't* kept out of the road. He advised the use of Indian red : the red in the human face being no brighter than that. Burnt umber, black, white, yellow ochre. But I see in Stuart's faces, vermillion; Waldo, also uses it, and Peale. Stuart's heads, that I have seen, are superior to any. Your two of Tuthill's, are superior to any he has left on Long Island : but to return to the gallery. There is there a picture, as I have before stated, composed and executed by Col. Trumbull when he was eighteen years old. The figures he took from prints ; but arranged them in the piece, in his own way, I shall not decide on its merits. The two principal colors are blue, and red. The subject is the death of Paulus Emilius at Canæ. It was made before he had any instruction. The figures being selected from other pieces, I cannot judge what he could have done at an original composition. When in Coleman's room, in New York, one day, I unfolded my fancy portrait, and he placed it on the wall. He thought it pretty well done for a beginner. • A gentleman entering, walked up and looked at it, and said that he took a fancy to it, and enquired the price of Coleman, supposing it to be his. I was then at some distance. O, says Coleman, that is not mine; that young man painted it, pointing to me. The gentleman turned away immediately, and looked as though he had lost time, and exposed himself finely, in being so imprudent, as to express his admiration of a picture, before knowing who painted it.

I cannot see into Col. Trumbull's preferring the fancy portrait to the Granicus; Waldo's preferring and apparently considering the little drawing I have of you a greater achievement than all my designs, and at the same time supposing I had copied them from the old masters. I remember, while unrolling them, of casting Hammond's and your's aside, remarking, that they were mere portraits, and at the sametime presenting the designs; without thinking of the fact that Waldo had, for forty years, diligently followed the making of mere heads. I have since thought that he may have been trying to instil into me a greater respect for heads than I appeared to have; for when, to show my regard for his especial vocation, I discoursed on the difficulty of getting the expression and contour of the human face, he evidently thought I was very reasonable, and gave more praise to my portraits than I could have rationally expected.

I did not return to New York until the time for receiving pictures at the Apollo, the 1st Sept., was passed. They must be received before that time to be registered in the catalogue. I did not know of this rule until my return to the city; but I do not regret it; for if I engage in the practice of the law, the less I am known as an artist the better. The fame of the painter is, like Napoleon's idea of history, an agreed fable, and I care not to be the subject of wrangling opinions, for the present. Your letter of July, which reached me at New Haven, mentions some persons on Long Island, whom you desired me to visit. I met with some of them; but not with Fanning and Woodhull, probably; though some called to see me, or my paintings, whose names I did not learn, or do not remember. Many of my customers there, would have been better pleased with a florid daub, than a painting. The best I made was the last, supposing I could lose nothing by doing it well, as it would not deter others from employing me, because I was just leaving the place. It was the portrait of Captain W——, in whose vessel I came to New York. He told me he would settle with me there. When we reached the city, he paid me all but eleven dollars, and he told me he was not satisfied with the painting, and that he was out of money. I shall request him to bring it to the city, for me to retouch. When I get it in my hands, I will refund what he has paid; as it is worth a third more than I charged for it; and take it to Ohio. It is worth, at least, forty dollars. I doubt whether I shall go to Boston, though I would like to see Washington Alston, to whom I have a letter, given me by Mr. Ridner, the President of the Apollo. Clevenger seemed anxious that I should see Alston, and that he should see my designs. If I go, I will send to you a newspaper from a town east of this place.

I went, about the 20th August, in a sloop, from Orient, across Gardener's bay, to Amaganset, and walked some four miles through the sand, to East Hampton, that looks out on broad Ocean, to see a cousin of your mother's, or rather the place of her nativity. My memory placed what you had said of the Hedgeses, of New Jersey, to the account of those of East Hampton. On entering the town, I asked some one where David Hedges lived ? He answered that there were three of that name in the place. The one, said I, that has a son in a medical college. He directed me to the David, late of the New York Legislature. I called, and to be certain that I was at the right man's house, asked him if he had a son at a medical college ? He replied, he had. I then told him who I was, and to quicken his powers of recognition, stated that you called on him, last summer. He said you had not called: that he had a remembrance of you, but had not seen you for a long time—not since you were a boy; and but for a book, handed to him by some one, of which you was the author, he would not have known even where you lived. He invited me to spend some days with him; showed me a portrait taken of him, by Spencer; and he and his wife seemed agreeable enough; but why he should deny that you had called on him, and say that he did not much like your passing by him, on the other side of the island, last summer, when I was sure that you had called on a Hedges, who had a son at a medical college, and be correspondently slow in comprehending my first allusions to you, brought on such doubts as to the propriety of accepting his hospitality, that I set out in two hours, in spite of remonstrances, for Sag Harbor, where I slept. The next morning, I crossed over to Shelter Island, which I traversed on foot; thence, over the ferry, to Greenport; walked along the shore, to Orient, and arrived at friend Griffin's in the afternoon, with well exercised limbs and a keen appetite. When Mr. Griffin informed me that you and mother went up the north side of the island, without going to East Hampton, I perceived that a Hedges, having a son at a medical college, did not necessarily make him the identical Hedges on whom you had called.

At Aquebogue, I found, in the graveyard, the tombs of your father and mother, that of his first wife, and that of the child, Sylvester, by his third. I took a pencil sketch of the homestead and the tombs, and copied the inscriptions.

Col. Trumbull says he has written to Judge Ruggles, stating the advice he gave me. He says a painter is made by practice, and cannot be taught; that painting is a dangerous sea to sail on; that of the numbers who had attempted, few had succeeded; that in his designs he had always dropped his imaginary figure, if he could not draw it correctly: which appears to me to be yielding to a difficulty that perseverance might overcome. I respect much the advice of Col. Trumbull, as it is such advice as comports with age, always cautious and considerate; but excessive caution is as injurious in its effects sometimes, as rashness. Old men have seldom attempted what requires the greatest possible vigor and perseverance in execution. When a youth makes a leap, he does it without thinking of all the accidents that may possibly attend it. If he were to consider all the consequences that might follow, he would never make the leap. Imagination can always produce difficulties without number, which ardent action and perseverance overlook.

Affectionately, your son,

S. GENIN.

The commentary of the father, on some matters in the foregoing letters, is contained in the following extract from a letter to the son, dated, St. Clairsville, Dec. 27, 1840.

DEAR SON:—Yours of the 16th, to Mr. Hugh Anderson, was handed to me, by him, on the 22d. Yours, to me, of the 19th, reached me on the 24th inst. Mr. Anderson seems to think Col. Trumbull has no good cause of complaint against this nation. There may be some petty vexations, such as the Connecticut Legislature's overlooking him, through notions of economy; but, considering the nature of things, the habits and education of the people, the infancy and poverty of the United States, just after the war of the revolution, the country has done as much for him as could reasonably have been expected. There is probably no man, whatever his success may have been, that is satisfied with it, or with the appreciation of him, or his works, by the world. Napoleon was not. His conversations with O'Meara, and Las Cases, are attempts to enlighten mankind on this matter. Benjamin West, it is said, died poor. There is a direct tendency to poverty, in all who pay but little attention to money after they get it; who adopt no measures to make it productive, and are deficient in economy and management. Heirs of large estates, without cultivating painting or poetry, frequently, soon find their patrimony evaporated. Great lawyers, notwithstanding the lucrativeness of their profession, have often died poor; for a leaky bucket will, at length, be found empty. Judge Ruggles has shown to me Col. Trumbull's letter of the 13th Dec., inst., stating that your friends have not overrated your talents as a painter; but on account of the nature of our institutions, and the uncertainty of popular favor, he has advised you, as his friends advised him, to make the study and practice of law your chief pursuit, and historical painting, the amusement of your leisure hours. There is nothing in this advice but what I expected. I would not advise one to attempt an epic poem, or even to cultivate poetry beyond a portion of one's leisure, yet I would not annihilate what I have done in poetry, or abandon its enjoyment, for any pecuniary consideration. I should dislike the responsibility of advising one to a course, in which the chances of failure so far outnumber the chances of success: and in which, success itself is scarce discoverable, except by posterity. The same feeling makes one distrust his own judgment, when he views what seems excellencies in the higher efforts of literature, and the arts, if made by a contemporary, as to whose merits the world have not yet agreed. I do not recollect of any one speaking otherwise than discouragingly to me of the NAPOLEAD, except De Witt Clinton, and Dr. Samuel L. Mitchell, who at the same time cautioned me against expecting any temporal advantages from it. My literary friends, of less capacity, while they professed to admire my short pieces, could see nothing but presumption in my attempting an epic. This is so natural that I am surprised to have found an exception, or a Clinton; for I am not sure but he determined the opinion of Dr. Mitchell. You have seen that Col. Trumbull's views accord with my own, as repeatedly expressed; consequently the object of your tour to the East has, to me, lost nothing of its importance. I wish you to see W. Alston, and the Bostonians: I do not insist on your going thither—do as you think best. I have a notion that Alston can weigh contemporary with ancient merit, unclouded by the vapors that annoy inferior minds, however honest in purpose. This idea may be erroneous; still, to be so near, what you term, the emporium of the arts, and not enter it, might be regretted. You should visit Baltimore and Washington. There are some excellent paintings in those cities. It is important that you should hear Henry Clay, in one of his high efforts. It would enable you to appreciate what has been said of Demosthenes, and Cicero; and to read the speech of the latter against Verres, with increased interest; to distinguish the orator from the bawler; nature from affectation; ardor, sincerity, and force, from mouthing, scowling, and emphasizing. It is astonishing how few of the vast number, at the bar, pulpit, and senate, become even tolerable orators. Marmontel has said, that nature, exhausted by the effort to produce a Demosthenes, or Cicero, seemed to need the rest of a thousand years. I want you to hear Mr. Clay, for the same reason that I did not want you to go too early among the mass of modern artists and connoisseurs. The contagion of lofty example will not dwarf one's genius; but give it energy. Much that is practiced and said, in reference to poetry and the arts, is not calculated to make a great poet, or artist; and should not be known or seen by the pupil, until, by keeping better company, he has acquired a strength of poetic, or artistic constitution, which cannot easily be affected, or corrupted. Your letter of the 19th inst. illustrates the ground of my objection to your earlier taking your present tour. You say, "you are confident, had you been born and bred in New York, you would never have painted a picture, of much value." Your experience has thus verified my apprehensions, founded on the history of the past; not doubting that there was a cause for the greatest painters, as well as the greatest poets, existing in the infancy of nations, or while in their ascent, and before their decline, and before stupidity, by tacit consent of the masses, is permitted to form rules for the government of the motions of genius. I would not inspire a contempt for mankind; but their boasted reason encounters so many disturbing forces, that she, with difficulty, sits uprightly on her throne. Envy, and jealousy, less often disturb, than weakness and pusillanimity. In my youth, knowing the range of the reading of some literary friends, I offered for their opinion, a few lines of poetry, from an author of established reputation, as if they were my own. They were considered faulty—even ungramattical; because the judges did not understand the application of what we style the adverbial adjective, which gives such force and beauty to our language. When I offered them some lines of my own, as the composition of the same author, they could discover no defect, though there actually was a small one, purposely left for experiment. The falibility of human judgment is such, that it should never be allowed to elevate or depress the spirits, but merely be used so far as the reasons for it have weight to enlighten the understanding. Follow nature, and, if human opinions cannot keep pace with you, it is their, and not your misfortune. One should render himself independent of patronage. It takes but little to support, in simplicity, the painter, while he executes immortal works. The real wants of man are easily supplied. Riches consist less in the number of dollars, than the moderation of desire. Since discovering your capacity, as an artist, I have been more careful of property—instead of leaving money in banks, I have put it out on interest; and for the last four years, have added something to my estate. The tenants excused my demand for security, because they knew so many had gone down the river, without paying me. There will be enough to support three painters as comfortably as a wise man could wish, and allow each to have ten children. I say this from confidence in your prudence, and moderation, believing you would live about the same, whether possessed of five, or a hundred thousand dollars. So the prospect of public patronage need not be an element, unless you choose to make it so, of the decision, as to what extent you will pursue the art of painting.

Our elections show how little mankind are controled by reason. The people are almost equally divided on every question, as if governed by the law of chances. A copper, tossed a hundred times, falls nearly as often on one side, as the other; and heads, or tales, by turns, get, a majority of one to four, in about the same proportion, as the political parties, notwithstanding the great amount of reasoning on either side. The cause of this effect, probably is, that people decide from feeling, or prejudice, first, and then, employ reason, as the slave of prejudice, to support the decision. Nineteen-twentieths of all reasoning, oral, and written, is slave labor. Could reason be emancipated the progress of man towards perfection, would be greatly accellerated. This being the case, it is manifest, that one must investigate for himself, and rely on his own judgment, listening to others for reasons, but not for opinions.

NEW YORK, Jan 1, 1841.

DEAR FATHER—Yours of the 27th ult is received, I am well and contented by a good fire. I do not like to travel in the winter, though I wish I was at home, participating in the benefits arising from the Moot Court, and Demosthenian Society. I am availing myself of the means of information here. The Mercantile Library is open to me through cousin Sidney C. Genin. I have been reading the work of Leonardo Da Vinci, containing many useful hints. It is an elementary work on painting, and gives details a slight notice. His ideas are such as common sense would dictate. He was leader in the restoration of the fine arts, and the greatness of Angelo and Raphael is attributed much to him. He looks at things as they are, and keeps the word *can't* at a distance. He never rejects ideas of figures because the drawing is difficult. I have concluded that one can do very little at painting, if he searches with a timid eye for difficulties; because the fanciful mind of a painter can see, if he has belief, a ghost in every stump and in an ant-hill an inaccessible height; so by the time our artists paint portraits for a living, finish their voyage of discovery for difficulties. and spend due time in regarding them with holy awe, it is no wonder they do not engage in historical painting. The substance of the information I have obtained from the painters, as to historical designs is, that none but the great masters ever succeeded in such things; that of the numbers that have tried most have failed; that it is presumption to conceive, temerity to attempt, and almost impossible to effect any thing of importance in this line; and I have reason to believe that a large portion of those who, on first viewing a picture, think it is a copy of the old masters, ever after, in their hearts, believe, whatever may be their professions, that the picture is a collection of plagiarized figures; because they cannot conceive how any one should be so rash as to attempt to draw a man or horse in divers contortions, when it puzzles even old artists to draw common postures. I am out of the notion of applying colours unmixed with white. By intercourse with several painters, I have obtained some useful hints, as to the chemical effects of mixing colors. What some knew, others did not. One said carmine always faded, while madder lake and vermillion lasted bright. Lake should not however be mixed with white. In this opinion, all have concurrred. Cole said that Prussian blue was a very doubtful colour, and, mixed with vermillion, always destroyed it. This is a good hint to me, as I have mingled these substances. It was not known to any other I conversed with, but I would take Cole's opinion on coloring to be entitled to great respect. Another said that chrome yellow ought never to be used mixed with white; it was sure to turn dark in time, one destroying the other. The Apollo was closed yesterday; it will be opened again on the first of March next. The association purchased several pictures, two or three of Huntington's which were good; but being short of funds, they bought some daubs, by way of premium, for unskilfulness, or haste; though the ostensible reason was to increase the number of prizes. In my opinion art would have been more encouraged by the purchase of one good than many bad pictures, for no inducement is held forth to spend time and labor on pictures, if less labored and inferior ones, of easy production are more certain of sale.

Young Huntington bids fair to be the best artist in the country. He has just returned from Italy, and has several fancy pieces and designs, all of them very good, and quite original. They are chiefly groupes of three and four persons. He drew them naked, first, and then clothed them. He says sitters of either sex are easily obtained in Italy for twenty-five cents a day; but he is in harness for portraits, and those on hand, and expected, absorb all his time, so that he cannot undertake any important work of art. He has fifty dollars for a portrait.

I called the other day, to see Cole's four pictures he has been painting for Ward. They are beautiful landscapes. Cole was quite affable : he explained the allegorical figures. During the interview, I told him that I had the pleasure of seeing his first performances. He remembered you; said you called to see some of his pictures; and that he had to struggle hard in those times. Captain W. came into port a few days ago, with his sloop, and did not bring his portrait; and says, he would not give a shilling for it. He offered to pay two dollars if I would relinquish all further claim. I did not accept his proposal. He is evidently pleased with his portrait; and is manœuvering to filch a few dollars. I would sue him here, were it not a small business. This is all that saves him for the present. He must disgorge at last, poor fellow. I think of presenting this claim to friend Griffin. He has a convenient apparatus for sweeping clean the pocket of W. of these coveted pence, in a son, who practices law in the county where he resides. The fact of his holding the claim, would, of itself, relieve the Captain from temptation, to such a degree, as to render the employment of the apparatus, perhaps unnecessary. This ill wind would, thus, help a friend, and repair a cracked fiddle, and put it in tune again; for the Captain has a considerable conscience, if I judge rightly from his words and looks, which gives him hard thwacks. He first said he had forgotten to bring the portrait. When rubbed against the grain, a little, he said, he did not feel bound to bring it. When in port before, and I showed a lamb-like passiveness in my disappointment, he praised the accuracy of my likenesses to a Pearl Street merchant, with whom he had some business relations, so much, that the merchant desired to employ me to copy a portrait of his uncle, at New London, and then cross over the sound to Mattatuk, and take another, from life, of his father. It seemed as if he was disposed to restore, in this way, what he had been tempted to unjustly withhold. I think therefore, that he is a sinner that may be saved. Though the temptation of eleven dollars seems small, yet the event shows it surpassed the poor Captain's powers of resistance. It was more operative on him, than eleven millions would have been on a great or magnanimous soul. I declined doing the painting for the merchant, as you wished me not to be diverted from the object of my tour, by an ambition to keep the balance of trade in favor of Ohio.

Mr Anderson should send on two or three of his maps to the principal book stores, and publish, or cause to be published, some paragraphs, praising, criticizing, and explaining it. A map, showing at one view, the ancient and modern boundaries of countries, and their ancient and modern names, few general readers would dispense with, after comprehending its utility. Reality, in simple dress, is unregarded, while often, the unreal arrayed in splendid guise, is sought with avidity. This is called the age of humbugs. It is probable human nature is unchanged. It seems necessary to spread your banners, and sound the trumpet. Unless a work, however meritorious it be, is assisted in its progress by some such means, it will not be known to the public, in time to do the author much good. A notice in some of the most popular papers of New York, with an influential name attached to it, would sell more maps than the offer of a large commission for obtaining purchasers. It is astonishing how the opinions of men are governed by such a thing. A few days ago, a notice appeared from the pen of S———, lauding a young artist very much; placing him even along side of Cole. I have never seen any of his works; but, they are said to be indifferent. Mr. R—, remarked, he knew some days before, what would follow the artist's presentation to the editor of two landscapes. Afterwards, on conversing of the arts, the young man was named as having made great advancement, and was almost equal to Cole; that his merit was such as to elicit the most flattering notice from Mr. S———, &c.,

Enclosed is an account between myself and my pocket book. It speaks for itself. The funds on hand are in pure gold. The board now due, makes a hole in the balance of seven dollars. My newspapers will keep you informed of my where about.

I left New Haven on the 21st of December. In the steamboat, Captain Luther Hildreth was a passenger. He left his sloop at New Haven, laden with two thousand bushels of oysters, which he brought from York River, Va. He thinks the profit of the voyage will be about one thousand dollars.

The growth of oak, which succeeded the pine, cut off by your brother John N., at Red Creek, about thirty years ago, was sold recently by his widow, for near twelve hundred dollars. It is said, when this black oak is cut down, it will be succeeded by pine. I was not aware that nature thus indicated a change of crops. If I visit the Island a few years hence, I will examine this tract.

PHILADELHIA, Feb. 1, 1841.

DEAR FATHER—I am thus far on my way home. I left New York on the 27th, after having visited our friends, in New Jersey, a couple of weeks, which I spent very agreeably. I there took a pencil sketch of Judge Wm. Woodhull, and his wife, Elizabeth Hedges, from their portraits in the old mansion, now occupied by his son John. I forgot the genealogical tree, whose trunk is in Wales, with the name spelled Woad'l. They equalled the Long Islanders in friendly attention. * *

While last in New York, I went with Mr. Butler one evening, to the New York University, to hear Senator Southard hold forth ; but you have seen an account of this speech. The hall was crowded when we arrived : a chair was procured however for Mr. Butler, which he required me to occupy, and another was then got for him ; so, I was very comfortably situated, for seeing and hearing, as well as gratified with the polite attention of one whom his fellow citizens treated with so much respect. I visited, with some members of his family, a private gallery of paintings belonging to a Mr. Reed ; it contains many fine paintings, and an admirable collection of engravings; among the latter is Raphael's battle of Constantine ; Leonardo Da Vinci's Last Supper ; for which Mr. Reed gave one hundred and ten dollors. It is considered the best engraving in the world, and is an extraordinary piece. Among the paintings, there are five, by Mr. Cole, representing the course of empire ; and fine pictures they are. There is a boldness of design, and richness of color in them that is uncommon. The first, represents man in a wild and barbarous state. In the foreground, a savage has just pierced a deer, with his arrow, and is running towards his prey ; while, in the distance, a group of savages is seen, with their implements for hunting. The second scene is on the same ground ; but instead of extreme savages, there are seen Shepherds with their flocks.— The third, represents a city, built on the same ground. It is beseiged, and troops, blood, and carnage, are exhibited. The bridges, surcharged, are falling with the weight of fugitives. A galley is sinking in one place, and burning in another. The horrors of war are well depicted, and forcibly strike the spectator. The fourth, represents a triumph ; there, all is joy, beauty, and grandeur. The galleys, with their painted sails, the soldiers with their glittering arms, among the waving of flags, and trophies, as they gleam in the sun, form a magnificent prospect. The fifth, is that city in ruins. The soldiers standards, and trophies, have disappeared ; rank weeds, and moss-encircled fragments of columns, have taken their place. The figures are small, without much beauty of drawing. They are remarkable only for landscape effect.

Rembrandt Peale was married lately, and will go to Europe in the Spring. I have shown him the Granicus ; it seemed to impress him as it has others. A suspicion of plagiarism from the old masters, succeeded by hesitation, and want of faith in its being my own design, was manifest. I begin to think that some suppose plagiarism convenient. Possibly it might be to one of barren imagination, who has access to a great variety of prints ; but I am sure if I had the prints, it would cost me four times the labor to make a piece with plagiarised figures, than with figures of my own conception, and the design, then, must be of small scope, if some of the figures were not burlesques on the end proposed. I scarce believed this method of design practicable in even any degree, until Col. Trumbull declared its employment in one of his early efforts. I certainly set a much higher value on my paintings than I did before I left home ; while my respect for the opinions of men has considerably diminished. My desire to see St. Clairsville greatly exceeds that of seeing Baltimore, or Washington, with all its attractions. But I shall remain here two or three weeks. I am copying the arms, armour and costume, of various ancient nations from a work in French, which I found in a public library of this city. I consider this work of more account than all I have hitherto met with. Before its perusal, and the copying of its plates can be accomplished, Washington will begin to be crowded with visitors, to witness the inauguration of Gen'l. Harrison, and instead of getting an opportunity to hear a speech from the head of the oratory of America, I shall probably have the luck to only see a profusion of silly heads, and incur the suspicion of being one of the number. I would prefer visiting Washington at some other time, when the prospect of getting an opportunity to hear the distinguished speakers is more favorable than now. Write what you think of it, I shall call to see S. Colwell, Esq., to-morrow.

Affectionately, yours, &c.,

S. GENIN.

He came home from Philadelphia by the most direct route on the 20th of February, and thenceforth earnestly pursued the study of the law, with occasional intermissions for painting, and seldom neglected any opportunities of knowledge, or mental improvement. He was a frequent, and sometimes, an instructive speaker at the Lyceums, in St. Clairsville, which have generally been attended by most of the members of the bar, and at times, by the Rev Clergy. His fluent elocution, flute-like voice, originality of conception, and force of reasoning, often witnessed, excited expectation, and drew attention whenever he rose to speak. These institutions are favorable to the development of mind ; and it is fortunate for the young men of a village if its elders join in the debates, whether it be for amusement, or to excite a spirit of inquiry, or improvement.

In the spring of 1841, he painted his family in a group, on canvass already occupied with valuable figures, which he obliterated rather than stretch another canvass on a frame, One of these figures, a listener, was spared at the intercession of his father, who saw its danger in time to save it from the threatening brush : It now stands in front of the group, a sample of the forms which he was accustomed to throw away.

In the summer of 1841, he designed the landing of Julius Cæsar, in Britain, with India ink, on paper, pasted on canvass, resembling an engraving, 46 by 27 inches. It contains some forty figures. The principal ones are Cæsar, and his standard bearer ; the former with an oratorical, as well as martial air, standing on a galley, directs the landing of the troops by means of flat boats, under cover of slingers and archers. Naked Gauls are acting as boat-men. Some of the soldiers, who have landed, are in deadly struggle with the Britains. one of whom, having run out on the shaft of his car between the horses, is wielding a club against a foe in front. The standard bearer, having leaped into the water, telling the soldiers to follow him, or betray their standard into the hands of the enemy, is bounding forward, but casting a stern glance behind, to see that proper support is accorded.

> With grace of Cicero's rival, Cæsar pours
> The sea-borne armies on the bristling shores ;
> From the beak'd galleys, grounded on the sand,
> The naked Gauls, in barks, assist to land ;
> The standard bearer, leaping in the waves,
> Breaks danger's spell.

In the same year he designed the Passage of the Red Sea by the Israelites. It is painted in oil, 21 by 21 inches. Moses, in front, extends, with his left hand, the wand over the sea, while he looks, and stretches his right hand towards heaven, as sincerely invoking, and confidently relying on celestial aid . Aaron, and the elders, near, behold him, with solemn confidence, as one on whom the safety of all depends ; exhibiting to the multitude an example of reliance on Heaven and their leader, well calculated to keep them in subordination to his orders. Others behind, not burdened with the cares of government, seem to have their attention bent on objects of curiosity, or danger. The following fragment has reference to this piece.

> His wand, stretched o'er the sea, he looks to heaven
> With faith's assurance, meek, but dignified.
> Those next in power, devout attention lend
> To that high invocation, big with fate,
> And teach the mass to reverence and obey,
> Whose grovelling minds prized freedom less than food.

The Death of Julius Cæsar is one of his most finished productions in oil. It is 22 by 27 inches, and contains some 20 figures. The principal ones are Brutus, Casca, four or five other dagger-brandishing conspirators, and Cæsar, near Pompey's statue: who, with one hand, is in act to throw his robe over his head; while he extends the other towards Brutus, as with mingled sorrow and surprise, he beholds him among his assassins, and resigns to his fate. In the back ground, are seen the variously excited vizages of the Roman Senators. The following lines are illustrative of the subject:

> The sculptur'd Pompey views th' assassin's knife
> Upraised to end brave Cæsar's glorious life.
> The hero's robe inveterate Casca holds:
> Th' approach of Brutus treason's depths unfolds.
> Then, graceful in extremity, he throws
> A mournful glance at one he sadly knows:
> "*Et tu Brute!*" exclaims, and o'er his face
> Swift draws his robe, to end life's fitful race.

The rescue of the American prisoners by Jasper and Newton, is a design executed on paper, in the Spring of 1842, with India ink, 22 by 18 inches in size. It contains fifteen figures. The two assailants attack the four soldiers on guard, two of whom have been prostrated; another is falling from the effect of a blow; and uplifted guns are about descending on the fourth; while the hand-fettered prisoners look on, with various emotions of hope and fear.

While engaged on this piece, he rode out one day with another young man, in a buggy. The horse run off. His companion jumped from the vehicle without injury, contrary to what usually happens in such cases; while the artist, holding the reins, thought to keep the horse in the centre of the road, and, at length, check his speed as he ascended a hill, some sixty rods ahead. But the animal took to kicking, while under great velocity, and disengaged himself from the carriage; its thills fell to the ground, and met an obstruction, which caused it to pitch over endwise, throwing the driver in advance, as a bullet is thrown before a wad. He struck the turnpike at an angle quite acute, and rolled over and over: a piece from his coat, at the shoulder, was torn by the percussion; the rim and crown of his hat were broken; but, except a slight scratch on the forehead, no wound was perceptible. He was apparently dead for some minutes, and it was near half an hour before any blood could be got from his arm. He was somewhat delirious at times, for a day or two after the accident. In a week, he was apparently well. His constitution and disposition were thought to be a little impaired by the shock. He exhibited, for a year or more afterwards, not the least inclination to paint, or to finish the piece on which he was earnestly engaged at the time he went out to take the ride.

In August, 1843, his nervous system received another severe shock from a dental operation, from which, as from the other, he, perhaps, never entirely recovered; for if the nervous energy —the main spring—be reduced from the quality of steel to that of iron, from any cause, it probably never wholly regains its pristine elasticity. Through the year 1847, he enjoyed pretty good health. On the 22d of Dec., of that year, he had sixteen teeth extracted at one sitting. This injured his health so manifestly that he did not hesitate to ascribe to the dental operation of 1843, and the percussion on the turnpike of 1842, his increased susceptibility to disease. After this third shock to his system, it seemed quite incapable of resisting the external influences of cold, and other enemies of life. A want of vigor was observed in him by his family, and felt by himself. He grew pale, and thin, and the first cold taken after the extraction of the teeth, caused a bleeding at the lungs, and came near ending his life at once. The usual doses of physic, as after the prostration in 1843, had not their wonted effect. Nature, depressed, struggled for relief by uncommon avenues, by breaking through new channels, or seeking new outlets for her obstructed secretions. The bleeding at the lungs began about the 1st of Feb., 1848, and continued about every tenth day for forty days; diminishing from two gills, at first, to a spoonful at last. By the 7th of April, he was sufficiently recovered to go by steamboat to New Orleans, in pursuit of a milder climate. He thence went to New River, in Louisiana, where he remained until the middle of June. In the last days of his residence there, he painted the likeness of the horse, Gray Medoc, and also a child for the Hon. D. K. Kennar. He took a copy of the horse as a model; then, ascending the river to Cincinnati, he spent seven weeks in that city, arranging some unfinished law business, and trying some causes of his brother Thurston, whose library and office furniture, on his return home in August, he brought to St. Clairsville; where, on the 7th of Sept., following, he saw that brother die of consumption, about nineteen months before his own dissolution.

His brother's ill health was preceded a few months by a severe tooth-extraction, which is supposed to have been the remote cause of his death. The first cold, afterwards, showed that he had leaped, in constitutional elasticity and energy, from 26 to 75 years of age, by some modern improvement, or progress. Physicians have, formerly, refused to pull more than one or two teeth at a time; but dentists are not always physicians; and if they were, they are exposed to temptation. The patient is more likely to consent to the extraction of a number of teeth, sufficient for a profitable job, before, than after enjoying the transports of having one or two wrung from his jaw.

The common error of consumptive patients is their persistence in acting as if they were well. The somewhat insensitive lungs not speaking to them in tones of pain sufficiently loud to rouse their caution in time, they go among the robust, and expose themselves to the same influences as others do, without reflecting that the heat which their constitutional energy ceases to supply, must be furnished by the fire place, warm clothing, and extraordinary care: and if they would take this care they often find their efforts thwarted by the thoughtlessness or indifference of the robust, with whom they fall in company; who. for their pleasure will keep a coach window open, though it lets in death to the invalid. The reason of the rule, that the welfare of the weaker should be preferred to the convenience of the stronger passenger, ought to be better understood. The healthy and hardy should reflect, that what is pleasant and harmless to them, is disagreeable and ruinous to the diseased and infirm; and that the strong can bear a little extra heat without injury, while the frail cannot endure the cold without endangering their health. As the strong can bear heat better than the weak can bear cold the claims of the weak should be preferred, being founded on necessity, while those of the robust rest merely on convenience. Thurston recovered from the first attack of phthisis to the surprise of all who were acquainted with his case; and as many thought his disease would prove fatal by March, 1843, it may be useful to note the means of cure: He confined himself to a room, whose grate night and day blazed with bituminous coal, from the 1st of Jan. to the 1st of June of that year. The chimney draft took all the air of the room away quarter hourly, as was judged from filling it with tar smoke, and noting the time of its vanishment. When at the worst, when redness could scarce be produced on the skin, sinapisms were applied to the breast, arms, and feet, a blister to the breast, and chafing to the whole surface; but this treatment was of short duration, not exceeding a week: the chief remedial agents were exercise and perspiration. Some determination to the surface was kept up constantly; but about every third day, for some twelve weeks, he took a profuse sweat, by taking a position near the fire, and drinking warm water made agreeable to the taste by milk or other harmless thing: as the perspiration increased, blankets were shouldered, and after an hour's endurance of the heat, the wet clothes were taken off and hot dry ones substituted with one motion, leaving no pause for the inroads of cold; this was repeated four to six times the same day: The effect, immediately perceptible, was an increased buoyancy of spirits, vivacity of the eye, exemption from irritation, soreness or stricture at the breast, increased energy and disposition to take exercise by walking the room, with folio volumes in hand, swinging and lifting them, so as to exercise the muscles of the chest, and not of the legs alone, that the weaker parts might participate in the motion, lest the stronger might throw morbid matter on the weaker. Magnesia and pulverized charcoal were occasionally administered to assist languid nature to perform her functions. His health at length seemed restored. He commenced the practice of law in Cincinnati in 1844, with spirit and success, gradually regaining a part of what had been lost in constitution, and as gradually forgetting the terms on which that constitution permitted him to enjoy health. In January, 1846, he wrote that he had never felt more robust; and about this time underwent another dental operation. Some six weeks afterwards he takes a cold, neglects it for three months and a half; then trifles with it, hoping to vanquish it without resorting to the inconvenient and tedious remedy of 1842–3, until it was entirely too late; though never doubting that if he thoroughly adopted that remedy it would prove successful. In its use, the head and hands should be protected from cold, and the face even, not be exposed to it long at a time. The disease may be aggravated by either of these parts feeling the sensation of cold for a greater space than the body would require for a tonic bath. Cold judiciously applied, is among the most useful tonics in this complaint. Before rising in the morning, the body should be chafed by the patient himself, to quicken his circulation, and enable him to dress without experiencing a chill. Warm water should be freely drank to aid the determination to the surface, and give greater fluency to the secretions. He should not sit down to write or read, without placing himself so near a fire, as to be safe against surprizes from cold, whose stealthy approaches are seldom noticed by the preoccupied mind. He should avoid repletion, indigestible food, and too meagre a diet; take regular daily exercise, being careful not to carry it to the point of fatigue, ever remembering that it is a disease of weakness, not of strength; a fire should be in his room the entire year: there are times when the air is warm but negative, in which the heat from the grate is much needed. Flannel and other woollen garments should not be thrown off, save temporarily, when exercise is more than supplying the heat they ordinarily afford, to be immediately resumed on its cessation. In short, the consumptive should treat himself as a sick person, but he generally treats himself in many things as a well person; and hence comes the notion of the incurability of the disease: night sweats hint that nature seeks relief by their means. To aid her judiciously in this effort gives strength to the patient.

Although Sylvester witnessed the beneficial effect of what may be termed the warm treatment on his brother, in 1843, and on himself, in the first paroxism of his disease, in February, and March, 1848, he persuaded himself that it was possible to so strengthen his system by exercise, chafing the surface of the body, and daily use of the cold shower bath, as to enable it to triumph over its infirmities. He disliked the confinement and the susceptibility to take cold, which the warm treatment implied ; and, if he would not permit the disease to restrain his action, the cold treatment was doubtless the best. At times it promised success. In October, 1848, he attended the Superior Court of Tyler County, Va, being sole counsel in several important land causes, and thence went into the woods to explore, survey, and ascertain the location of lands, and returned home, on the 9th of November, in very cold weather for the season, after an absence of 37 days. The first 28 of these days his health improved ; then, by too much exposure to cold, he not only lost what had been gained, but the disease got an additional hold on his vitals. He continued his attention to business as if he were well, and argued several causes in the Autumn of 1849, in such way, as to leave the impression, that his lungs were probably not much impaired—though his pale, and lean aspect, showed that his hold on life was very weak.

Thinking he had been benefitted by the climate of Louisiana, in the spring of 1848, he left home for the Island of Jamaica, on the 17th of November, 1849 ; stopped two days at Cincinati, and six at New Orleans, and reached Kingston on the 28th, of December. His passage thither, from New Orleans, was rendered uncomfortable by sea sickness, dampness and cold. He speaks in his letters of having been treated with great kindness by the inhabitants of the Island; and of the judges of their courts, sent from England, as men ot deep erudition, and polished manners ; and of the climate, as debilitating and unfit for consumptives ; and of the Island, as retrograding from the effect of emancipation. On the 28th of March, he arrives in Kingston, from Mr. Fleming's of St. Thomas, East ; and appears desirous of the arrival of a Steamship, that he may go to New York, and try the cold water remedy ; but took to bed on the same day, at the house of Mrs. Mary Ann Munford, the widow of the Law Reporter of that name, and died on the morning of the 4th of April, 1850, at nine o'clock, and was buried in the Episcopal burying ground, in the suburb of the city, where a stone has been erected to his memory. The Jamaica Gazette, thus notices his death. " Died in this city, on the morning of the 4th, inst. Sylvester Genin, Esq., from the state of Ohio. To personal respectability, and high attainments in his profession as a lawyer, Mr. Genin added very respectable talents as an artist. He was a victim to pulmonary disease. His friends at home will be gratified in knowing, that while he had the best medical advice, and most careful nursing during life, every attention was paid to his remains on his decease, by the venerable, and estimable American Consul, to whom his country owes a debt of gratitude, not to be estimated for his urbanity, kindness, and unremitted attention. The funeral was attended by the Revd. Dr. Ferris, of New York City, the Revd. Mr. Radcliffe, of the Presbyterian Church. Col. Harrison, the American Consul, a number of American gentlemen, and many merchants and inhabitants of this city."

The following letter, from the Revd. Dr. Ferris, chancellor to the New York University, relates to his last hours.

NEW YORK, May 21, 1850.

DEAR SIR—Permit me to tender my condolence with you and your family, on the bereavement you have experienced. I doubt not you will feel his loss deeply, as he was undoubtedly a man of unusual attainments and capabilities, and whose promise in his profession was all a father could wish. It was not my privilege to know your son until within a few days of his death. I was myself at Kingston, as an invalid seeking shelter in its fine atmosphere, from the severities of the March air of my native city. But though an invalid, I was able to visit my countrymen there; and I confess my heart was tenderly drawn to those who seemed going down to the grave, as was your son. I had an interview with him on the day the American Consul was called in to take his last wishes. Drs. Ferguson and Campbell, had just frankly informed him that all their skill could not avail, and suggested the propriety of his arranging his affairs without delay. He was cool and collected, and seemed to have an apprehension that his case had been misconceived by the Doctor. Our interview was of a general character, and brief. The day before he died I saw him again; he was quite feeble, and evidently failing fast. Our conversation was solemn, and referred to the value of a hope in the gospel. I asked him if he was a professor of religion; to which he replied negatively; but added that he had aimed to live a Christian life, and set an example to others. He confessed that his mind had been too much in the world; and he assented cheerfully to my remarks on the blessedness of the privilege of casting our case on the arm of a gracious God. Through that day he sunk rapidly, and the next morning, soon after nine o'clock, he died. I understood that his last remarks were about his home, his parents, and especially his mother. Just before he expired, he failed from weakness to be able to make himself understood in something he wished to say, and burst into tears which flowed freely. It was thought from his last preceeding remark, that he wished to say something of home. He was occasionally flighty; but at the last entirely himself. Without a sigh or a struggle he passed away. Dr. Campbell, who especially attended him, is an eminent physician, and a kind friend. He made a post-mortem examination, which I understood, fully confirmed his previous judgment of the disease.

Your son enjoyed the entire confidence and affection of the venerable Consul, who seemed indeed to visit him as a son. The funeral occurred on the evening of the day of the death;

the law, it was said, making this necessary. I attended as a Clergyman, and performed the services which are usual among my own people. The Rev. Mr. Radcliffe kindly volunteered to be present with his own conveyance. To me it was a solemn scene, to be gathered, as we were, a company of Americans, far away from home, some far gone with the same disease, mingling our sympathies over the remains of a countryman. At the grave, the service of the Church of England was read by the chaplain for the day, the Rev. Mr. Chandler. The grave yard is one of the Episcopal Church, and is on the outskirts of the town. The place of burial was a few paces within the gate; I think on the great Central avenue; Mr. Hitchins has marked the spot particularly. Your son had gained friends every where; and even in death his countenance indicated a mind of very high order, and great amiability of character. The American Consul appeared as chief mourner as if he had been the aged father, burying his son, and that, a son dearly beloved.

If his remains were to be removed, which could be done, or if a stone is to be erected on his grave, Messrs Hitchins and son, who took an active part in all relating to him, would be the persons to attend to either.

My dear sir, one who was at that funeral, an attendant, is now in his grave at Baltimore. Thus we are reminded of the uncertainty of life. I trust a gracious Saviour, will sanctify this loss to you and your family, and that we may meet in a world where parting and sorrow are unknown.

Respectfully, yours, &c.

ISAAC FERRIS.

At a meeting of the Bar of St. Clairsville, June 20 1850, J. A. Ramage, Esq., was called to the chair, and Henry Kennon, Esq., appointed Secretary. The following preamble and resoutions, reported by a committee : composed of Miller Pennington, R. J. Alexander, and C. C. Carroll, Esqrs., were, after being supported by some appropriate and feeling remarks from C. C. Carroll and Judge Cowen, unanimously adopted.

Whereas, we have learned with the deepest regret, that while in the spring time of life, and in the hope of a bright future, Sylvester Genin, Esq., a member of this Bar, died from home at Jamaica, on the 4th day of April last ; and for the purpose of expressing the high regard we have for the memory of one whose talents so well fitted him to adorn the profession of which he had been so short a time a member; who has left for himself, a name bright and durable as are the many productions of his rare genius in the fine arts, and whose private virtues qualified him for the confidence and esteem of all who knew him, therefore

Resolved, That we do severally express to the parents, and only brother of the deceased, our sincere condolence for the great affliction that this melancholy event has brought upon them.

Resolved, That the Court be requested to have the proceedings of this meeting entered upon its journal.

Resolved, That a copy be furnished to the parents of the deceased by the Secretary of this meeting.

On motion the proceedings were directed to be signed by the officers, and the papers of this place requested to publish the same.

J. A. RAMAGE, *Chairman.*

H. KENNON, *Secretary.*

The following obituary notice published in the St. Clairsville Chronicle, on the 10th of May, 1850, and written by the Hon. Benj. Ruggles, for 18 years Ohio's Senator in Congress, and one of the old men whose age and experience gave pleasure and satisfaction to the youthful artist, may here be introduced not only as a suitable peroration of this narrative, but as an act of justice to the deceased, who chiefly esteemed the approbation of the wise and the good.

" SYLVESTER GENIN—When a young man passes the threshhold of life, and enters upon the busy and active scenes of the world, the public as well as his immediate friends, take a deep interest in his future fortunes. Mr. Genin, whose recent death in a foreign land, is deeply felt and mourned by all his acquaintances, commenced his career with brilliant prospects before him, and the strong hopes of a long and useful life. He possessed talents of a superior order, which were cultivated and improved by a liberal education and extensive reading. He early qualified himself for the profession of the law, and was soon admitted to the bar, and commenced a successful practice. In conversation, Mr. Genin was remarkbly gifted, and could always draw upon his varied fund of information for proper material to entertain, interest, and enliven his friends, or the social circle. His manners were those of a well-bred gentleman, dignified, but not ostentatious, easy and courteous, free in his communications, and obliging and respectful to all. In his associations he was not confined to the company of youth alone, but sought society with age and experience, in which he enjoyed much pleasure and satisfaction. His systematic manner of doing business, excellent moral character, and uprightness of conduct in all transactions of life, are models worthy of imitation.

Mr. Genin possessed a natural taste and genius for the fine arts. In early youth, apparently unaided and without instruction, he employed his pencil in drawing portraits, landscapes and historical scenes, which he continued at intervals to the close of his life. His productions have been pronounced by competent judges, as finished specimens of painting, and do great credit to the art as well as to the youthful artist. Among his works the writer of this notice has observed the battle of the Granicus—the landing of Cæsar in Great Britain—the battle of Arbela—the death of Cæsar—the passage of the Red Sea by the Israelites—the rescue of the American prisoners by Jasper and Newton—the woman of Monterey, and others, containing from 6 or 10 to 70 or 80 figures, in varied and expressive attitudes, harmonizing with the leading idea of the design.

The combined oratorical and martial air of Cæsar, directing the descent on Britain—the intense action of Bucephalus and his rider, rushing over the Persians—the mingled sorrow and dignity, with which Cæsar views the steel of Brutus—the meek but, dignified assurance, with which Moses looks to Heaven, while extending his wand over the sea—the calm intrepidity of the Mexican woman, and the gratified expression of the wounded soldiers, receiving water at her hands, evince great strength of conception, and power of execution in the artist.

I have been told that he aimed at anatomical accuracy, and

would draw first the skeleton, and then gradually clothe it with arteries, veins, muscles, and skin ; to impress on his mind, an exact idea of the human form.

For some years before his death, Mr. Genin's health began to decline ; and although every thing was done, that parental affection and tenderness could do, no change for the better could be produced. He determined to take a journey to the South if possible, to regain his health, believing that the sunny skies of the tropics, and balmy air of the sea, would arrest the disease. But it was all in vain. The great destroyer had marked him for his own. He spent the winter at Kingston, or in the Island of Jamaica, gradually sinking away until the 4th of April, when, at the age of twenty-eight, death closed his earthly existence. He was thus cut down in the morning of life, and the ardent hopes of his friends, and the presages of future eminence and distinction, were blasted forever. Although he died among strangers, in a strange land, yet he was not without friends. His goodness of heart, and urbanity of manner, created for him the warmest attachments. His dying bed was surrounded by anxious and sympathising hearts, until the last pulsation of life announced the fact, that death had done his work, and that his spirit had fled from earth to heaven. He was buried in the most honorable manner. The Consul of the United States, the Rev. Clergy, all the Americans in the city, and a large concourse of strangers, followed his remains to the grave, and deposited them in their last resting-place upon earth.

Who can invade the sanctity of family sorrow to assuage its bitterness? Paternal and fraternal love can never die. The agony of severed ties will be felt. Grief must have its outpourings; and nothing but time, submission, true philosophy, and the fortitude of the Christian and his hopes, can give consolation. An afflicted community sympathize with the bereaved family for their irreparable loss.

The Wheeling Argus of May, 1850, edited by the late Dr. John Dunham, says, among other things of the deceased, that "as a gentleman, few young men ever had a more enviable reputation—as a lawyer, he was sound and practical, and rising daily in the esteem of the older practitioners; as an artist, he produced many works that procured him the friendship of our most respectable painters and sculptors."

He exhibited great skill and eloquence in the trial of causes. In special pleading, he was well accomplished and uniformly successful; and though few were more capable of forming and illustrating general rules, from elementary principles, he always fortified his positions with authorities, not omitting the use of principles however, especially in illustrating the unity of object of the authorities, which he generally brought to bear with great force on the end proposed.

In the argument of land causes, in Virginia, the lawyers who were present have averred that he displayed great ability; and other spectators expressed their admiration, by declaring that their Court House never before witnessed such eloquence; a declaration not strictly correct perhaps; but showing that the speaker's manner was impressive.

General Jackson, of Parkersburg, Virginia, in an address to the Circuit Superior Court, in Marshall County, at a special term in December, 1852, assumed the impregnability of a point, because it had not been overthrown by the "ingenuity and erudition" of Mr. Genin. "I had occasion," said the General, "to argue this question in another county, some years since, in opposition to the younger Genin, a man whose extraordinary talents and research commanded my highest respect and admiration, who usually cast upon the subjects he discussed, all the light which authorities could bestow, and whose genius I have witnessed in the skilful dispositions and elaborate display of authorities in the case in hand; for I am informed that he prepared the general outline of this defence; yet even he, with all his ingenuity and erudition, could not bring authority to bear efficiently against my position."

Ex-Governor Shannon, when at Kingston, remarked the favorable impressions made there by his neighbor, whose death was considered, as the American Consul declared, a loss to mankind.

The compositions which are offered to the reader in the following pages were found in the rough draft, with few exceptions, and scattered in so many places, on the backs of letters and obsolete business papers written often with lead pencil, that it is doubtful whether he ever thought of their collection and publication; but his family being disposed to gather into one parcel the many artistic sketches known to exist, while searching for them, occasionally found a piece of poetry, or prose, and threw it on a heap by itself, out of which the following pages have been compiled. The subject of the pieces respectively, was not named. This has been inferred from reading each piece, and placed at its head. The time of the composition can only be judged by the subject, and the handwriting, as it gradually changed from a plain stiff to a running hand. The first two-thirds of the Day of Judgment, from this criterion, is supposed to have been written in his 17th or 18th year; the translation from the Ænead in his 16th. The first half of the Ode to the Wind between his 16th and 18th; the last half of it at a much later period.

He had little hope of recovering his health in the spring of 1849, when he wrote the piece, entitled, "The Dead;" and again in the spring of 1849, when the lines on "The Transient Nature of Things", and "The Spouse", are supposed to have been written. In the summer of the latter year he seemed to think he might live to visit Rome; but from the following lines, written with a lead pencil, it appears, he expected never to return from such an excursion.

> Soon in Italian dust I lay my head,
> I go to sleep among the Roman dead
> In the mild radiance of Italia's sky,
> Life's drama closes on my longing eye.

He was deterred from leaving home until late in the fall of 1849, by the supposed necessity of his attending to the trial of some law suits, in which he was sole counsel.

Certain members of the St. Clairsville Bar, were desirous that he should be made President-Judge of the 15th Circuit, in the winter of 1846–7. He so far listened to the suggestion as to visit the Capitol of the State, and reconnoitre the ground; but seeing it occupied by Mr. Cowen with considerable force, and disliking to annoy him, on account of his willingness the previous winter, when a member of the Legislature, to support his brother Thurston for a Judgeship in Cincinnati, he did not advance his pretensions. He being a moderate free soil whig, and the free soilers holding the balance of power in the Legislature, it was thought he might be elected by the joint support of the democrats and free soilers. He staid less than a week in Columbus, and continued his journey to Cincinnati, to which place he professed to be going when he left home. While there he attended and addressed a meeting of the citizens, in favor of the establishment of a Western Art Union : in the success of which he took much interest, and continued a member of it while he lived.

Besides the ten designs already mentioned he executed 22 others.

In the summer of 1847, he painted *The Woman of Monterey* in oil, 44 by 39 inches, containing ten figures. The Woman holds in one hand a bucket, in the other a gourd shell, out of which a soldier is drinking, with an expression of grateful earnestness, as he leans upon a dead horse and lifeless companion. On the other side of her, another soldier with his hand on her bucket, supporting himself with his elbow on the ground, is looking in eager expectation for his turn at the gourd. In the distance are seen Mexican lancers spearing the wounded, and the legs of troops under fire, whose heads are shrouded in the smoke of battle. The hills beyond Monterey occupy the back ground of the picture.

Jepthah's Daughter, with India ink, on paper, 13 by 12, contains nine interesting female figures, representing the daughter and her maids, in various graceful attitudes, descending the steps of a palace. The daughter of the man of the rash vow, is in advance, with her hand at her ear, listening with the utmost attention to catch the distant sounds, that announce his approach with the triumphant army.

The Entrance of Napoleon into Russia, is done with India ink, 6 inches by 9; and contains seven or eight figures in the foreground, and others that become indistinct as they recede in the background. A Cossack, with his spear, on a horse, in swift motion, darts from a forest in front of the cortege. The

Emperor's horse, at the moment, is stumbling, while the Cossack is asking what the French want in Russia. The French are in fine order, and apparently animated with glorious hopes.

The Retreat of Napoleon from Russia, is of the same size and executed with the same material, exhibiting about the same number of figures. This piece presents standards and clothing in shattered condition; wo-begone countenances; abandoned wheels of carriages; some soldiers marching; some sitting down in despair; some prostrate in death; and a strong wind sweeping the sleet, Napoleon's robe, and his horse's mane and tail, in one direction, as they labor over the wintry landscape.

Gorgcud intercepting the blow aimed by the Cossack, at Napoleon, at Brienne, is a sketch on paper, in India ink. The Cossack's arm is raised just behind the Emperor, prepared to strike; Gorgaud, at full gallop, has his sword lifted, to defeat the Cossack's intention; Napoleon's steed is rearing, and stands upon his hind legs; his rider is looking intently in a direction different from that in which Gorgaud and the Cossack are operating.

The Mother and Infant Child, is a bust of the size of life, in oil, on canvass. The lovely mother holds the babe in her arms, on her lap, contemplating his features, with maternal delight, while he looks out from her fond embrace with vernal freshness, infantile mildness, and attractive vivacity.

The Twin Sisters are, likewise, in oil, on canvass of the same dimension. Their style of beauty is prepossessing, and their relationship strikingly manifest.

The Negro Child and Dog are in oil, of full size. The child, with his arms around the neck of the dog, looks at the spectator with gleeful satisfaction, while the dog, of the fyst species, disliking the liberties taken with him in rude familiarity, stands upon his dignity, and unveils the white of his eyes very majesterially.

BIOGRAPHY. 71

The Horse, *Gray Medoc*, in oil, is, with the landscape surrounding him, very well executed, as are several other pieces in oil, containing a single figure;—such as *The Fancied Beauty*, No. 1 and 2; *Little Girls;* the portraits of himself at 17, 20, and 27, and three of his father and mother; and as many of his brothers, at different periods.

The Sketch of the Throng referred to in these lines—

> Close by the gate, within the jaws of hell,
> Revengeful cares, and sullen sorrows dwell.

contains a dozen figures, with countenances and attitudes in accordance with such an unpromising locality. It is on paper, with ink, 6 by 9.

The Reckoning between the Lord and the Steward is of the same size and material. The expression is in harmony with the particular business in hand. Both have hold of a paper, on which the Lord has his eyes fixed, with the air of one who seems to think he is not to be deceived: while the Steward, in the confusion of detected delinquency, looks up enquiringly, as if studying its effect, or contriving a subterfuge.

The leap of Alexander from the tower, into the fortress, of the Malli, is a sketch, with ink, on paper, 8 by 9. The king is contending with the enemy, on the floor of the fortress, with his sword: stones are on wing from above: arrows are aimed at him from within. There are some eight figures. The piece is rough and unfinished.

Christ enjoining the rendition unto Cæsar the things which are Cæsar's, is a sketch with ink, 5 by 8, on paper, containing 6 or 7 figures, rough and unfinished; but quite expressive. The mild dignity of Christ: the surprise and wonder of the Pharisees at the easy dexterity with which he evaded their snares, and their thwarted expectation, are apparent.

McCullough riding down Wheeling Hill, is a sketch, with ink, on paper, 12 by 10. McCullough, with his gun in his left hand, and his right holding the reins, is descending a steep declivity, of between fifty and sixty degrees.

Horses Playing, are on paper, with ink. The front horse, with his weight on his fore feet, looks behind at the other, who is reared on his hind feet. The sketch is spirited and natural.

Samson rending the Lion's Jaws asunder, is a sketch on paper, 10 by 9. He is running at full speed at the moment of grasping the jaws. His weight is on his right leg: the other is extended behind—not having overtaken its fellow; the hind part of the lion's body is on the ground: the forepart and head are nearly on a level with Samson's. A striking idea of velocity and force is afforded by the picture.

Lazarus asking Alms of Dives, is on paper. The humble diffidence and pity-invoking air of the one, is in striking contrast with the supercilious and contemptuous scowl of the other.

The Ploughman and his Team of Horses, is on paper. The team and its rustic lord are apparently moving over a partly ploughed field, on one side of which is a hay-stack, and other signs of effective husbandry.

Anthony exhibiting Cæsar's Robe to the People, is on paper. The lurking duplicity and cunning of the demagogue shines through the affected indignation, and bold attempt to assume the appearance of candor and sincerity, made by the incipient triùmvir.

The Dispute between Achilles and Agamemnon, is on paper, 8 by 10. The former is about to unsheath his sword, as he sternly eyes the King, seated above: while Ulysses, sitting behind Achilles—not seeming to notice the menace—may be supposed to be calculating the consequences of the quarrel.

Dido on the Funeral Pile, is a sketch on paper. The mournful beauty, reclined on the pile, casts a longing glance at the ocean, and the receding ships of Eneas.

The Mamelukes attacking a French square, is a sketch on paper. A line of soldiers is seen, partly enveloped in smoke:

the horses of the Mamelukes are throwing their heels into the faces of the soldiers behind them; being backed upon the bayonets of the French, by their riders: who, with uplifted sabre eye the foe in the rear, to guard against his thrusts.

He had some hair-breadth escapes, involving lessons of prudence. In his third year, standing before the wheel of a wagon, loaded with straw, as it started, he raised his hand against it, and was thrown to one side, just far enough for the wheel to pass, without crushing him.

At another time, he passed under an axe, while the operator was bringing it down with all his power. He escaped by scarce an inch, in distance, and about the thirtieth of a second, in time.

Awhile afterwards, accompanying a thoughtless milkmaid to a cow, with a young calf, she rushed at him, furiously; he pushed himself to one side, by throwing his hand against her head; her horn passed outside the chin, wounding it slightly— a half inch more, and the horn would have taken the jaw.

A cart, in which he was riding, was overturned on a sidehill. He was within an inch of being crushed under it. A fall from the top of one of the loftiest hickory trees, was only prevented from being fatal, by his grasping at small branches on his descent.

On emergencies, he showed great presence of mind and decision of character. The relieving of cattle in distress, or subjecting them, if refractory, and the disentangling of perplexities of all kinds, often exhibited his efficiency and skill.

One cold morning, in his 15th or 16th year, he was found in a distant field, with his coat off and shirt sleeves rolled to his shoulders, assisting a distressed cow. The calf was dead, but his practice was successful.

On one occasion, a heifer, enraged on account of her offspring, pursued his brother, Thurston, down a road. He followed close behind, at full speed, calling to Thurston to quicken his pace; for she was overtaking him; and threw his hat in the direction she was running, over and beyond her head, to withdraw her attention from his brother. This tactic saved him: she stopped to horn the hat, while Thurston escaped.

He soon got a noose over her horns, and tied her to a tree. This was in his fifteenth year.

His perception was quick, and hand steady. Mr. James Brower, his instructor in the use of the sword, averred that in this he excelled.

These matters have been recorded, as interesting to Mr. Genin's relatives and friends; and as to which a few others, as members of the human family, will not be indifferent. The object has not been to make a book for sale; but to preserve what is valuable, and to erect a monument to one, whose merits appear in the work itself, and in this respect, is better than a structure of marble.

SELECTIONS.

ON GREATNESS.

THE truly great so act as to command respect. They may be sometimes in error ; but their sincerity still invests them with dignity. They prove themselves equal to what they undertake ; and their actions are in accordance with their position. They seem to have an instinctive perception of the harmonious relations of things—judiciously adapt means to ends—and perform appropriately and well, the duties of their station.

Whether beheld wielding the destinies of nations ; influencing senates, guiding the rage of battle, acting as parents, companions citizens, artists, mechanics, farmers, doctors, lawyers, or preachers, they appear great in every station ; earnestly, ably, and faithfully performing its duties.

The same mind, the same energy, the same sincerity, exerted in whatever station man's reasonable wants have created, commands the same regard from the just and enlightened observer.

Angels may view with reverence the patient, industrious, frugal wife, or husband, making the best use of their means, their reason, and wealth, for noble objects; the nurture and education of their children in virtue and knowledge ; or the mechanic, or artist, elevating the taste, and relieving the wants of mankind to the greatest extent and perfection of which his art is capable ; or the farmer, using all his faculties in increasing and refining the bounties of nature ; or the jurist, vindicating justice, with all the arms which the law supplies ; or the physician, supporting tottering humanity with all the lights of long experience ; or the divine, wielding all the splendors of rhetoric and the force of reason to exhibit, motives of virtue in time and eternity ; or the citizen resolved on the most exact obedience to, and complete enforcement of, the laws of his country ; for each of these possesses the elements of greatness in as high a degree, as if acting in a wider sphere.

Seated in a log cabin, several bundles of yarn gracing its sides, the sugar trough, cradle, and eight or ten children, dressed in homespun apparel, before me, and the surrounding land bristling with stumps of huge trees, recently swept away by the hand of industry, I have thought to perceive in the occupants, the patience of Job, the energy and perseverance of Hannibal, the virtue and independence of Cato, and the energy and decision of Napoleon, exerted in a humble sphere ; but not the less worthy of admiration : they had suffered without despairing ; they had encountered difficulties, which they had surmounted ; and when the mother recounted the signs of usefulness, which she had observed in this and that child, I participated in her hope, in her pride, and rejoiced in her triumph of victory : no train of captured princes, or bright array of spoils, could have increased my emotion and delight. Greatness was unveiled : Ulysses shone through his humble garb.

POSSIBLE CAUSES OF LEGISLATION

The Legislature of Ohio has seemed at times to be a lever in the hands, now of land speculators, within her borders ; now of foreign bankers ; now of cotton-planting States ; and now of a nobility that exercises political power, without sharing in the burthens it imposes; and now of the principle of evil, tempting the honest to be dishonest.

It has taxed the whole state to raise the value of land in certain localities, by rail-roads and canals, of which a large portion of the state, bordering on, and intersected by rivers, would know and care but little, if it did not *hear* of their benefits, and *feel* their evils, in oppressive taxation; consoled however, by the reflection, that the burthen was not imposed by the union of the benefitted *few* with a nobility *above*, but with a nobility *below* the tax payer, on the score of *social*, not *political*, importance. Whether it is better to be governed by a poor privileged class, that votes, but pays no taxes, than a rich, educated, privileged class, that also wields political power, but pays no taxes, I will not now express an opinion; nor do more than allude to the end of the beggar on horse back. It is strange however, that a people, who suppose themselves the most enlightened on earth, while expressing their aversion to privileged orders, should voluntarily create a numerous one; arm it with power to impose burthens it does not share; and humbly bow to its decrees. I desire the happiness of all mankind; but would tempt no portion of them to be tyrants. Taxation by those who did not share the burthen caused the Revolutionary War. I am in favor of internal improvements, and the education of the people; but would not be unjust in order to effect these objects. Injustice can never do good. The Legislature can never repeal the laws of God and nature. The coveting the ox, or ass of the neighbor, or the robbing of one, for the benefit of another, cannot end well; whether it be for the purpose of digging a canal to raise the value of lands on the Scioto; or for the purpose of slackening the energies of the father to provide for the welfare of his offspring; or to release the debtor from performing his promises; or to lessen the value of home products for the benefit of the foreign purchaser; or to crush our own banks, to make room for the circulation of the paper of irresponsible foreign banks: Justice is the only safe foundation of Governments. The depression of Ohian banks, apparently to make Ohio the field of circulation of the paper of banks of neighboring states, banks irresponsible to us, is an act of such kindness to foreigners, and disregard of our own interests, as inclines a philosopher to look to the foreign states for causes of which Ohian legislation is the effect, it being difficult to account for its charity's extending its journey so far from home. If our law makers are disposed to be thoughtless, a neighbor might think for them; but he would think to his own advantage. Our privileged non tax-paying class might care little for the interests of stockholders of banks, yet even this class is concerned in having sound banks at home, and would have them there, if its action were not an effect of foreign causes. The bankers of neighboring states, would be benefitted by the discontinuance of our banks. The cotton and sugar planters would get agricultural products at lower prices, if all banks were swept from the Northern and Western states ; but because these are reasonable inferences, it does not follow, that foreign statesmen influence the Legislation of Ohio. If her legislation is without thought, it might, by chance, help others more than herself, all parties being entirely guiltless of design ; yet a series of measures, all tending to one object, leads to the suspicion, that the intelligence which originates them, has only that object in view. It is scarce practicable to enlighten those whose desire to sustain a political party, is stronger than their desire for truth ; hence statesmen, who would lead men against their own interests, first enlist them in a party ; rouse their animosity against the opposing party ; then, being in their confidence, gradually educate them in doctrines false to their interests ; but the falsity is not perceived, or, if seen, they will not believe their own suggestions, if they do not accord with party views : thus farmers vote with a party, whose measures tend to make wheat bring forty, instead of eighty cents per bushel ; and this state of things is inevitable ; and must continue, notwithstanding a general diffusion of the means of knowledge, so long as prejudice is capable of being made stronger than reason. By this force, governments exceed their limits ; wander from the object of their creation, civil protection, and military defence, to legislate on all things, and become the tools of cupidity, whether acting for the benefit of Macedon or Persia *without*, or speculators, or thieves, *within* the borders of the state,

ON HISTORY.

HISTORY is perhaps among the first causes of civilization; for by tradition, before the invention of letters, the advantages of good, and disadvantages of evil actions, were perceived by mankind. They, thus learned to shun the evil, and pursue the good; and adapt means, the most suitable for the attainment of the end in view. The historian is to the uninformed what the wise adult is to the simple child. The adult's superiority over the child is not owing to his having a better mind, but to his having more experience; and if the experience of some thirty years gives him a striking superiority over the child, would not the experience of many past ages still give a greater superiority? The possession of the experience of the past, implies the possession of more than the knowledge of past transactions: judgment as well as memory are essential elements of experience; which is not only the remembrance of facts, but the conclusions drawn from those facts. The recollection of the facts recorded in ancient and modern history, would be almost an useless incumbrance on the mind, unless just conclusions could be drawn from them. One may therefore know many things, and be very old, without having much experience, or a proper perception of the causes of results; so, one may be quite young, and yet possess considerable experience. When one has attained his twenty-first year, he has already observed a great many phases of motive, in short, the broad world in miniature; and though, with knowledge necessarily limited, for want of time for large acquisitions, yet his observations were made with, probably, about the same volume of mind that he will have in a more advanced age. Much that is observed in after life is merely confirmatory of what has been often witnessed before; as years increase we more easily distinguish the true from the false from repeated observation; but our field of knowledge it more slowly enlarged. Alexander Pope published his Essay on Criticism at the age of twenty-two. Many have lived eighty years without attaining the experience which this work displays in its author. We may justly infer, that he who reads industriously, and judges soundly, may soon reach a great age in experience, as did Clive, Pitt the younger, Napoleon, Scipio Africanus, and others. The unnumbered developments of selfishness, as disclosed by history, sufficiently indicate the principle which chiefly governs mankind, nationally, and individually: founded on want more or less; as luxury or simplicity prevails, it steadily urges events with more or less force. It makes monarchies the tools of courtiers to advance families. It makes republics the tools of demagogues, land speculators, and office seekers; and compels the people to fly for shelter from robbery, to regal government. Their rights are undermined by the sweetest siren melody that selfishness can breathe. The land holder deems it very reasonable, that he should be made rich by what is termed an internal improvement, at the public expense. The house-holder thinks nothing more clear, than that he should be maintained, and his family educated by the public; for, says he, above half the convicts cannot read and write. The learned rogues mostly escape, and the ignorant ones, their cats-paws, are caught. The zealot wonders that tythes are not exacted for the support of stated preaching. Written constitutions in vain oppose this principle of selfishness. In all forms of government, it operates with more or less force; but in republics, without virtue, it breaks out into undisguised robbery. A thief on the bench, or in the legislature, delights in the indulgence of his natural propensity, under the forms of law. The force of selfishness, modified by fear, honor, virtue, patriotism, temperance, luxury, &c., determines the duration of governments. These endure in proportion to the exemption of the people from its rapacity. A few drones in a despotism may be supported a long time without exhausting the masses; but in governments, where great numbers succeed in reaching the public treasury, they hasten the downfall of the nation, by exhausting its resources in countless ways. Excuses for imposing taxes are never wanting—the honor of the State, the glory of God, the advancement of true religion the promotion of learning, the improvement of the country, in short, for every thing besides, as well as the true objects of government, civil protection, and military defence; and these proper objects of government, are, at times, perverted, to give employments to favorites. These workings of selfishness, history unfolds, and teaches to guard against its rapacity, and to promptly check the first deviation of government from its proper objects; which John Locke, and after him, Mr. Jefferson, says, people are not disposed to do, until the repetition of abuses becomes intolerable.

TARIFF.

The advantages of a protective Tariff have long been understood in Europe. The protective policy is the permanent policy of all European Governments. Its utility is no longer a debatable question among their Statesmen. We may safely infer that their anti-protective, and free trade speeches, and documents, are made for exportation, and foreign consumption: so great is the difference between their precepts and practice. Their practical Statesmen have endorsed the writings of the free trade theorists by word, not deed, to give them currency abroad; and the history of the United States, shows these political abstractions to have been the dearest of our imports. We have seen our prosperity increase, or wane, with the increase or diminution of our Tariff; yet many seem resolved not to be benefitted by the experience, and wilfully shut their eyes on the discrepancy between the theory and practice of foreign Statesmen. Some actually pretend to question the power of the National Government to establish a merely protective Tariff, or one which has not revenue for its sole object, overlooking the deep foundation of such a power in the nature of things. This power is founded on the right of *self-defence*. The exercise of this right is not affected by the nature, or the manner of the aggression. It matters not, whether we are assailed by hostile arms, or hostile policies. If we have a right to self-defence, we have a right to exert it in all cases. If an enemy send a ball against buildings, in one of our harbours, he must redress the injury, or feel our vengeance; but may he plunder us by an inimical policy, and destroy our commercial prosperity with impunity? A bull-dog could comprehend the case of open violence, and there is need of but little more sagacity to understand the other. If the Federal Government has not the power to regulate commerce, under the constitution, by express provision, still, could we rationally infer that it has not the faculty of self-defence in a matter of such vital importance? Has not a nation natural rights, and is not its Government bound to guard them, whether the duty be expressly enjoined or not? The Government of a nation must, in the pursuit of the object of its institution, defend its people against attacks of every description. In the face of this natural right of self-defence, and the express grant to the Federal Government to regulate commerce, is it not an extravagantly audacious experiment on the American understanding, to attempt to convince it that there is no power in that Government to establish a protective Tariff? If the Federal Government cannot exercise that power, the power remains in the States; but it is not claimed that the State Governments may regulate commerce. The power is in the National Government, if any where; and while this Government neglects to regulate our intercourse with foreign nations, those nations will regulate it at our expense, and keep us in debt to them, selling to us more of their productions than they buy of ours. If the Federal Government, swayed by sectional jealousy, neglects to protect us, we should, by fixing the price of lisence to sell goods, or otherwise, endeavour to protect ourselves, by State laws, which is scarcely practicable, since the same influence that controls the Federal governs State legislation, by party tactics, and Federal patronage. The slave and free States are in a condition of rivalry, rather than union: the former wield the general Government, and form commercial alliances, compromitting the interests of the latter; saying, by acts, to England take off your duty on cotton, and rice, and we will, in return, take off so much of the duty on iron, and cloths, and impose such a duty on dye stuffs, raw silks,

&c., as to give your manufacturers a decided advantage in the American Market.

It is the policy of monarchies to favor capital, and labor, as its adjunct, to sustain a noble class ; and all the advantages their laborers derive from our errors, go to swell the incomes of their nobility and capitalists. While we choose to be co-laborers with their paupers we share, in some measure, the evils of their oppression, and they enjoy a portion of the benefit of our freedom ; for it is a natural law of commerce that the tendency of unrestrained trade, is to equalize the wages of labor. —What a consolation for the devout democrat! If he grows poor, for the want of protection against the pauper labor of monarchies, his losses have gone to increase the incomes of nobles !

To claim that our manufacturers may flourish, without protection, is to claim that an infant may successfully wrestle with an adult.

Foreign Governments, by giving premiums on articles exported, many ruin the manufacture of such articles here, if unprotected. Protection, to be efficient, should be permanent. To claim that a market for our agricultural products, three thousand miles from our shores, with its exposure to interruption from wars, accidents, and cost of freight, is preferable to a market at home, or that protection cannot be accorded without an unjust partiality, or that foreign commerce diminishes with the increase of articles of trade, is to claim an absurdity.

The cost of freight adds to the cost of production. The Ohian takes five dollars worth of flour to England at an expense of one dollar and a half. The Englishman takes five dollars worth of woollen, or cotton goods, to Ohio, at an expense of ten to twenty five cents, according to the quality of the goods. Thus, the distance of the market, adds but little to the cost of producing the goods ; but a great deal to the cost of producing the flour. It is plain, that the expense of freight, in the exchange of productions, falls some fifteen fold heaviest on the Ohian. He must employ fifteen ships to carry to England as much flour as will pay for one ship load of manufactured articles. He therefore should try to get the manufacturer's loom nearer home, even adjoining his farm, that the more perishable products of the garden, orchard, &c., might be exchanged for goods without cost of freight. In every article of foreign manufacture which he buys, he purchases, in effect, as much agricultural produce, as the manufacturer consumed while fabricating the article : But I have hardly patience to group arguments in support of axioms, self evident propositions, that have been illustrated, besides, by the practice of all civilized nations, and sanctioned by all our Presidents. It is probable, that in every hundred millions of goods imported, we purchase from eight to twelve millions of foreign agricultural products, and thereby injure our own agriculture to more than double that amount, by depriving it of market to that extent, and forcing manufacturers to become farmers.

NATIONAL DEFENCE.

The arts of peace, provide for defence in war. By those arts, the physical and intellectual resources of a people are developed, and the acquisition of money is facilitated ; which has been considered so necessary in the contests of states, as to be termed, "the sinews of war."

The general education of the people increases the intellectual resources ; the equal encouragement of commerce, manufactures, and agriculture, by increasing the wealth, furnish the physical resources for the successful prosecution of war. As war is only a trial of strength, whatever makes a nation powerful, best prepares it for war. Whatever weakens a nation, disables it for this trial. The arts of peace give strength. Large standing armies, and heavy taxation, give weakness. When the occasion finds a people well supplied with the "sinews of war" and a sufficient leaven of intelligence to skilfully direct the physical mass, armies and fleets suddenly rise. Railroads, Turnpikes, and Canals, are our best fortresses. These may throw large armies on a given point, as well as aid in furnishing the sinews ; Their capacity to concentrate men and supplies, will enable a defending nation to precipitate an overwhelming force on an invader, in a time so brief, that each soldier might carry his own food for the campaign.

A foe from the ocean would select his place of landing on our extensive coast, and might take a fort, by assault, and use it, as a shield, against our attacks ; but, if he were obliged to land on a naked shore, he could only find shelter in positions afforded by the configuration of the ground ; and from these positions he might be more easily dislodged, than from a fort. Still, there should be forts at proper points : This view of the matter might limit our reliance on them, without dispensing with their use. All things have a tendency to beget their likeness : anger excites anger ; a warlike attitude begets a warlike attitude in others. A peaceful attitude would produce similar results ; and soon create interests entirely opposed to a state of war ; so that the whole world would be a social body, with nations for its members, whose general welfare, would be promoted, by the soundness of each of its parts. If there were no pauper labor in Europe, it would not affect our industrious poor. We feel a part of the miseries of the English people, in spite of occasional protective tariffs. The prosperity of each nation would soon be found to be beneficial to all the nations. No one should wish to injure himself, by harming his neighbor, and impairing his capacity to be a good customer. Stocks owned by a belligerent, have saved cities from bombardment.

The United States need but a very small navy and army— The elements of both should be provided ; that is, military knowledge should be diffused, and materials for ships should be accumulated, ready to be put together in case of war. A flourishing commerce, agriculture, and manufacture, would supply the sailors, the soldiers, and the sinews of war. A state of continual preparedness, for immediate war, on a large scale, costs far more than all its advantages are worth—admitting these to be considerable. In peace prepare for war ; but preparation is ill made by exhaustion of strength in bearing armour ; withdrawing large numbers of men from those employments that enrich a state, making them a burden instead of a support to it. Still, the governing class in Europe are tempted to keep large armies on foot ; else, one might hope to see the general interests of humanity more consulted. The European states might disband three fourths of their armies, without fear of being crushed by a sudden assault from without, and the remaining fourth would be as efficient to repress rebellion, with the aid of rail roads and electric telegraphs, as the whole force formerly was. The holders of office, might be provided for in a way less expensive to the state, and more advantageous to themselves than drilling soldiers.

Lest evils should result from disbanding great masses at once the nations might stipulate to discharge ten per cent of their troops annually. After they become interested in the avocations of peace, a large influence would be withdrawn from war.

The war of eighteen hundred and twelve found the United States, who declared it, quite unprepared for immediate action. A navy was built on the shores of lakes Champlain and Erie, which vanquished the enemy. Militia were soon made available : They won victories—The French republic, in seventeen hundred and ninety, were without regular troops ; but they had good officers, and abundance of men ; these were soon taught to form in line, fire, and run to the rear, where they again formed in a line, reloaded, and repeated their discharges, until they penetrated the well disciplined phalanxes of the Austrians. History abounds with evidence that military knowledge, or skill, can act efficiently with the most raw materials. Provide this leaven of skill, and a prosperous people will easily supply the physical force of men and money. It was chiefly with soldiers of short experience, that Napoleon won the victories of Marengo, Lutzen, Bautzen and others, which immediately followed the Russian campaign of 1812. A Samson, or a Hercules is easily armed ; so a nation grown strong by the arts of peace, will readily make its strength available on the exigency of war.

FALSE VIEWS OF SELF-INTEREST DEPRIVE MERIT OF REWARD.

It has generally been the lot of those who have benefitted mankind, by their genius and talents, to be treated with cold neglect; or become the objects at which are aimed the keen darts of envy and malignity. Mankind reserve their gratitude, if it may be so called, until it cannot be enjoyed by those towards whom it is pretended, they wish to show it. Why pile useless marble, and erect the magnificent mausoleum over the graves of the departed great? Is it to honor them, or to exalt the living? Is it not a trophy raised to reflect honor on the builders, though founded on the merit of the dead? A beacon which attracts the attention of the world to the living, on account of the dead, and the more their glory is displayed the greater is the honor their fellow citizens derive from it. Why then do we not fan the living blaze of genius, at least not endeavor to extinguish it, nor give a helping hand, until, by its native vigor, it overcomes our endeavors to smother it, and its mortal tenement has become lifeless clay? 'Tis not because we are more able to perceive the merits of the dead than the living. Their works, or our capacity to judge them, do not improve by time: Why is it then, that we withhold our gratitude to our benefactors; to those men of genius, to whom we are indebted for all the blessings knowledge and science can bestow; those men who have braved the malevolence, ignorance, superstition, and prejudice of mankind; the hardships of poverty, to cultivate knowledge, and benefit the world, until they descend to the grave, oppressed by all the evils thankless ignorance can inflict; where they feel neither the fangs of envy nor chill gripe of poverty; where the trump of fame, and the serpent hiss of malignity are alike to them. Does this come from false views of self-interest, entertained by their contemporaries, and survivors? Is it feared that the meritorious, if justly appreciated, and rewarded, will take too many loaves and fishes; but after they have ceased to need the things of life, do their neighbors, their nation, their race, then admit the height and breadth of their merit, merely to share its glory? False views of self-interest inclining man to deny the claims of merit before and to admit, them after its possessor has descended to the grave?

The assumption that such views are false, is, at least, as correct, as the maxim, that honesty is the best policy. The proposition, that it is no ones interest to be unjust, is too plain to need illustration: Nine tenths of all who succeed well in life, owe their success to a certain confidence in their honesty of purpose. The success of those who seem to form exceptions to this rule, may be traced to such confidence; and if the abuse of it is unpunished in time, it may be inferred from the nature of things, that evil and its consequences, will ever be evil in whatever state of existence man may be The fruit of injustice, though its external appearance tempt the palate, will, in the end, prove to be bitter ashes. Wealth is what contents the conscience as well as what supplies physical wants; both are essential to hapiness.

Certainly, those who throw obstacles in the path of genius struggling with adversity, from apprehension of its rivalry, do certain evil for a doubtful transient advantage, and do wrong under less temptation than the thief, who steals an article, which affords immediate benefit, and must stand self-condemned forever for the deed.

Doubtless, all the greatness of the truly great, is not discoverable at a glance: Owing to this, in part, Homer, Milton, Shakespere may have been neglected; but how could those next in intellectual power, who influence the masses below, have failed to appreciate, in a considerable degree, such transcendent geniuses! and why was such appreciation without voice or effect on public opinion? May it not be inferred that the secondaries rather concealed than disclosed the merits of their superiors?

THE SOCIAL IS THE NATURAL STATE.

The natural rights of man, may be defined to be such rights as are necessary to the *perfect* enjoyment of life. These rights embrace all the powers, or liberties, necessary to the exercise, and cultivation of all his mental and physical powers ; the perfection of these being necessary to the perfect enjoyment of life. Cannot these rights be said to be properties inherent in the constitution of man ? Is society (which necessarily implies Government) a natural state ? The desires, the passions, the weakness, in short, the kind of being man is, says yes : God, therefore, formed us for Society. One man is but a part of a whole, and that whole, a community ; this community is a thing, a whole being, and is, like all other natural things, governed by natural laws, formed in harmony with its nature, and elements ; for God never formed a being, or thing, one of the properties of which, was not the law controling its existence. Society, as well as man, is an emanation of nature, or God, having his own constitution, and laws peculiar thereto ; the obedience, or disobedience of which, in either case, produces perfection, and health, or disease, decay, and death. The rights of man, and the just laws of society come not in conflict. All nature is harmony ; there is no discord in God's laws ; man, of course, surrenders no rights when he enters into society ; but acquires rights he never could have enjoyed in the unnatural existence of a wandering savage ; for what the writers call the natural state, is the most unnatural state ; for the natural is that which is best adapted to his nature, which is society, it being the only state in which man can reach the greatest physical and mental perfection. The argument is life ; its main propositions are pleasure and duty. If we properly understand, and pursue undeviatingly our happiness, we perform all the requisitions of God. He only requires, that we benefit ourselves. If we did not cultivate vicious appetites we would be prone to do right.

The sanctity of the right of property is the basis of human improvement. It induces youth to provide for old age ; causes frugality and industry to make provision for years of famine ; for the cultivation of the arts and sciences ; for the support of the poor, or those who cannot help themselves : but the abuses of legislation may incline the social towards the unnatural state, by tempting to sloth and dishonesty ; taxing the industrious and frugal for the benefit of the idle and prodigal ; protecting the sluggard's thistle patch from satisfying a just debt, and preventing its transfer into industrious hands ; thus obstructing the natural process of purification, and inflicting disease on the state. How pitiable is the condition of a people in the hands of quack statesmen !

ON ROTATION IN OFFICE.

There are but few offices in this country that require a change of occupants, because of the power they confer. The mass of the offices are of a nature, which confer no power on their possessors, but are the instruments growing out of, and dependant on the general departments to perform the functions of the government. A capacity for, and a willingness to attend to official duty, with fidelity and honesty, is all that is necessary in the incumbents of such offices. A want of any of these requisite qualifications unfits an officer for the discharge of his duties ; he should therefore be dismissed, because of incapacity to perform his duties ; which alone would justify the rejection of an officer ; because the object of the office would not be obtained ; and the Government lose the necessary assistance of one of its functions.

All offices should be necessary ; and the claims to office, of right, are founded on superior capacity and honesty, if the object of the office is the public good. The pay of such office holders should be proportioned to the skill required, and labor to be performed, in their respective duties ; and should be regulated by the common reward, such skill and labor would produce in other pursuits ; and capacity, and honesty should be the test, in the selection of an officer. Would this not be urged with equal reason for his continuance ? And does not a long discharge of the duties of an office, capacitate the officer for a more perfect discharge of his duties ?

If an office is unnecessary it should cease to exist ; as its support is an unnecessary expense. But, if necessary, there can be no right to office in reason, unless founded on superior capacity to perform its duties If the existing officer is faithful, and capable to discharge his duties, none has greater right to such office. If offices are sinecures, I reason unsoundly. Every cent paid to an officer, beyond the common reward for labor and skill, is an unnecessary expense, and is a patronage of Government, which, all equally have a right to receive or share, and it is this excess alone, which may strictly be deemed patronage ; and this, alone, that creates the desire of rotation in office ; and only this, can be urged in its favor.

Who wants rotation in the post of private in the Army ? None ; because no more is received for the service than for other labor requiring similar skill. If the compensation of the soldier were ten fold greater than such skill and labor commonly received, would not a certain class call for rotation in the army, and claim, that all are equally entitled to share, not in the reward of labor, but in the advantages of the position ? And would not such expectants be most devout adherents to the dispenser of the favor ? How dangerous to liberty might such patronage prove ? All power to remove *from* and appoint *to* office is a power to bribe for support. A power to pay with public funds for partizan services ; a power to pervert, what belongs to the whole, for the benefit of a part of the people. It is a fearful power, over which, public opinion should have the restrictive authority of law, to paralize, and make odious, him who abuses it.

The excess of recompense beyond the value of the labor performed by the officer, which aggravates the evils of patronage, it is difficult to guard against ; for what is a scant reward to a competent and accomplished officer, is a munificent reward to an incompetent and ignorant one. Suppose the salary fixed according to the labor and ability needful in the incumbent ; it would soon be found, that though the men to whose capacity the salary had been proportioned were indifferent to getting or retaining the office, yet it would be eagerly sought by persons of inferior capacity to those for whom the compensation was determined. These inferiors seeking to serve themselves rather than the country, could consistently demand rotation in office; as the very expression implies, that offices are for the benefit of the holders, and not of the public ; that is, a sort of gratuity to the individual officer, and not a labor, yielding no greater profit, than the same skill might acquire in other labor. What is gained in patronage, therefore, by those who remove from, and appoint to office, tends to the injury of the public, by the offices falling into incompetent hands. As it is only in proportion as the labor of the officer is compensated more than other labor, that the office is desirable, rotation tempts the unskilful and incompetent to slander and supplant the skillful and competent, and aggravates party strife for party rewards, from which the public interest must necessarily suffer.

It may be assumed, that in a confederacy of states, the state that most disregards the principle of rotation, will have the most influence ; for her affairs will be managed by abler men, than those who are called into service, not because of their experience in public matters, but because it is their turn at the public crib. And it may reasonably be suspected that the principle of rotation in office, is the suggestion of a rival to facilitate his ascendency. Its adoption is certainly an act of self-degradation.

NATURE IS THE ART OF GOD.

We would be Atheists if we could believe that matter exists without a God. All the changes and varieties of organization, found in animal and vegetable existences, may be the nature, or qualities, of the matter; and the harmony therein perceivable may result from the absence of antagonistic matter. We, as parts of this mass of matter, cannot determine otherwise; because we cannot rise above our nature. Suppose another world of matter, entirely different from our own, were joined to ours; might not the union create new existences, new combinations, new organizations, to the destruction of all present organisms? Such consequences might follow: for nature would be changed; and that all her parts might be in harmony, we would also be changed; for we could not live in opposition to nature, then, easier than now. The new existences might act on different principles—obey God by conforming to other rules of action, morally, mentally, and physically. What these new combinations would produce, we are unable to conceive; for we cannot comprehend ourselves. The utmost attainment of man, is, to see in the several harmonics, with which he is acquainted, the greatest influencing element of nature, or of the mass of matter of this world, and of the system of which it is a part, what we call God: or, in other words, a something, incomprehensible and infinite.

In corroboration of the above, I might refer to the effect produced by the influence of another ball of matter upon us, viz.: the Sun. If this luminary were withdrawn, our globe would still retain all its elements; but the organizations resulting from the combination of these elements with the Sun's rays, would not exist; there would be no living animal or vegetable existences: the sterility of the poles would be found at the tropics: and that strange phenomenon of nature, called life, would disappear; because the discontinuance of combination with that other globe would cease to produce it.

APOPHTHEGMS.

No man should acquire the art of reasoning sophistically; it perverts the judgment.

The acquirements of a man should keep pace with his capacity to use expertly, and to tell what he knows. Nature seems to demand more time to learn well the use of knowledge, than to acquire it. How many disobey her; they do nothing but acquire—acquire.

That expression which is the most beautiful, is the most lucid and forcible.

THE form of greatest beauty possesses the greatest strength: other things being equal.

THE brain, or head, of greatest power, is the one which is most symmetrical in form, and of most beautiful proportion to the rest of the form. Such is the harmony of nature.

THAT philosophy is false, which teaches us to despise the pains and pleasures of life. If we are perfect men, we feel them; and to despise them is to despise ourselves, as also the God who made us as we are.

GLORY and "public honors," which some call empty, and mere baubles, are not follies; because they are the source of pleasures; as substantial, nourishing, and invigorating to the mental man, as pork and potatoes are to the physical man; and are the elements of mental and patriotic action.

To be wise is not merely to see our own follies and weaknesses; but rather our perfect adaptation to our position in nature:

IF it were the necessary lot of the wise to see the imperfections of their nature, without a more than proportional amount of perfection; of course to feel them more strongly than others, as some writers assert, wisdom would only confer unhappiness. This is unnatural. Happiness is the object of life: and happiness is the result of perfection; and it is the end, or object, or effect, sought by the operation of all the laws of nature: and wisdom is essential to perfection.

OUR passions are, as they should be, our guards, guides, and friends. We are charged with their education, and must not corrupt them, or they will prove our greatest enemies.

THERE are two classes of religious persons; one worships the principles of his religion, and his God; the other worships the forms of religion: this class persecutes all who disregard the forms of religion. The other class pities those who disregard the principles of religion.

EXISTENCE is a condition between the individual and nature, who will not perform her part, if we do not perform ours.

THE ATTRIBUTE OF STRENGTH.

Power seeks the strong, as stones fall to the earth, or water seeks a level. It is the attribute of strength. It always crushed Pygmean shoulders; always fell from the hands of the weak, in whatever sphere its action.

What availed it that in the Athenian republic the assembly of the people gave sanction, and effect to, or annulled the decrees of the Senate. The populace did not, for all that, govern themselves. The weakness of their natures gave them up to stronger minds: who controlled their every action, as the nurse does the babe. Human law gave them all the power it could confer; but nature's law transferred it from the weak to the strong: breaking the cobwebs of human forms.

If you educate the subjects of a despot, or, in other words, strengthen the power which is exercised in governing, the power passes virtually into the hands of the people; and though the forms of government may exist, the despot becomes a subject, or rather a servant to many masters, courting their favor, and pandering to their caprices. Thus power will only be found in the hands of the strong; it is nature's law, and human law cannot affect its operation. Statutes may give it a nominal residence, but nature's law gives it a virtual one.

The successful termination of the Revolutionary war, would have only exchanged a foreign for a domestic tyrant, had the Americans been as ignorant as the serfs of Russia. And the chartered rights, or rather civil and political powers of Englishmen, are the result of their intellectual strength, and not of royal concessions, or acts of parliament; they being the mere effects of such strength.

In what way can we distinguish the good from the bad, but by their acts—their deportment in their business with other men? If words and professions were the index, liars would have a decided preference over the good. If acts that do not conflict with interest, or passion, be received as evidence, hypocrites have a manifest advantage.

The laws of animal creation and existence cannot be accident, though our individual creation may be; because the action of nature's laws may by accident have been brought to bear on the particular case.

RELIGION.—There is nothing which has had greater influence on mankind. Nothing which has appeared in more various shapes, or been more abused and perverted from the purpose for which it was designed. It has been the instrument equally of goodness, vice, avarice, and ambition; by it, the warrior has inspired his troops with confidence. Priests, kings, and knaves, have, by its means, attained their ends, whether good or bad. And why? Because it makes stronger impressions than other things. Religion has always tended towards one end; but its forms and its results are various. It is in its forms, that the abuses alluded to have been effected. Its modes of action, therefore, should not be disregarded. The fire that warms, may consume, if ill directed.

VIRTUE has various forms, and is the subject of disputation. According to the common opinion, it is moral goodness: that term prohibits the doing of any act that is bad in itself, to effect a good purpose. Thus they cite the idea, which barbarous nations had, of revenge being a virtue, and show the effects it would have in our social state: without considering that acts may be good, or bad, according to circumstances, and that the end may be of more importance than the means. An amputation of a limb may save the whole body. Where general laws fail to protect, it does not follow that wrong must triumph. The right of sanctuary, has made the use of the stiletto, in Italy, frequent. The revenge of individuals supplies, in some measure, the defects of law. The avenger of wrongs being viewed in the light of a public prosecutor, he would be thought to disregard his duty, if he let offenders escape punishment. Those who have lived under the common law of England, have been the least inclined to avenge their own injuries; because the law purports to remedy every grievance. There is no wrong without a remedy, being one of its maxims, every one hopes the law will give him relief. Among savage tribes, the general safety is concerned in the certainty of revenge. As all is well that ends well, possibly that is virtuous, which conduces most to the public good.

SLAVERY IS AGGRESSIVE.

The reception, by a free state, of the vicious, degraded, ignorant, and infirm outcasts of slavery, is unjust to the state; and cultivates slavery by diminishing the expense of supporting its infirm members, and of governing its vicious and ignorant outcasts; the worn out tools of a selfish and heartless institution; which would not fail, according to its natural instincts, to prey upon the magnanimity of any policy adopted by the free States towards the negroes. The free States should not allow themselves to provide alms houses for slavery; but, as far as practicable, require it to bear its own burdens, and retain within its own limits, its degrading emanations. The laws of most of the slave States require the free negroes to leave the State, within a certain time. The intelligence which originates those laws, would naturally suggest to its tools in the free States, to facilitate the admission of such victims to all the rights of citizenship there. This, with colonization in Liberia, would do much towards weeding the garden of slavery, and giving this man-degrading institution, a more vigorous growth. This institution is, in its nature, aggressive. It is difficult to restrain itself from acts of hostility; and, consequently, truce or peace with it cannot long be maintained, more than with hunger. It robs others, by insolvency, or conquest, to supply deficiencies. One half of the population, laboring reluctantly, cannot well support the other half in idleness and extravagance. It is always hungry, and must always prowl; as did Roman slavery, which, after there were no more neighboring nations to rob, commenced taxing the provinces, or devouring her own extremities. Its basis being the destruction of human rights, the superstructure must exert a malign influence on all within and around it. It is necessarily a curse to the master, to the slave, and to free labor. The latter feels its blighting breath in its action on the Federal Government, abolishing tariffs of protection of home industry, making wars to extend the area of slavery, &c. Its control of the patronage of the Federal Government might enable it to pervert the legislation of the free States to its purposes, and even to introduce itself there, with all its evils. It has fastened itself on Texas, notwithstanding the immense capital in land, and small comparative capital in slaves, existing there; showing that her interest in excluding slavery from her limits, was incalculable; for that peculiar institution peculiarly depreciates land. Yet the good of the many has been set aside for the convenience of the few; not the few of Texas, it may be presumed, but of other States, who have slaves to sell, and a balance of power to maintain.

When the Texans comprehend their true interests, they will abolish slavery. The act would treble the value of their lands. In a confederacy of States, those most monarchical may get control over the rest, as did Macedon. Their veteran will relieve apprentice statesmen from the labor of thinking, while rotating in office; provide them with maxims of conduct, and political teachers, paid with federal offices. The free States might thus be furnished with false guides, in their own citizens; by whose direction their legislation might benefit others more than themselves. Party names gild the pills of false doctrine, and "subject the policy and will of one country to that of another."

CELIBACY attends luxury; because luxury makes wealth indispensable; throws society into grades; and as men think they have reason to fear their means will prove insufficient to maintain their grade, and support a family, they choose to remain single.

MATRIMONY attends simplicity, frugality, and economy; for one may hope to be able to supply all the real, or natural wants of a family, as these are limited; but artificial wants are without end. The human race would become extinct, if *luxury* were universal. The simple, industrious, and frugal, are the conservators of humanity; they are its body and soul; the luxurious and slothful, are its excresences, warts, or tumors, continually inflaming, suppurating, and disappearing.

WEALTH has power, mostly, because of artificial wants. He who can satisfy these wants, holds a strong lever, by which to influence human actions. He governs, with the magic wand of gold, a world, misled by the siren voice of desire. In the natural, which I claim to be the social state, a degree of exercise necessary to the healthy condition of the body, would supply all real wants. But in the artificial state, imaginary wants make men dependent on those who possess the means of satisfying them; for these wants are as urgent for gratification as those which are real: When Dr. Franklin ate his sawdust pudding, in the presence of his patrons, he exhibited his independence of wealth, in the moderation of his desires; as did, also, Diogenes, when he wanted nothing of Alexander, but that he would not intercept the rays of the sun. Both are extreme cases; but illustrative of the independence of those who have no other than natural wants.

With moderation of desire, one could seldom feel poor; without it, one could never be content: it is indispensable to happiness. What folly, to torment ourselves with artificial wants.

HAVE ALL THE SAME PROPENSITY TO GOOD AND TO EVIL?

THIS is a mere question of *fact*, determinable by observation alone. If I were asked whether the natural propensities of the tiger were more dangerous than those of lambs, I could only answer, yes; look and you will see. So with the question we now discuss. Does the history of the past—does your own observation of the present time, afford no answer to this question?

Does not all time teem with instances of men, having instinctive tendencies to good and evil, varying in degree from high to low? Has that Nature, whose laws produce such variety; who gives to one, beauty; to another, deformity; who now brings forth a Solomon; and now an idiot; a Hercules and a dwarf; a bold man and a coward; not given to one a greater propensity to do good than another? Had not Washington a greater propensity to do good than Robespierre? Had not Howard, who periled his existence, expended his property, and devoted his life to the prosecution of benevolent objects, a greater innate desire, or propensity, to do good, than a Cataline, who made the same sacrifices for lawlessness and injustice? It may be said that circumstances form the character: they have their influence; but a thief is a thief, wherever you place him; clothe him in purple or in rags: as a ruler, he robs a nation; as a pauvre, he robs a hen roost.

So, with the Philanthropist: as a man of wealth, he establishes a school, a hospital, or alms house; as a man of genius and talent, he urges reforms in law and in morals; and, if he is without wealth or talent, he still gives the widow's mite. Station makes no difference as to the manifestation of the propensity; though it does, as to the effects of the manifestation. Virtue comes, sometimes, from the filthy haunts of vice, uncontaminated by the immorality that surrounded it; and sometimes vice is engendered under the shade of altars. It is said the consciences of the wicked are seared, as with a red hot iron; thus a restraining power, which influences materially the propensity, is impaired. The propensity to crime, by the occasional partial loss of conscience of the parent, is transmitted to the children, by the law of hereditary transmission of qualities; thus, " the sins of the parent are visited on the third and fourth generation." As to the cause of the different propensities for good and evil, it may be found in a different cerebral organization; an organization, in some measure, the effect of influences, operating from and before the first moment of existence; but the question is, " Is there a difference?" not what is the cause of it.

INJUSTICE RUINS.

The purifying, or sanitive tendencies of the operation of nature's laws, are evinced in all her works. Diseased action of the functions of animal, or vegetable organizations, or of governmental organization, in the political, or of religious organization, in the moral world, results from an effort of nature to expel some noxious influence from the system. The effort is always proportionate to the amount of the obstruction to healthy action ; and it may be assumed, that the duration of the contest, and its evil effects upon the system, are in the same proportion : whether it is so, or not, one side, or the other, gains the victory ; and death, or health, though often, with impaired organic action, is the result of the contest ; which is often procrastinated by an equality of strength in the contending powers.

The history of ancient and modern nations is all confirmatory of the proposition, that the constitution, laws, and administration of all governments, must be founded on justice ; it is the element of their strength, prosperity, and duration ; while, injustice is the cause of continual disease, and final disorganization, or death ; being, from its very nature, anti-organizational ; and though tyrants of every kind and degree, whether existing in democracies, or monarchies, limited, or absolute, may strive to maintain their unnatural relations, by every support, which human force and ingenuity can give, yet the strong hand of nature, or truth, will prostrate all their puny barriers on the least relaxation of the artificial force. A nation may be said to have lost its liberty from the time that it looks upon the invasion of the rights of its citizens with indifference, although it may not discover the loss, until the unjust invasion has become a precedent, or rule, by which other invasions are justified, no more illegal than the first encroachment, but less expedient, and more difficult to be endured. If, in violation of the tenth commandment, A's property may be taken for B's use, for one object, it may for any other : If it may be taken to enhance the value of B's ten thousand acres, by railroads and canals, it may be taken to erect for him public baths, a church, in short, there is no end to the abuse, on pretext, that it is for the good of the public. If legislation is permitted on subjects beyond its lawful and proper range, civil government and military defence, individual rights will be the sport of its power, until the repetition of abuses drives the people to throw off the disease, and resume their natural rights, and teach their rulers to confine their action to the objects for which man enters into the governmental compact. If the first invasion of the rights of the citizen is tolerated by the people, it is certain to be followed by others, which eventually prove fatal to the government. Whose first unjust movement should therefore be effectually rebuked : It should not be allowed to tempt citizens to be unjust, nor to become, itself, the tool of cupidity. Ought not the Chaplains of legislatures to explain the great iniquity of what is called log rolling ? The sinfulness of combinations of the few to rob the many ? That injustice cannot prosper, and necessarily leads to destruction ? and that man cannot repeal God's commandments ? The disease of injustice has never failed to prove fatal to States. Its approaches are stealthy ; offering present advantage, at least to somebody, for eventual ruin ; and soon becomes formidable from neglect.

THE PUBLIC SUBJECT TO PRIVATE INTERESTS.

THE public interest is ever exposed to be sacrificed to private interest. Generals have been accused of prolonging wars, and statesmen of occasioning wars, merely to promote their private fortunes. In the United States, large investments were made by individuals in forest land. To enhance its value, emigrants from Europe were invited by favorable laws to come and govern us. The land speculators were willing to risk the infusion of foreign habits and monarchical principles into our masses, if it might advance the value of real estate.

These foreigners now hold the balance of power, and can decide elections. Negro slavery, by all admitted to be a curse to the States where it exists, and the trade in alcoholic liquors, and their manufacture, so ruinous and degrading to mankind, began and continued for private advantage, and for public sorrow and shame. And we may infer from the past that there are men who would annex Russia to these United States, if their individual interest would be benefitted thereby—if it would increase the value of their lands, or negroes, or if Russian influence, or votes, would give them power to rule their fellow citizens.

Cupidity is the great disgrace of this nation. It seizes Jonathan by the crown and crushes him down upon his knees to beg for the offal population of darkened Europe to come and govern him: he covets the slavery for the sake of the increase of his dollars. It thrusts him towards Mexico, and kicks him into conflict to obtain (at an expense of twenty millions besides) an opportunity to present his bare back to be striped by Mexican votes. He forces Mexico to govern him at the instance, not of mere land speculators, but of holders of stock in negroes, and of political power founded thereon. These, wishing to enlarge their power, based on slave stock, are willing to risk the entrance of Mexican ignorance, and prejudices, into our system of government, for the sake of so partial an object. The State and Federal governments are constantly wielded for private and for sectional purposes. Where a railroad, or a canal, promise great profits, capitalists can scarce be kept from making them ; but where they present no prospect of gain the public crib is appealed to for their construction, by interested individuals, who seek to enhance thereby, the value of their town plats, or large tracts of land, and are willing the public taxes should be increased, that their individual interest may be improved. Property is taken from one to enrich another by legislative robbery. The frugal, industrious, and self denying, who accumulate a trifle for old age, see that trifle heavily taxed for the benefit of the fortunate large property holder, or the poor and the idle, the lazy, the drunkard, the glutton, who indulges all his passions, and denies himself nothing ; who gets in debt, and then skulks behind bankrupt laws, assignments, exemptions, &c., enacted by kindred spirits, though elected by those they rob, through sheer carelessness and wanton disregard of the plainest dictates of common sense. Thus public are made subservient to private interests in a way to make questionable the proposition, that the interests of "self and social are the same." The industrious middle class are taxed, not only to increase the value of the property of the extremely rich, but to increase, and promote idle habits in the poor ; and so long as the people mistake the tools of knowledge, for knowledge itself, they will probably progress from absurdity to absurdity, without suspecting that they are the soil, which cupidity cultivates for its own purposes. The love of virtue, and the exercise of a sound common-sense, is the obvious remedy, but chiefly the latter ; for when will monarchs, especially tyrants, cease to combine with the extreme low, to oppress the middle classes ? Speculators and demagogues do the same : Tyrants, demagogues, and speculators, consider the industrious middle class, as their prey, and are too much under the power of temptation to listen to the voice of virtue. The middle class, then, must not depend on the moderation, or virtue of the speculator, the tyrant, or the loafer ; but exercise a sufficiency of common sense to avoid divisions in itself on comparatively unimportant matters ; such as party names ; and the election of this, or that individual ; and maintain a firm union in support of all measures that affect its true interests, and in confining government to the objects for which it was instituted, viz : the protection of person and property, and military defence ; for if allowed to transcend these limits, there is no point at which it may be required to stop more than another ; on pretext of promoting the public good, the industrious will be taxed to build babels, wash the faces of loafers' children, educate them, build houses for demagogues, dig canals to increase the value of the land of speculators, &c., &c. When it was decreed that man should live by the sweat of his brow, avoid theft, and covet nothing of his neighbor's, it was not implied that he might, without sin, legislate in contradiction of these commandments—or lead the people into temptation contrary to the policy of the Lord's prayer. In republics, their principle of life being virtue, such legislation is suicidal. The children of the rich are often paralized by the prospect of being able to live without labor ; and in proportion as a government relieves any class of its subjects from exertion, by imposing the burden of its support and education on the industrious, it treats them unjustly, violates the divine commandments, corrupts the class it assumes to favor, by giving them a taste for enjoying what is not their own, and in so far as they are relieved from living by the sweat of their brow, it takes from them that incentive to exertion to which humanity owes its chief glory. The best specimens of mankind have generally been found on comparatively barren soils, whose cultivation required much labor. Human wisdom would promote human happiness more, if it would not lose sight of that which is divine ; nor deviate from the path of justice ; nor tempt to be vicious the people, whom it seeks to imbue with knowledge. To make them wicked, while enlarging their power, facilitates the march to perdition: one educated rogue can do more mischief than a hundred ignorant ones. Republics progress into monarchy, by gradually departing from the rules and principles of their founders, and seeming to forget, that virtue is their life, and vice their death. The writers have dwelt less on the need of knowledge, than virtue, probably, because virtue is instinctly correct, and accomplishes the end. Knowledge can only make virtue more efficient, not more right ; still, the government should, by *just* means, take care that the people that are really poor, are taught reading, writing, and arithmetic ; for the rest, a proper respect for scholastic attainments—the laurel wreath—will inspire an ambition, and do more to advance knowledge, than all other expedients.

THE SOURCE AND SUPPLY OF VITAL ENERGY.

THE brain is probably but one organ, and performs but one function ; that is, feeling. Thought, sentiment, memory, &c., are but different modes of that feeling. When excited so as to feel, the blood flows into its vessels, causing a boiling motion, more or less intense, and proportioned to the strength of the feeling. Each kind of feeling results from a different motion. Thus, destructive, or vindictive feeling, is the result of latteral pulsation ; while reverential and kind feeling is the result of vertical pulsation. The pressure against the skull, and the frequently repeated pulsations would cause it to protrude ; thus, giving an outward evidence of the internal action.

The brain is not the source of nervous energy ; but rather the place of its deposit, a point, where nervous energy is expended.

The nervous energy enters the brain by the spinal marrow, and is collected by all the nerves of the system ; being the highest rarefied material fluid, resulting from the digestive process. This fluid reacts through the system to give muscular movement and propel the various machinery of life. This action of the voluntary powers denotes a centre of force and action, or will. The muscles that involuntarily move seem independent of the brain, and indicate a distinct nervous apparatus: These muscles, then, may be the points of expenditure of a distinct ramification of nerves, whose activity is not governed by the variation of mental disposition ; but only affected by the physical ability of the whole system to generate the requisite stimulus : This distinct arrangement may be owing to the vital importance of their continual action.

The mental and muscular exercise, then, should be regulated by the capacity of the body to produce the nervous stimulus : If more than the proper amount be absorbed by the nerves of motion, in the muscles, and in the brain, the drain prevents the muscles of involuntary motion from receiving the requsite amount; they become debilitated, and a general langour pervades the system. The proper measure of the nervous fluid that is permitted to be abstracted from the involuntary powers is denoted by a sense of weariness in the brain, muscles, belly, or other purloining members. After that feeling of weariness to continue action, is disobeying the voice of nature. It is robbing life of its proper aliment. The first expenditure of the nervous energy, is to supply the organs necessary to the existence of life : Second, to create mental and muscular action. This latter action, for the above reasons, should not reach the point of fatigue; but should be continued periodically until weariness begins to be felt; because it is an organic law, that parts or organs strengthen in proportion to the requirements made of them; and diminish in size and power in proportion to their disuse. It is this law that has wrought organic bodies into harmonious proportions ; the useless members withering and disappearing ; and the useful strengthening, in proportion to their wants, and shaping themselves in conformity to their uses. This conformity being the result of compromise between the member and the vital and other organs ; it takes that shape which would require the least vital stimulus to enable it to perform its appropriate function in the animal or vegetable economy. In conformity to this law, the mental and muscular action should reach periodically the point, where weariness begins, that the functions, creating the nervous energy, may grow strong, and be capable of supporting vigorous vital action; and also, of amply supplying the brain and other organs of voluntary motion. Unless such a course is pursued, the supply of nervous energy will dwindle to a bare sufficiency to continue the action of the vital organs, and finally cease : vital action itself not being required ; for action is the end of life ; and in conformity with the law of nature, above alluded to, unless the continuance of life is demanded of nature, by action, life will dwindle and die.

DEEDS CONFUTE WORDS.

The Foreign Reviewers, and their American Echoes, more deserve our pity than indignation.

The European comes here, where the sun of liberty warms into life, and stimulates into activity the latent seeds of genius, that dark ignorance, chilling poverty and all the man-debasing influences of transatlantic despotism had kept dormant. Here he walks in the light of knowledge ; here all the virtues of his being are quickened by vivifying incentives. Should he not be a better, nobler creature here, where the god-gifted virtues can find nourishment and develope themselves ? No : say the European reviewers. But do they not see, that in reviling and attempting to belittle the Americans, they are debasing themselves ? If there is a defect here, it is a family weakness : We are the offspring of the European nations : In throwing stones at us they hit themselves.

The Genius of the American people has been turned into those channels, which circumstances required ; and it has shone preeminent. The extent of our territories, variety of climate, and diversity of interest demanded a peculiar form of government ; and American Statesmen furnished a more perfect one than any other people can boast. The immense extent of our rivers, and the vastness of our internal commerce, made us need a more efficient, and powerful means of transport ; and American Genius produced the Steam Boat. The extent, and exposed condition of the maritime border, required the means of defence ; and an American has put it in the power of the government to defend the whole sea board at a small expense ; and another American has provided the electric telegraph, by which intelligence is conveyed in a moment from one end of our extensive country to the other ; thus enabling the government to bring our wide-spread resources into simultaneous and united action : besides, the patent offices of this Country, France and England show, that there are more inventions in this Country, than in both France and England.

This does not show that we are better and they worse; but that there are more minds here disenthralled from ignorance, enjoying freedom of action, and having incentive to exertion.

AVAILABILITY.

Among the corrupting errors that fasten their harpy claws on Republican humanity in these times, and in this country, is the idolized doctrine of availability; whose undisputed supremacy of control in American Society, social, and political, seems to enforce submission, without resistance, even from those who are unwilling to become its slaves. Its ascendency is complete; it is the great paramount, who dispenses all posts, be they of honor or profit. It makes, supports, continues, or destroys relations, social, and political. Availability is the ruling genius at the nominating caucus; over the Editorial corps; at the stump; in the bar-room; at the fireside, and ballot-box. Not content with dictating who shall, or shall not be the nominee, or representative, it extends its mastery over the minds, and consciences of men.

Availability issues its Bull; commanding what principles shall be adopted, what doctrines shall be preached, and what issues taken.

Availability is "a monster of such hideous mien, that to be hated, needs but to be seen," in its true character; " but seen too oft, familiar with her face, what we abhorred, we pity, then embrace,"—and alas! does the community openly and shamelessly embrace this digusting principle, the flagitious parent of iniquities. Is a man objected to? a thousand tongues proclaim: be still, be still; he is the most available candidate; popular follies; popular prejudices; sectional feelings; party grudges, and party preferences must be consulted. But your man is unfit; he is too old, or bigotted; ignorant, and idle; diseased in mind and body ; of doubtful morals ; and ten thousand voices shout : true ; but he is the available man; and the world say Amen. Thus availability outweighs all other considerations ; and reason, and argument, vainly attempt to breast that most conclusive of conclusions; and an available can only be set aside by presenting, in the way of set off, another Mr. Available!

Is the course of Republics always downwards, with greater or less declivity into Monarchy? Does the nature of popular government require, that ignorance, and prejudice should be regarded more than knowledge, and wisdom? Is it impossible to enlighten a people so that a majority shall be intelligent, wise, and virtuous? Though more weak than strong minds exist, if the strong would unite, in the support of correct principles, they would uniformly prevail. It is the want of virtue in this class, more than the ignorance of the multitude that has ruined so many republics. If God's attributes are impressed on the laws, or rules of action, governing the moral, or social, and political conditions, or relations of God's creatures formed for such conditions, then virtue, intelligence, capacity and individual fitness should be the only passport to public consideration, esteem, confidence, and trust : then, merit, confident of the meed that awaited it, would leap fearlessly, and ardently into the arena, animated with noble purposes, and press forward in a career productive of public utility and advantage, and the fields of science would witness the same energies, and the paths of useful, and peaceful labors, be trod with the same ardor, that has urged military aspirants to death or glory.

Availability is likely to exert a pernicious influence on the individual and national character of the American people : It is founded on the short-sightedness, that prefers cunning to wisdom ; on that folly which sacrifices the greatest future benefits, to obtain a supposed present advantage. The youth steps forth in the morning of life ; he looks in upon himself; communes with his heart, glowing with upright purposes ; feels his own instincts, and pure motives ; he looks out on nature ; grasps at God's truths ; judges, adopts, and inscribes on his

,standard, his principles, his image: that standard waves over him, blazoned with his beliefs, and fired with sincerity, he will bear that standard, and die under it, rather than admit any thing to be more available than justice, goodness, wisdom, and truth. He will not sacrifice any of these to popular error, for the sake of office, or gold ; but when he sees almost a whole nation yielding to the tempter, he will need the firmness of Abdiel to breast the corrupting torrent.

WHAT DEPRECIATES LABOR,

The price of labor is depressed by the supply exceeding the demand for it. In this, labor does not differ from every other thing. What then increases the supply or lessens the demand for labor ? Were every cent of capital annihilated in a country, few could hire laborers. What tends to diminish capital, therefore, tends to lessen the demand for labor. Among the causes that depress and diminish capital, is, taxation ; sudden changes of measures or policy, occasioning its derangement, or holding it in suspense ; banishment of capital, by unfavorable laws ; shifting, or transfering it to new pursuits ; and annihilation of capital by fires, earthquakes, foreign insolvency, unprofitable canals, rail-roads turnpikes, &c. For when invested in anything, it ceases to be the means of payment of wages, except from its dividends. Wages are low in all heavily taxed countries. A high tax is just as injurious in a democracy as in a monarchy. Oppression is most felt at the pocket, under all forms of government. 'Tis the same to the tax payer of a high tax, whether the money goes to build a babel, or pay a sinecurist. If the tax is only moderately high, capital may stand its ground, and continue to employ labor, at reduced prices ; that is, in some hands ; in others it changes its pursuit ; takes flight to other lands ; or it may remain suspended, waiting opportunities : but in all these cases the demand for labor (which must depend on capital) is diminished ; for where capital changes its pursuit laborers are discharged : the same occurs when it takes flight to foreign countries ; or remains suspended ; or is annihilated. This discharge of the operators increases the supply of laborers beyond the wants of the capital that remains employed ; and, by an irrevocable law of trade, a slight supply beyond the demand, occasions, not a slight, but a great depreciation of the value of the article with which the market is surcharged. As capital is the basis, the food, and the market of labor, the latter has reason to protect and cherish it as its mother. No blow can be inflicted on capital without injury to labor in an aggravated degree ; as the capitalist *can* travel, but the laborer *must* live. As to dividing profits between capital and labor, nothing but the nature of things can govern the matter : To provoke labor to war on capital, is to prvoke a seller to assault purchasers, or his customers, in his only market ; because they will pay no more for his commodity, than the price, which the relation of supply and demand has fixed upon it.

THE CREOLE CASE.

The Creole departed from Richmond, Virginia, bound to New Orleans with a cargo of slaves, under the charge of one Merrit. While out at sea the slaves arose, killed Merrit, and took the ve-sel to Nassau, where they now remain. They have been repeatedly demanded by our government ; but the British authorities will neither surrender the negroes, nor make compensation to their owners. We claim, and England refuses. Are we right or wrong ? To determine this, we must apply the principles of existing laws, and not form new ones, as interest, or convenience dictates.

The laws of nature give to men dominion over all things ; but to all men equality and freedom.

Every man, being by nature free, the power that enslaves him cannot spring from the same source as the law, which gave him freedom and equality of right ; but must be arbitrary, and hostile to the law of nature ; and is the offspring of force·

Nor does the fact of being born of slave parents alter the position, that force is the foundation of slavery. As every man is born free, by the law of nature, it is at his birth that his freedom is wrested from him, by the force of local laws. This force of individuals, exercised singly, or collectively, must be the only right (if it deserves the name) which institutes, and the only law, which sustains the unnatural relation of master and slave. The negroes of the Creole were placed in the condition of slaves by the force of the municipal laws of Virginia, the jurisdiction of which was necessarily limited to the boundaries of that State. Having passed beyond these limits, the authority of her local law ceases, and the collective power of the State of Virginia ceases to sustain the relation of master and slave. We now view them on the common territory of the world—the great deep, where the laws of nature, and of nations alone bear sway : beyond the jurisdiction of the local laws, that made them slaves, they were to continue as such, only by their own consent, or the superior force of those who had them in charge. With no power to support the existing relations of the two parties but their own force, to that they appealed. The law of force, which had subjected them formerly to slavery, now gave them liberty. This decision of arms reverses the relation of the two parties ; and the negroes had as good a right to take the whites to Africa, as those whites had, previous to such decision, to take them to New Orleans. But the negroes did not exert, to that extent, this prerogative of force ; and sailing into the waters of the British dominions, they, of course, relinquished those rights, which force had given. They came voluntarily, and with intent to remain within the jurisdiction of the British law, which recognises no property in man, whether it be acquired by the force of those large collective bodies called nations, or by a troop, or an individual. Had the negroes held the whites in custody, as property, they would have been compelled to release them on a writ of habeas corpus ; if the whites had held the blacks on similar grounds, the effect of a writ of habeas corpus would have been the same ; for a claim on a man, as property, is no sufficient cause to justify a duress under British law. The magistrate, therefore, had no discretion ; the law was positive ; and nothing, but the Supreme power of Parliament, could suspend, or abrogate it. Had the negroes, therefore, asserted the claim to the persons of the whites as their property, because the exertion of superior power had made them such, or had the whites of themselves, or through their government, made the same demands, founded as they must have been, on similar grounds, the magistrate could not have granted the request of either party ; nor could Parliament ; unless it acknowledged a principle repugnant to, and hostile to the whole system of British law.

Should either of the two parties claim indemnification of the British government on account of loss of property, supposing the government to have recognised a property in man, and of course the principle, that force is the foundation of such right of property, would not the claim of the negroes, as being the last owners, give them an equal, if not superior title to that of their white competitors ? By whose force, but that of the negroes, would the parties be found in the Island ? a force still operative, if rights could emanate from it.

The claims of our citizens, through the government, for indemnification, founded on a right of property, are therefore without foundation ; for they have no right of property in the negroes ; and if such right could exist, it would not be in the owners of the Creole, but those persons, who last owned such owners themselves.

What is demanded of England ? Is it merely the paltry sum of compensation for a few negroes, or those negroes themselves ? No, it is to admit a principle by such restoration or compensation, which is unknown to their statutes—and this we claim in violation of that well established principle of law, confining the jurisdiction of states to their own limits, where their own, and no other laws are of force. We claim that the political and civil disabilities of the Virginia negro shall follow him into the British empire. This is giving local law wings to fly, and lungs to breath in an atmosphere, that is not its own, in some unnatural element. And it is to establish this principle, that we are to go to war with the most powerful of the nations of the earth! Well, we propose a difficult end. Great Britain is not the only nation that will refuse to accede to an unjust demand, and that will sustain the existing legal principles, that govern the subject. The Americans will have the glory in the Presidency of John Tyler, of having at least attempted a difficult enterprise—if not an unjust one.

Thus much for the claims of the owners of the Creole negroes through the Government. Let us consider on what grounds we may claim them, as persons, amenable to our laws. A government may claim to exercise a jurisdiction over her citizens, wherever they go, and may hold them amenable on their return, for the violation of her laws; but though a government may claim such right, yet, it cannot enforce it, while the citizen is within the jurisdiction of another power.

France claims to regulate the conduct of her citizens wheresoever they may be, yet none will declare that the civil, or political rights and disabilities of Frenchmen follow them here.

It would be giving the local laws of France a general force, not consonant with the sovereignty of other states. We therefore cannot demand the Creole negroes, as citizens, or persons on whom the United States government has claims. If we may claim a citizen because he is amenable to our laws, is not our claim equally good, when we demand the service of an absent citizen in time of war? Surely it is, unless a right of a government to the possession of the person of a citizen for service in war is inferior to a right to the possession of his person in order to punish him; if, therefore, we can succede in establishing that principle, the European governments will retain such jurisdiction over all Europeans in this country, or would make a demand for their service in time of war effectual. It therefore behoves all foreigners resident here to fight well to support the principle, that would enable their respective governments to draft or to demand them for service in China, India, or some other theatre of war. It is not denied that all governments have a claim on their citizens, and also, that one country as a mere matter of comity, has often surrendered fugitives from justice on the presentation of the claim of their respective governments. Although I know of no instance of a government surrendering a citizen for services in war, because demanded by his government, the justice of the claim being questionable, as it involves the right of expatriation.

Thus even admitting that the negroes on board the Creole were guilty of mutiny and murder, it is quite evident our government, on the principles of law and the usages of nations, has no right to demand their surrender from the British government

But is it certain that the negroes did commit mutiny and murder, as is alleged, supposing the negroes to have been within the jurisdiction of the general government? Its powers are limited, and it has only such as the states gave it; they never gave it the right to hold slaves. It can assume no right; it has not, then, the power to recognize such right. No law therefore of the general government was violated by the negroes when they took proper measures to escape from an illegal duress; consequently, they did not commit mutiny. If in so doing there was a necessity to take life, they committed no crime; it was not murder; but justifiable homicide.

This appears to be the situation of the case; and the British government, in answer to the demands of our government, have but to quote the decisions of our own courts.

To engage in a war, where our own courts declare us wrong, would be but a silly pretext, if we even desired a quarrel. We have many and serious causes of complaint against England, in which we are unquestionably right. The line between right and wrong is boldly drawn, and distinctly seen, in the case of Oregon, where the flag of England waves unmolested over the territories of the United States. And in the Maine boundary question, where England lays claim to a soil which she once declared was ours. Why do these questions, which so deeply affect our national honor; which are so injurious to our rights, remain unsettled? Which are so important, which need no nice legal distinctions, no judicial decisions to determine their propriety or impropriety, remain in the back ground, and the poor, petty, trifling case of the Creole, be the all engrossing subject, the great point of dispute between this nation and England ? Indeed we see and hear of nothing but the Creole ; our other causes of complaint being mentioned apparently for form.

Is it not because our Government is in the hands of those whose interests are more affected by the Creole case, than any thing that might affect Yankee boundaries, and Western territories ?

Is it not because our Government is ruled by those who regard their own interest, more than the nation's honor ? whose hearts are so filled with the love of sectional and peculiar interests, that general patriotism cannot find room to dwell therein ? Is it not strange that this patriotic sectional love should so craze the brains of these Government worthies, and their own Secretary of State, that they could not see the right inclination of the scale of justice ; for the eye of reason is dimmed when men are strongly prepossessed on one side : therefore it is not wonderful that the darling object of their hearts should by them be made the ostensible cause of war with England.

The people of that part of the country, who have not those peculiar sectional feelings should exercise a self-constituted guardianship over those official gentry ; for it is of some importance to those, who have to support the expenses of war, and fight its battles, that the grounds of dispute be distinctly understood ; that we may know what we are to gain, if we succeed ; or loose, if we fail ; and insufficient causes ; mere pretexts, should be discarded ; for to have just, and unjust causes commingled, taints the whole. The disgusting deformity of our unjust claims, will first attract the gaze of men, and prejudice rightful claims. And is it not of importance, that a cause of war, be considered just, by mankind ? When we have hitherto appealed to the God of battles, our cause has been just : let none other be ours ; and let us show to the world, that the descendants of the fathers of the Revolution have inherited there virtues, as well as their valor. May the world never point to America and say " she bled, that injustice might triumph."

EACH excels in that which most pleases, or engages his attention; or in that for which his mind has affinity, or taste; and taste springs from the conformation, or disposition of the mind, inclining it to particular forms and styles of beauty. One artist copies the form accurately, another the color, a third the spirit, energy, and passion of a scene. Taste should be regulated by reason, lest the mind should be unbalanced. He approaches nearest to perfection, who is equally pleased with all, and equally able to comprehend all; whose imagination never soars beyond the sight of his reason; who equally perceives the sublime, the beautiful, and the true: such was Michael Angelo, Leonardo Da Vinci, Raphael Urbin, Virgil, Homer, and Milton.

SOME who would imitate their superiors, accomplish only the imitation of their faults.

WISE men do not adopt the weaknesses, but emulate the perfections of the great.

WHAT is done, should be done well. Do your best, if you would improve.

ON USURY LAWS

READ IN THE ST. CLAIRSVILLE LYCEUM, DEC. 26th, 1841.

AN Usury Law, is an attempt to change the natural relation of things, and to fix the price of money without any regard for the demand and supply. As well might legislative wisdom attempt to determine the relative value of every thing, as to fix that of one.

The controling influence, which the supply and demand exerts in regulating the value of money, and every thing else operates as continually as the law of gravitation; and as the attractive power of that law, determines the specific weight of any particular article, so the relation of the supply to the demand, determines its relative value.

The *weight* of things is fixed by the one law, their *value* by the other. The laws of gravity, always acting with the same power, the specific weight of things remains always the same; the supply and demand continually changing, changes as continually their relative value. Nothing is valuable, but that which the desires or necessities of men demand. As it is the supply and demand which determine the value, *that* must be the natural law, which governs it.

An Usury Law, attempting to fix the value of money, should prevent the fluctuation of demand and supply, or it necessarily fails in the end proposed. One, who, contemning the laws of gravity, walks over a precipice, but makes an exposition of the power of that law, he affects to despise.

In the creation of an Usury Law, do we not equally disregard an established law, governing value, which fixes interest at one price, while Usury Laws declare it to be another? Here is an issue between a law of man, and a law of nature: this declares the use of money worth so much; that says otherwise: which law prevails is best seen in the effect. The first effect of an Usury Law is to increase the value of money, by diminishing the supply. It diminishes the supply by destroying the inducement to loan; in not allowing capitalists to receive that value for their money, which the relation of supply and demand gives to it; charges it with insurance in proportion to the risk incurred by lenders; drives it from its natural channels; expels the moderate lenders from the money market, leaving it to sharpers, unchecked by competition, and paralizes much of the capital of the country, or, at least, prevents its being invested in loans to animate the business, and aid the exertions of the industrious. It increases the profits of money-lending in proportion, as it decreases the competition of lenders. It creates an odious monopoly in favor of that class of usurers who, by high interest, insure themselves against the penalties of law. This class is not composed of the most conscientious : these are no longer in the field ; but it is composed of the sagacious and adventurous usurers, who, despising a statute that violates their rights, prove to the necessitous borrowers at an exorbitant interest, that the relation of demand and supply still regulates the value of money, notwithstanding the existence of the statute.

Does not an Usury Law fail to produce the effect it seeks ? It is intended to prevent extortion. It increases it. It appears to seek the relief of the borrower : It inflicts on him the tax of increased interest, and superadds that of insurance against penalties. Necessity compels him to borrow. The improvident law closes the door against the attainment of his ends, and leaves him to perish, or to pay to extortioners increased interest ; and woe betides that man, whose poverty incapacitates him to insure these violators of law against its penalties. This insurance can only be afforded by the rich, whose interests, as also those of the lawless extortioners, this law peculiarly favors by increasing the value of their particular commodities, (money, and land.) The sharper, without competition, gets what he pleases to ask of the borrower ; and the moderate lender, not willing to accept the legal rate of interest, invests his money in land, which consequently rises in value, in proportion to the demand for it, thus created, and surely this Usury Law affords a most signal proof of the superiority of the law, which nature has established to govern the value of things.

Our situation in regard to others may, also, increase the pernicious effects of Usury laws.

If we are surrounded by states, whose policy differs from ours in that respect, we drive the money of the country to the markets of our more liberal, or rather wiser neighbors ; for capital, in common with produce, seeks that market, where it is most valuable.

British capitalists held stock in the Bank of the United States ; because it divided more interest than the Bank of England.

Flour, in 1836, was imported from Europe, where it was

needed, to America, where it was not; because the inflated currency of this country made it more valuable here. If the demand made money more valuable in Virginia than an Usury law in Ohio allowed, Ohio capital would seek investment in the Virginia market, and Ohians would be compelled to go thither to borrow. Suppose Ohio should attempt to regulate the price of produce, and, as in an Usury law, disregarding the demand and supply, fix the value of wheat at one dollar per bushel. Should the limited supply, and great demand, increase its value to three dollars per bushel, where would our wheat market be ? In Ohio, or the surrounding states ? Our farmers would sell their produce there. Our consumers would be compelled to go thither to buy.

What would be the effect of a different policy? Suppose the legal amount of interest were six per cent, without contract concerning it ; but contracts were permitted to be made for any amount : Thus giving a legal remedy for the violation of the contract.

The apparent liberality of the terms would attract so much capital into the state, from states where Usury laws exist, that the increased supply would reduce the value of money far below the price sought to be given to it by usury laws.

If our commercial interests require the freedom of contracts, which Usury laws restrain, our future welfare, as a nation, demands the rejection of those principles, which such laws admit. They declare the contract to pay interest, over a stated amount, a crime, punishable by a penalty. It requires two to make a contract, which, if illegal, makes all the contractors equally criminal ; and it is a principle of law, that all parties engaged in the commission of crime, are equally liable. This principle an usury law disregards, and punishes only one of the offending parties ; the other party, it bribes, (by giving the lender no remedy against him) to violate the law, and to act unjustly. Thus, in its unequal operation, disregarding justice, and encouraging crime.

An Usury law affects the rights of property. The right of property is a right established by the laws of nature, and as sacred as that of liberty or life.

If nature has bestowed on us a right, she has given it perfect, and its valuation is necessarily the exclusive prerogative of its posessor. The borrowing majority, by an Usury law, attempt to deprive the lending minority of this prerogative : thus assuming to such a degree the right of property, as to declare the price, at which its owner shall give it to them ; and, in proportion as the real value exceeds the legal price, that proportion is endeavored to be legislated out of the hands of its owner. The principle, which admits the assumption in the majority, of the right of property, to such a degree, as to determine its value, not the value which they will give, but that which the owner shall take, would sanction a further assumption of property, and would lead to an equal distribution of wealth. The principle that admits the infraction, permits the destruction of the right of property, and of those other equally sacred rights of liberty and life. What usurpation, what injustice, does not such a principle sanction ? If the political disadvantages, which result from the passage of an Usury law, do not argue sufficiently against it, the admission of so unjust a principle, a principle so pregnant with future ills, should, of itself, be sufficient to outweigh any selfish motive, or vulgar prejudice, that could be adduced in its support. The principles, which any law embraces, should be carefully scrutinized : Let not an imaginary present benefit, resulting from its passage, induce the admission of an unjust principle in legislation ; lest there be reaped the fruits of folly, in the deadly harvest, that springs from the seed of injustice.

Laws emanate from principles, and sound or unsound, the law partakes of the nature of its source.

Principles precede, and laws follow : Principles are the rule of action in the formation of law.

Having seen that Usury laws do not prevent, but aggravate Usury ; that, to decrease the interest of money, we must encourage, and not discourage the making of loans ; and thus, increase the supply of money as, also, induce competition, whose tendency is to diminish prices, we may infer that such laws, are the unwise creations of misguided, and ignorant legislation, at war with the interests of those they are intended to protect; in opposition to sound principles of political economy, and the nature of things, regulating value, and ought to be rejected.

MAN MAY BELIEVE CONSISTENT WITH HIS REASON.

OUGHT one to believe anything inconsistent with reason? Reason means *right*, as distinguished from *error*, or *wrong*. Reason is truth, as distinguished from falsehood. All nature is harmony; and truth, and right, and reason, are but the consistency of thing with thing, as part of nature. But error and falsehood are unreasonable, unnatural, inconsistent with all other things, and discordant in their nature. This must be, if nature is all harmony; for truth, nature, right, and reason, mean the same thing. They are the component parts of nature. How then can a belief in anything, inconsistent with reason, be but a belief in error? And what good is produced from a bad? What right is born of wrong?

If all nature is harmony, and has, as is demonstrable, a principle of self-preservation, that harmony is disturbed by the consequences of an unreasonable belief; and that principle of self-preservation is exerted against the offender, to rectify the disturbance; and this exertion is always proportioned to the flagrancy of the violation: and this is true throughout nature; in the physical, metaphysical, and etherial parts, or divisions, of the great, perfect, and harmonious whole. It is useless to produce examples: it must be self-evident, that all beliefs contrary to nature's self, or nature's laws, are equally absurd; and actions resulting from such beliefs, are proportionately pernicious: For beliefs are of consequence, only as they control actions: Belief is the principle whence actions spring: and can good, or useful actions come from bad, or mistaken, or erroneous, or unreasonable principles? If a man believed that wood was harder than iron, and tried, influenced by his belief, to chop an iron log with a wooden axe, he would break his axe, without gaining his object. If a man were to believe it best to hate men, and not love them, and act accordingly, it would render his path of life a path of thorns; and thus, force him to discard his unreasonable belief, and, in a measure at least, to adopt the more reasonable doctrine of Love. The several parts of a machine must move in harmony with each other; and man, his body, and his mind, are but parts of the machine of nature. Unless he can control nature, he must act as a part of nature: and, as such, act in harmony with the laws of his own nature, and of all things beside—that is, with reason: for it is a part of the universe. God made the world; it bears the test of his hand, and evinces the high attributes of its Creator; and God is not an unreasonable being.

Man ought, then, only to believe things consistent with reason, as any other belief is error, and injurious in its effects.

But what is belief? It is a conviction of the mind; an impression, produced by perception, or reflection, or both; a result of causes, over which we sometimes have no control. Belief takes possession of us, independent of our will, and we cannot escape its control. It may be unreasonable, or reasonable; yet, be it what it may, it has possession of us, and we cannot reject it by our will, for the will is the creature of belief. It can only be removed by causes, similar to those that produced it.

The perfection, or imperfection, of cerebral organization, or of mind: Or the sufficiency, or insufficiency, of the facts, or circumstances, or materials of thought, control the nature of beliefs, and render them more or less reasonable, or unreasonable. What, then, ought man to do? Believe, he must; if he sees, or hears, or feels, or thinks, he must have impressions, and reflections, and, consequently, beliefs: and all try to believe right, and reasonable, according to their perception of right, though they may deny their beliefs. Yet, even then, they may believe it best to deny. Ought man, then, to believe what is inconsistent with *right* reason? Yes, he ought to do that which he cannot avoid doing: It is consistent with reason that he should: He must believe, sometimes, what is inconsistent with *right* reason, if it be consistent with *his* reason, or his power to distinguish truth from falsehood.

ON PAINTING, AND BALANCING THE MIND.

EXTRACT—ST. CLAIRSVILLE, JUNE, 1841.

TIME has fled, almost unnoticed, since I left New York. I arrived here on the twentieth of February, and earnestly commenced the study of the law. In the latter part of May, feeling a strong desire to design, I began the landing of Julius Cæsar in Britain; and completed the draft in the month of May. The piece contains some forty figures. The subject is a good one, as it affords variety of action. On one side can be displayed the wild fury of a disordered mass of barbarians; on the other, the determined courage of the Romans in the endeavor to advance. The confused disorder on the beach; the descent from the gallies to the small boats; the rowing, pulling, struggling, and the great variety of posture that would necessarily attend an engagement so circumstanced, might be embodied, with effect, in a painting, had the artist skill adequate to the undertaking. But the grossness of the material, with which the painter recreates the creations of his fancy, destroys the vivacity of the original conception: his field is measured, and he must confine himself to it, however extended be his ideal range: he cannot paint the roar of conflicting hosts; nor the sightless swiftness of action; nought but the visible emotions of the actors can be painted; while the invisible, but more interesting, cannot be depicted. There is much to be learned, in every science and profession; so much, indeed, that the author of the Essay on Man, is almost justified in saying, that
> One science, only, will one genius fit,
> So vast is art, so narrow human wit.

This might appear true, had not the Creator bestowed on us

different faculties, fitted to different pursuits, whose cultivation, or neglect, strengthens, or weakens, those faculties, or powers of the mind, which those callings respectively employ. There is scarcely any science, whose study does not require an unequal exertion of the faculties of the mind. This unequal exertion will, in time, give the powers exerted superior vigor, and strength, and thus destroy the nice balance which Nature has given: and thus it, to me, appears impossible to arrive at a high degree of perfection in any branch of useful knowledge, without the acquisition of many others. What acquirement is not useful to a lawyer? If he were prosecuting, or defending a general, or an admiral, would not a knowledge of military, or maritime affairs, be of great use to him, in conducting the prosecution, or defence? Would he not be enabled to elicit, and to see the bearings of the evidence, in a clearer light, in such, and in all other cases, whose facts lie within the sphere of his previous studies? I believe it may be safely assumed that the more one knows of many things, the more capable he is of understanding and illustrating any one thing; yet the study of many things, with a constant regard to their bearing, on a particular thing, is but the study of such particular thing, and its relations to other matters; and, consequently, the student's proficiency in a science, would be in proportion to the relation which the aggregate of his studies bore to the science, whether his mind were bent on the particular science, exclusively, or on sciences illustrative thereof. Thus, by the study of languages, though they are afterwards mostly forgotten, one is permanently improved in the knowledge of his native tongue: The explanation of the foreign, by English words, impresses these on the memory, in association often with the words from which they are derived, and though the student indifferently understand the foreign, he finds himself advanced in the English language: Still, this is not the best way to learn it; though the surest, the cost exceeds the utility; if the object be to obtain a knowledge of the English alone.

ON THE ADMISSION OF THE INDIANS INTO THE UNION.

LYCEUM, 1838.

MIGHT we not admit the Indians, after duly preparing them for the event, into our Union, with all the social, and political privileges appertaining to the whites? The time of admission should be determined by their capability to assume the duties of civil government, which can only be ascertained by their advance in the arts, and sciences, which are essential to the prosperity and happiness of civilized communities : a condition which it is our moral and political duty to attempt to produce. That it is practical, as well as just ; that the Indian possesses those mental qualifications and capacities, which, by cultivation, may become suited to such a condition, cannot in reason, admit of a doubt : the same capacity that can plan, and execcute a campaign ; the same force of thought, that has distinguished many an untutored son of the forest, in debate with the white man, at numerous councils, and treaties, held between the two races ; the same hardihood of constitution, command of feeling and ingenuity in the adaptation of means to ends, that he has evinced in his connexion with his pale faced exterminators, and which has won for him, even from his persecutors, the appellation of "noble Indian," would, under the influence of civiliza'tion, when impelled by different motives, and improved by cultivation, be manifested in a different, and a stronger manner. Thomas Jefferson, to remove the prejudices, that existed in Europe, against the insalubrity, and deteriorating influences of our climate on the mental and physical constitution of man, called the attention of the world to the Indian character, and capabilities ; thinking it doubtless, a strong and irrefutable argument to remove the prejudices of the Europeans against our climate. The unlettered Indian has had no historian from among his own people, to tell mankind of his virtues, and to rescue his deeds from oblivion; but the perpetuation of his memory has been left to his foes. Yet, even the faint and imperfect outline, which they have sketched, present him to our minds, as not naturally inferior. In forming our judgment of his capacity, we must weigh the circumstance of his condition. His intellectual force, as evinced under the unfavorable influence of the savage state, admitted to be considerable, by the common consent of his white neighbors, afford a sufficient guaranty of his usefulness, as a citizen, as also of his capacity to assume that condition. Yet, the Indian has his vices, and who has them not? "Judge not, lest ye be judged." The prisons; the gibbets; the navies; the armies, marshalled for war; the bleaching bones of a thousand battle fields; the clanking chains of enslaved millions; the squalid pauperism of oppressed masses, bear most mournful evidence of the selfishness, violence, and fiendish vices of people calling themselves Christians. Let them not arraign the Indian; nor refuse to share with him the benefits of their science and virtue, because he partakes of their vices; vices which have sorely afflicted him; and which may God pardon us, for bringing upon him.

Though the Indian partakes of our vices, we find him endowed with many virtues: he is constant in friendship; has a noble sense of justice; is confiding in his nature, and generous in his disposition; and has, in an eminent degree, the religious sentiments; for whose exercise, and gratification, he has, without the aid of revelation, formed a religion for himself, which, in the opinion of Red Jacket, was productive of more practical utility, than what seemed to flow from the professors of Christian creeds.

Apart from the question of practicability, arising from a supposed intellectual and moral incompetency of the Indian for citizenship, the Indian's rights and our duties, demand his admission. It is a debt claimed by justice, in his behalf; and which we should pay, though it should give us some inconvenience; and give to the few remaining Indians the privilege of having a civil equality in a country of which we have deprived them by purchase, for an insufficient consideration, or by open violence.

If no claims of justice can move us to give equality of privileges to the Indian, self interest, and sound policy, require that all the inhabitants of a country should have identity of interest therein. Where one class has greater rights than another, that other, is, of necessity, an enemy : and civil discord, and national weakness, are the necessary consequence.

When you refuse to another, equality of civil privileges, you oppress him : he justly considers you his enemy ; and he is yours ; and if a foreign foe, in contesting with us, should offer to the oppressed inducements, he would fight for his foreign friend, and our enemy. It would be right that he should do so ; for, should he fight for us, his oppressors, he would war on himself ; his every effort would be suicidal ; and the suicidal spirit is prohibited in Holy Writ ; and charity required to begin at home. All classes composing a nation, should be united in its support; and wise Statesmen will be careful to cultivate such unity of action, remembering, that " a kingdom divided against itself shall fall."

ON BANKING.

READ IN THE LYCEUM, AND PUBLISHED IN THE ST. CLAIRSVILLE GAZETTE, APRIL 29, 1842.

The increase of Bank paper decreases the value of money, and increases that of commodities ; in effect, therefore, it operates as a depreciation of coin, and is injurious to the money holders ; because it depreciates the value of their property, while it increases the relative value of the property of those who are possessed of land and other commodities.

About one half of the wealth of a country is in action for debts due, on contracts to sell at a given price ; these contracts are based upon, and these debts owing, in money. The amount of the value represented by the money is known, and it is for this *value* the contract is made, and the debt owed ;

the amount of value, however, is designated by a stated amount of its representative, money.

As the issue of Bank notes varies this relation between commodities and money, it alters the obligation of all monied contracts, and lessens the amount of the debt by causing a direct loss to the creditor ; it is thus, that all rights of action on debt, all property in *transitu*, by contract or otherwise, through the medium of money, are affected by the emission of bank paper, and one of the contracting parties is released from obligation in proportion to the loss of the other contracting party. The unjust effect of the issue of bank paper is best seen by presenting an extreme case : If the issue should be so excessive as to make a hundred dollars represent what one represented at the time a debt was contracted, would it not amount to an absolution from all debts contracted previous to such inflation ? It is therefore an indirect way of cancelling debts, and releasing obligations ; and such is the effect of the least issue of paper money, so far as it has any effect at all. Is not this a dangerous power in the hands of demagogues ? What is there to insure the nation against its abuse ? Parties in power have heretofore bought the favour of the people by gratifying their *avarice*, and parties, yet to exist, will abuse it more. As the evil complained of is aggravated by every new charter of a bank, the above reasons could be urged why no new banks should be created.

To injure the capacity of the banks, already created, to pay their debts, by an unnecessary severity of law, or to shorten their existence, would throw on the debtor that injustice, which their creation did to the creditor. When we view the question in this light, justice, as well as policy, would require the most *imperious necessity* to justify this disregard of individual rights, or some great national advantage to be gained : here is a direct injury to the money holders, and loss to the creditors ; which loss is a gain to the debtor and borrower. The supporters of the system of banks of discount and circulation assert, that the issue of three dollars in paper for one in stock, is justifiable ; because the institution is thereby enabled to loan at one third the market value of money ; and thus, the law, by giving the bank credit, enables it to extend the same benefit to others in an equal degree. This is self evident and needs no argument to support it ; there is more money loaned and at a less interest, than would otherwise be, and consequently *money* is more accessible to the mass of the people. Here, I would observe, that it is necessary to make the distinction between money, or rather the representative of value, and value itself. If the issue of bank paper created value, the benefit conferred on the borrower would be as great as the amount of money he received; but the value, which money represents, is not increased with the representative, it therefore represents less value than it did before the issue increases its amount. He, therefore, who pays less interest through the effect of bank inflation, must observe, that the same cause that decreases the interest, decreases, also, the value of the money he receives ; for the commodities it represents do not become more valuable, but the money less valuable. He who paid eighteen per cent for thirty three dollars, to buy one hundred bushels of wheat, before the issue of bank paper, paid no greater interest on the actual value received, than he who paid but six per cent, on one hundred dollars, to buy the same amount of wheat, after such issue. In both instances the same per cent, is paid on the amount of wheat, or value received, but not on the money. Thus it is, that banks, of themselves, do not give *credit* any advantage over that it hitherto posessed ; as no more *real value* is loaned at a less interest for its use.

There is, however, an advantage to credit, by the effect which the competition in loaning exerts in diminishing the rate of interest on all loans made by private individuals ; this indeed is the great and only benefit to credit, which the banks exert. But from whom is this benefit to credit derived ? From that class of citizens, whose property was *reduced* in value, by the emission of bank paper, the competition of which now reduces its profits. This loss by the moneyed interest of the country, first, in the depreciation of the value of their property by the issue of paper money ; secondly, by the loss of its profits by the paper competition, is all that is gain ed in favor of credit by the present banking system. Poor argument that, which is drawn from *injustice*, and odious is that credit system, whose growth depends on the infringement of *rights*. The money invested in *stock* is not decreased in value ; because its representative, the paper, swells with the decrease of the value of money. If the proposition be true, that the emission of bank paper changes the relation between money and the value it represents, unless there is a correspondent increase of commodities to the amount issued, the conclusion is unavoidable, that the amount of value first represented by the original stock, is all a bank can loan, no matter how much paper they issue ; for each new issue makes the prior one less valuable.

Those who borrow of the banks, in the first of their issues, received an amount of value, which decreased at each new issue. It is then in the power of the banks, by expansion, or contraction, to regulate the amount of interest received on their stock, or value, which is loaned. As the borrower has no control over this expansion, or contraction of the representative of value, which the bank loans him, he cannot regulate the interest he pays on a stated amount of the value he receives. Viewing banks of circulation in this light, does it not appear that all bank stock is a fund established for *usury* or *extortion*. ?

This usurious interest on the amount of value, or stock, which is invested, enables the banks to divide large dividends: twelve, to twenty per cent, was not uncommon in states, where private loans produced but six or seven per cent. It is for this reason, bank shares sold so high above par. It may be objected to this argument, that all have the power to become stock holders : The objection is unsound, unless there are banks sufficient to receive, as stock, all the money of the country : a point heretofore sufficiently proved, by the willingness of many to pay sixteen per cent premium, on shares, for the privilege ; showing, that if all had an equal chance, no one would have to purchase it.

For the reasons alleged above, I cannot conceive of any commercial necessity, or advantage, that would justify the state legislatures in the retention, or exertion of a power so fraught with injustice, and so dangerous, if abused ; which, if used with moderation, lessens the obligation of debts ; if immoderately, in some measure, cancels them. Finally, it is the power, indirectly, used, of releasing monied obligations. If the states would enter into a compact not to use it, there would be no surrender of right ; the people would have a security against injury, which they have not, as long as they admit the existence of such power. As there are many, who excuse injustice, if it conduces to convenience, or appears to be a source of profit, I deem it necessary to prove that the Banks of discount and circulation do not supply the necessities of trade, any more than banks of deposit ; nor do they give that energy to trade, which is ascribed to them ; for they are a source of loss to the nation ; or if productive of any incidental advantage, they are injurious to the people as a whole. I know no better method to prove this, than to recur to the causes, which make a currency necessary, and that have had some influence in producing the changes it has undergone ; as also to answer some arguments urged in support of banks being necessary, convenient, and profitable.

The necessity of trade first introduced money to settle balances due, or to purchase with, when the buyer had nothing to barter to the seller, which he wanted. Its great value, compared with its bulk, facilitated and gave energy to trade ; its solidity prevented much loss by abrasion &c. ; the difficulty of obtaining it from the mine, secured its possessors against any great depreciation of value by increase beyond that of the commodities it represented ; and the ready exchange it always offered, made it safe to hoard. The commercial world, however, had long felt the inconvenience and danger of transporting large amounts of specie, to supply the difference of exchange. The wants of commerce were supplied by the introduction or obtrusion on the world of a Deposit Bank, viz : As the hoarding of specie tempted robbers ; the rich merchants of Amsterdam, made deposits with the police, and took certificates thereof; and these were transferred from man to man, and passed as money. By the creation of similar Deposit Banks at the great commercial points, the certificates of each were transferred instead of specie ; thus facilitating large dealings, as the metals had formerly done in smaller transactions.

These Deposit Banks gave the first idea of those of discount and circulation ; for men observed, that one third of the specie deposited, sufficed to redeem all such certificates, as were, in the common course of business, presented to be cashed. This discovery showed that one third of specie on the amount issued, was sufficient to maintain the credit of the paper ; though it did not prove that the amount could redeem all the paper; but only such amount, as in the course of business, would be presented for redemption, during the existence of the bank, and that too in good credit. If, therefore, necessity should ever require the use of *credit*, this accidental experiment showed a way to use it to suit a sudden emergency. It might possibly be justifiable in a nation to make such issue on credit, in case of war ; when its existence depended on obtaining a supply of money, as its future revenues (which would be applied to the redemption of such paper) would be represented by that paper ; and might give energy to the contest, and safety to the nation. *Credit*, thus, is a *tax* upon the future ; it calls into action future resources, which nothing but the most urgent necessity can justify ; because every age should support itself ; and future times may need as much as the present. The experience of the Amsterdam Bank showed a nation how to extricate itself from difficulty, arising from want of funds ; by means it would be improper, as also unjust to use, unless such emergency created necessity.

But while the Amsterdam Bank gave this useful experience to the world, it also showed *avarice* the means of gratification : it saw that one dollar, in specie, could sustain the credit of three in paper ; but should a necessity arise, to redeem all the issues in a short time, one-third in specie would be insufficient. The future resources, on which credit is based, the bank had not; the calls of *avarice*, therefore, could not be satisfied, unless means could be found to supply the deficiency between one, and three. These means were supplied by a self protecting principle in the banking system, which appears to be the following : The banks issue an amount of paper ; for this, they get the amount of value represented by that much money at the time the issue was made ; this is all correct: the holder of the paper money can get it redeemed, in specie, on presentation. (I allude only to specie paying banks.) Another issue is made, and another ; each succeeding issue *decreases* the value of the money of the former one ; while it does not diminish that value which the bank received in lieu thereof. By this operation, that value, which the banks received for, say one hundred dollars by the first issue, in the change of the relative value of money by increase, say of three dollars to one, would redeem three hundred dollars, merely by the operation of this self-protecting principle. This, however, is based on the supposition, that the value received by the first borrowers is immediately vested in something of substantial value. It was thus, that *avaricious desires*, or acquisitiveness, induced the creation of banks of discount and circulation ; while the necessities of commerce, induced the adoption of metals, and banks of deposit.

Avarice, like all other passions, wants not specious pretences to justify its gratification. It is said by the supporters of the banking system, that the increase of commodities, being more rapid than that of money, the wants of commerce require legislative provision to supply the deficiency. In answer, I would say; first, that the inability to determine the amount necessary, prevents a proper remedy. Secondly, it is untrue, that such increase of commodities creates a want of representation, as it only alters the relative value between such commodities and money ; and it is not material, whether a given amount of value be represented by one, or two dollars. It is said banks of circulation facilitate exchanges : For the reason given above I cannot give them any preference over deposit banks ; but the depreciation of their local paper, may increase the cost of such exchanges. It is said the small notes, such as ones, and threes, give an activity to the currency, which gold, and silver cannot. I admit it ; but would not the issue of one dollar certificates of deposit be of equal benefit ? It is urged in favor of banks of discount and circulation, that they increase the amount of money in a country, and that where money is plenty, it is easier for the poor to get their share of it; that where money is scarce, and wages low, the laborer must remain poor. If man lived on money, and drew sustenance from it, I should think so too ; because the fare would be more plenty : but as it is a representative of value, and as the laborer works for value, it is of little account to him, whether that value be represented by twenty-five cents, or a dollar. Here all the supporters of banks abandon argument, and attempt to sustain themselves by matter of fact. In Europe, they say, the laborer gets but a few pence a day, and is, and must remain poor. This is attributing to a *specie* currency, what should be attributed to those laws, which, in all monarchical countries, exalt the rich, and depress the poor. All these countries have an idle and expensive *nobility* and court to uphold ; and it will impoverish any class of men who are charged with their support; and who but the operative is it, that supports or enriches any nation. If the property of his employer is taxed, it comes indirectly out of the wages of labor; if he is taxed directly, it is but taking from him, what in the other instance, it prevented his employer from giving him. It is therefore the amount of *value* the laborer gets, and not the small amount of money, that impoverishes the laborer of Europe.

Yet this is the argument drawn from facts, that Governor Davis, and others, have advanced to support the proposition that the amount of money received, determines the riches or poverty of the laborer. Do not the facts show truly, that the amount of money received as wages is immaterial, provided the laborer receives a sufficient amount of value ? Governor Davis also asserts, that the *tea* and *coffee* and other foreign productions, are bought with gold and silver : that it will take more time for the laborer to earn the money to buy them, if his wages are reduced to a specie basis ! This is a *sophism*, taken in totality, of which the component parts are truths. I do not think those productions could be imported cheaper than they are; and if it took the same amount of money to buy them, that money would be harder to get, at reduced wages. But as those commodities are not bought with bank paper, its value being merely local, they are obtained by exchange of productions, or by specie ; so that they are got only by giving real value for them now, and cannot be obtained hereafter, but by the same means: so that it is immaterial whether there be bank paper or not; they cost the nation, as a whole, the same. But will the capacity of the nation to purchase such articles be increased by having an exclusive metallic currency, or what is the same in effect, a mixed circulation of specie and certificates of Deposit Banks ? I aver it will not have less, but even greater capacity for such purchase. First, there will be more *specie* in the country to represent that value, which is now, in a measure, represented by the *paper:*—it being the nature of a representative to seek that place, where most value is represented by it. This is the nature of all money, and its continual operations to equalize representation every where : it is from this cause that the gold of Spain, sought representation in the other European states. Considering bank paper, therefore, as good money (and it is as good as any, where it brings specie on demand) its effect is to give property a greater representation than the same has in countries, which have a metallic currency : The tendency of things is to keep a continual drain from such country, through a thousand various ways until such representation is equalized. As the paper has only a local value, it is the specie that will leak out of the nation, through every chink, gap, and crevice. If we adopt the metals as a currency, and have not our share, the reverse will be the case, and it will *flow in*, until we get such share. It is thus by the natural operation of money, because of its being a representative of value, that we would have more specie to purchase the foreign necessaries of which Governor Davis speaks. But I contend that there would be less necessity to use such specie for such purpose, as our exports would be greater, and the exchanges might be in our favor ; and specie would be paid to us by other nations, instead of its being exported to pay them.

We have a productive soil, and more can be produced with less labor, than in most countries of the world : There is less requisition in the shape of taxes, tythes &c. on the products of labor, than there is in any other country ; therefore, what is consumed by bishops, kings and nobles in other countries, could here be given to the wages of the labourer. Thus our operatives would be better paid, and our capitalists reap golden profits, in successful competition with all the hard money countries of the world. But this we cannot do, while we have an *inflated paper currency.* We cannot export so much, or to such good advantage, for the monied cost of production, (unless the exceeding fertility of the soil makes up the difference,) and this cost prevents exportation to countries, where there is but, comparatively, little money to represent value. Here it may be said, we did export during our greatest inflation. If we did, were not the commodities, so exported, sold at a profit? and would not we be able to sell those same commodities for as much, if we had a *metalic* currency ; and could not the exporter afford to pay as much specie to the laborer, who produces them, as he now receives of paper money ? I aver that his profits would be *greater*, all things considered. First, there would be more demand for labor ; because all the commodities now exported, would continue to be exported. Many articles that cannot now be exported would then be exported. Second : The expense of living would not be so great : because the money now expended for imported manufactures would not then be paid ; because those articles would be made at home, and furnished cheaper, as the expense of transportation would be saved, and the cost of maufacturing be less, or only equal. The excessive profits, received on our productions, are owing to the natural advantages of our country ; which have enabled us to export, notwithstanding the counteracting influence of an expanded currency. We have not such great manufacturing advantages, and are not able to compete on such disadvantageous terms. If however all things are equal, we can compete in manufactures, but not otherwise. It is for the above reasons that with a *specie* currency, we can compete in manufactures with the European nations, without reducing the operative to the degraded condition of theirs ; for, I repeat it again, our natural advantages, and the comparatively trifling burden of the government, enables us to give *more value* to the operative than he receives in Europe ; and it is immaterial whether that value be represented by a *little* money, or a *great* deal. But I shall be told, that those advantages, represented as arising from manufacturing competition, can be obtained as well without a metallic currency, as with one. This cannot be proved by argument; and Governor Davis again has to resort to matter of fact, and says :—

"That England, with a paper circulation, has competed triumphantly and successfully with the other states of Europe, who had a specie currency." This is true ; but I consider it an unfair example to prove the effect of a similar policy in this country ; nor will the policies pursued in monarchical governments, always produce the same effects in republics.

The operative in England gets more *money* for his labor in England, than in any other country of Europe. But the unremitted toil of old and young, and their wretched poverty show conclusively, that the operative of England, if he gets more money for his labor, than the operative of the rest of Europe, does not get more *actual* value if as much. What is taken from capital for the support of most Governments of Europe, in England, is taken from the operative for the same purpose ; as also to favor capital. In confirmation of which, I will instance one law, viz : That which compels the dead to be buried in woolen. This is but detracting from the poor man's wages to advance the interest of his employers.

The poor operator thus virtually gets less for his labor, though he nominally gets more than the operatives of the rest of Europe. And the commercial prosperity of England, is owing to the great industry of her inhabitants, and amount of commodities produced by unpaid labor.

Her merchants have grown rich, her kingdom powerful, on the unrequited industry of the poor—wretched prosperity that, over which a people mourn, and a class rejoices ! Notwithstanding the United States exported during the inflation, by means of her natural advantages, I have reason to believe that the unpaid labors of millions, assisted her much to maintain such capacity. So much for Governor Davis's argument, founded on *facts*, to show that an inflated currency is not detrimental to commercial competition; and for the favorable inference he would give to the Banking system ; because of its having been adopted by two of the most enlightened nations of the world.

In this Essay I have considered the Banks as well conducted, and able to redeem their paper dollar for dollar, in specie. The evils that have been attributed to them are such as are *inherent* in, and *inseparable* from the system, leading to the inference, that they are *unjust*, or unnecessary, and impolitic, and that their benefits could all be secured in *state* deposit banks, which might issue their certificates of deposits, as small as they saw fit. I have said nothing of those expansions and sudden contractions that can be said to be more than probable ; nor of the many and dear interests of the people that are made to suffer by the mismanagement of the banks ; nor of the effects, which a mutable currency produces, in damping the energies of a people, and preventing the employment of capital.

ADVICE ON ADDRESSING A JURY.—EXTRACT.

THERE is no difficulty in trying a cause, if you understand it well. In addressing a jury, remember your object is to convince them; dash into your case; explain it; present it, so they cannot misunderstand. Do not think of the spectators, as whether they are pleased, or displeased, with your manner; but only think of gaining your point: keep your eye on victory, and push on, and all will think that you are an old, experienced, and crafty speaker. It is the infantile timidity, and fear of failure, that makes many a man, endowed with natural talents for speaking, miscarry. Speaking seems to me like swimming: some swim well at the first trial; because they are not afraid of sinking; others require years of practice. So with public speaking. Some leave the anvil or the plough, without much education, and surpass in eloquence hundreds of well-educated tremblers. Be filled with your case, and pour out what is in you, in the humor you are in at the time of speaking: talk as you feel, and act as you feel, and you will talk and act naturally: and you may throw all the rules of the writers on the shelf, if you adopt that natural rule: It is the rule of rules.

THE memory of all the parts of a case is strengthened by uniformly considering all subjects systematically. The mind thus may be habituated to arrange, remember and recall, at pleasure, whatever is needed. Habit thus may be made an index to all the stores of memory.

To have a readiness of recollection, on occasions, one must be able, by a memorandum, or sign of some leading feature, to bring the whole subject before his mind, as if it were a human image, with its head, arms, legs, all in their right proportion and place.

ALL GOVERNMENTS ARE *EFFECTS* OF WHICH THE PEOPLE ARE THE *CAUSE*.

THE Government, as the head, partakes of the nature of the body of the people. All Governments must suit the condition of the people; for their existence depends on the people: the people are the roots from which the tree of Government grows: It is the moral condition of the people that determines its nature and form. Governments are purely dependent: Every change in the moral condition of the people, produces a corresponding alteration, for better or worse, as the case may be, in the administration of the Government; or, if the case demands it, in the form of the Government. Every Government is necessarily a representative Government. Yes, every Government that now exists, or ever has existed, has represented the intelligence and virtue, or the ignorance and immorality of the people.

It follows, that every Government has been the best Government, all things considered, that its people, under the circumstances, could possibly have had. Russian barbarity is well represented at St. Petersburgh; and so is Russian energy. Increase, to a high degree, the morality and intelligence of the subjects of any Autocrat, Sultan, or ruler, whatever, and his Government becomes gradually modified, in accordance with their improvement, being borne along on a sea of moral power. Mark, at Washington, the faithful representation of the profligacy of a portion of our people; of the principle, that " might gives right," threatening encroachment on other nations. In the face of the world, we hear cries for plunder; and the Government is about to second the call. The virtuous and intelligent of the land, though represented, are out-voted by the mammon-worshipping class, and its servile dough-faces—vile slaves, that throw themselves into the snaky folds of injustice, and barter for a mess of pottage, the priceless inheritance of liberty, of which they are unworthy. The influence of the vicious is preponderating in our system, and portending evils; for Justice has never failed to strike down the pirate flag with the force of combined nations, if it did not fall of its own inherent tendency to dissolution, before overtaken by the avenger.

The death of Julius Cæsar could not remove the causes, of which his dictatorship was only the effect: these causes were deep-rooted in the condition of the Roman people; and continuing to operate, other Cæsars succeeded to his power. The tide of millions, tending towards arbitrary Government, could not be rolled backwards by poniarding a bubble on its surface. What had been the life of the Republic, its virtue, was gone; consequently, the safety of person and property was sought in the strength of the executive arm. Could the death of Cæsar have " restored the ancient virtues; thereby fitting the people once more for republican Government, then something had been gained by his death, favorable to liberty, instead of merely displacing one Dictator to make room for another: an arbitrary head being necessary to a vicious political body.

THE INSUFFICIENCY OF PHRENOLOGY TO DETERMINE THE COMPARATIVE MENTAL POWER OF TWO OR MORE INDIVIDUALS.

PHRENOLOGY furnishes rules, by which to determine the mental powers of animals: It teaches that the brain is the group of organs, whose action is attended with thoughts or feelings, of a moral, intellectual, sentimental, or animal character; that each kind of thought has an organ, of a certain ascertained locality; that the comparative strength of each organ is determined by its comparative size; which is always attended by a corresponding development of the skull; and that the appearance of the head evinces the comparative strength of any organ; or, whether the animal, moral, intellectual, or sentimental predominates. To determine the truth of this, we have only to open our eyes: All animated nature furnishes confirming testimony on this point: the voice of the lamb is equal to that of the lion, and the idiot as convincing as the sane.

Phrenology fails in attempting to do more than determine the comparative strength of organs in the same head. For there is no known rule, whereby to judge of the comparative mental force between individuals.

The temperaments afford some indication of an inclination to activity or repose; that is, whether the individual is likely to exert the powers which he possesses. This, however, does not determine the strength of those powers; the phrenologists admit, with truth, that a man of a lymphatic temperament may have a powerful mind, but be too slothful to use it.

The temperaments only show what degree of mental activity may be expected, and not the slumbering secret power, which, as yet, can only be manifested by acts. Men who have distinguished themselves by great deeds, have had good temperaments. This only proves that a good temperament must accompany a good organization, to produce greatness of intellect: yet an observation of men, in regard to this point, proves that an apparently good temperament and organization is not always attended with intellectual superiority. Many good heads, with apparently good temperaments, are floating in the slack water of society, like splendid steamboats, without a boiler. I have long observed this, and also, that the evidences of superiority of head and temperament, in men of giant minds, are not as marked as the superiority of their intellects. I felt that there must be some deficiency in phrenology, in not accounting for this. The writers on Phrenology have felt similar misgivings: Stretching and contracting heads, to suit their theory: but the calipers have failed to afford demonstration. Mesmerism, at length, seems to elucidate the mystery: though it furnishes no rule whereby to measure the power of mind.

Mental action seems to result from an effect produced upon the brain by an electric fluid, called *neuaura;* and each variety of feeling and thought to come from a different kind of neuaura. This appears from the fact, that when a person is in the mesmeric sleep, he is senseless; because the neuaura has been withdrawn from the brain, by the manipulations of the operator, passing from the head to the extremities; and from the fact, that the person who is in communication with the magnetized individual, is capable of transmitting any feeling he is possessed of at the time of communication, while a person who has not such communication, cannot produce a similar effect on the magnetized person. Thus, is manifested both the existence and the effect, or office of the fluid, and also, that it is of various kinds or qualities; for how can communication exist, mental action be suspended, or excited, and moreover, particular kinds of mental action be produced, without some such agent serving as a medium of communication, or as a cause to excite action.

As there is no mental action, if the neuaura be withdrawn from the brain, which resumes its wonted action, when, by transverse passes the neuaura is restored, can we not infer, with reason, that the neuaura is the immediate cause of mental action? Phreno magnetism further proves, that the violence, or strength of mental action, is increased, by increasing the amount of neuaura. Experiments in phreno magnetism prove, that mental strength and vivacity are displayed, and great force and energy of animal feeling evinced by even the stupid while under the influence of the neuaura which emanates from the nerves of the operator. When we behold these facts, we are led to the conclusion, that intellectual force and greatness, chiefly depend on a superior capacity in the body to generate neuaura; it being the power that puts the organization of the brain into action; whose abundance confers strength and activity of motion, producing a corresponding force and vivacity of thought and feeling; a power whose diminution is marked by a proportionate inaction and dullness.

Where, then, is this neuaura generated? Not in the brain; that is but a point of expenditure. The Physiologists consider that the digestive organs are the great laboratory, where the crude materials of food are elaborated into those conditions suitable for the various purposes of life. Here is the root of the mental tree; and without good organization in this region, however perfect may be the phrenological developments of the man, we must expect to find in him a fruitless mind. He may look like Jupiter Tonans around the brows, but be weak within : probably the feeling of incapacity, of which men of acknowledged genius sometimes complain, may arise from a temporary derangement in this laboratory. Even an ordinary cerebral organization, well supplied with neuaura,(not blood, as Mr. Combe says,) will display a force far superior to what the phrenological developments seem to indicate, yet, far inferior to what it would be, if the cerebral organization were more perfect.

It is this hidden power, that is wanting in those individuals, that we often see possessing fine phrenological developments, and an apparently good temperament, yet, bearing no fruits. How different from the geniuses, who seem to rise superior to the accidents of time, place, and circumstances, borne aloft by an innate energy, which no labors can tire ; a native force of intellect, that bursts the chains of form and precedent, bearing down all opposition, and leaping beyond their age, leaving their fellow mortals to labor on through centuries in their track, in a successless effort to overtake them.

The shape and development of the most perfect head, and of the various cerebral organs, are ascertained by phrenologists, to a degree of accuracy, sufficient for practical purposes ; so that it is now possible to determine the sort of mind a man possesses ; that is, whether the animal, intellectual, moral, or sentimental predominates; but beyond forming a judgment of the comparitive powers of the organs of the same head we cannot go ; the force of the mind being measured by the capacity of the body to supply the neuauric power, to measure which, we have, as yet, no certain rule ; as the temperaments and apparent robustness, or health of body, furnish no certain criterion ; for history informs us that Demosthenes, Cicero, Cæsar, Pope, Ames, and others, were of sickly habit, and had weak bodies : Still, their powers of endurance are proved by their works.

I am inclined to believe, that the power of generating neuaura depends more on a perfection of the organs that elaborate it, than on their apparent strength. I am more fully persuaded of this, when that temperament, called lymphatic, is seen so seldom attended with mental vigor ; so much substance being warehoused in the system, that it is not manufactured into neuaura. The digestive or lymphatic temperament may result from a deficiency in the refining powers of the digestive organs, as often as from their capacity to supply a superabundance. Milton was thin in his youth, assuming corpulence in his old age ; Napoleon said, that until he was twenty five, he was "as thin as a slip of parchment" ; but in the latter years of his life his temperament seemed to change towards the lymphatic.

THE NEED OF OBSERVING CORRECT GENERAL PRINCIPLES.

It was remarked by Julius Cæsar in his speech concerning Lentulus, and Cethegus, that time might show the ill tendency of measures, which seemed to be of great present advantage to the state; that certain principles were dangerous, and many evils had sprung from acts, which, at the time of performance, were generally approved ; but, being founded on wrong principles, were pernicious in their consequences, as precedents, when the administration fell into bad hands.

In illustration of this, he instanced among other things, the conduct of the thirty tyrants of Athens ; who began their power, by putting to death, *without trial*, such as were remarkably wicked, and universally hated ; for which, they were greatly applauded by the citizens ; who, having thus sown the seed for usurpation, reaped the harvest of their folly, in suffering a bloody proscription of both good and bad. He argued from this, that the execution of Lentulus, and Cethegus, though just, would set a precedent dangerous to the liberty of the people.

The necessity of correct principles of action in all the affairs of life is so great, that much peril is incurred in venturing to act without their guidance, especially in what affects the state. This necessity is indicated in the works of the Creator of the universe. The laws, which govern the existence of organic bodies, are general. The conditions of these bodies change ; but the laws of their animation are unchangeable ; and as the organism observes, or violates these laws, it lives or perishes, flourishes, or decays ; and the same principle, which produces motion in the minutest object of animal existence, gives action and vitality to the whole chain of created beings ; and extending its influence to the mightiest objects, propels globes and systems in their prescribed course through the abyss of space. The law which attracts all substances to a common centre, operates in every system. Legislators would do well not to neglect this example of the Lord of Nature, in his Government of the Universe. Philosophy has not discovered one instance, in which even infinite wisdom has used a discretionary power in that Government; or deviated from, suspended, or violated his laws of action, even when benevolence and outraged justice have seemed to require it. Let not man, then, with his proneness to err, and consequent need of a guide, reject the example of the Creator; but, as far as he is able, apply to that comparatively minute and insignificant mass, a nation, those correct general principles of action, that are well, because they end well. When infinity teaches, by the great tutor, reason, when experience proclaims the necessity of such principles, how eagerly should they be adopted, and how carefully guarded from violation! Every individual, in whatever sphere he moves, would find in them a light and guide. If his memory fails, he infers from his principle of action, what must, under the circumstances, have probably occurred. Thus, too, his judgment is aided, and general consistency maintained. Even those who wield arbitrary power must find it greatly to their convenience, and advantage to never deviate from a just principle of action: such a course inspires the public with confidence in the Government, that adds to its strength and permanence, and relieves it, in some degree, from the imputation of tyranny. The domestic parental Government is seen to be respected in proportion to the justice and certainty of its action: threats unexecuted; rigour at one time, and slackness at another; severity or leniency, as impulse inclines, uniformly brings it into contempt, and consequent inefficiency.

TO COMPREHEND A SCIENCE ITS PRINCIPLE MUST BE UNDERSTOOD.

ONE's progress in any science will be in proportion as its animating principle is understood :—If this principle is not ascertained, it will not be comprehended as a whole, but only in disconnected parts—mere details will be learned, by toil of memory, without discerning their source, and dependence on a common parent: The limbs and leaves of the tree will be seen, without noticing the trunk and root from which they spring, and without knowing whether they emanate from one or many trunks. Each detail, without a knowledge of its principle, is, in some degree, a mystery, being seen in a state of isolation and without the link of dependence on its principle. Before any department of knowledge can be viewed as a science its general principle must be known, and being known its details are seen almost intuitively ; it is known what they must necessarily be.

I do not know that the general principle of history is ascertained, agreed upon, or conceded. It appears to me to be the narrative of acts of man individually and collectively, governed by self interest, and that its events are evolutions of selfishness under the various circumstances detailed. The steady action of this principle embraced in the word selfishness, might determine the duration of governments. The force of its action as modified by vice, or virtue, knowledge, or ignorance, affecting the length of their respective existence. When, for instance, republics are founded, the founders generally consult public interest only. They have the same desire to guard as to establish the government. Their interest in founding is equally consulted in guarding, and they provide checks against abuses, such as requiring a property qualification in voters, that those, who, by voting, impose burdens, may share a part of the burden imposed, not meaning to create a privileged class, either rich, or poor ; requiring judges to be elected by a legislature to exempt them from the effect of popular passions and prejudices, &c. Afterwards, those who seek power in the state, consult their individual interest, and seek popularity with the masses, by promising to remove those checks.

They next destroy the principle of equality : remove the public burdens from the shoulders of the majority on to those of the minority. These bear the injustice as long as it is tolerable, then they consult their interest by calling in a Dictator, who yokes the licentious masses, and restores law and order. Afterwards, he, or his descendant, is required at a Runneymead, or elsewhere, to relax a part of his hold on arbitrary power, according as the same intelligence that created his, or his ancestor's power, deems it consonant with the public interest. Thus, the action of selfishness has urged all republics into monarchy, and, afterwards, modified this form of government.

To so act, as not to offend, but to please, is the animating general principle of politeness. The details might fill a hundred volumes, embracing dress, fashion, motion, sentiment, manners, grace, awkwardness, &c.; but one sees intuitively from the root and trunk, or principle, what the limbs or details must be.

And so of other matters. One is incompetent to teach, if he cannot explain the principle of the science in which he would instruct. He can only show how to memorise, not how to comprehend. He can only treat of effects not causes—load the memory, not enlighten the understanding.

ON FLYING.

MAN might construct wings to fly, if he could increase his muscular power, or supply its place by machinery, so as to obtain power in proportion to his weight, equal to the power of a bird. The sinews of a bird are not stronger than those of a man; but they have more power, on account of their structure, and attachment to the arm further from the elbow joint. The muscle being attached to the hand, or near the end of the limb, gives the contractile power of the muscle great influence over the limb. The bird at the point, I will call the hand, has the same power as a man at the elbow. At the shoulder, man is as strong as a bird; but the lever and fulcrum disposition of muscles is such, that his power diminishes as the hand is approached. It may be possible to obviate this weakness by machinery, perhaps an artificial sinew. The slowness of motion might be compensated by length and breadth of wing and tail, whose proportion to the weight could be accurately determined by arithmetical calculation, of which the elements would be, the weight, size of wing and tail of birds, and motion of their wings. A partridge has a wing much smaller, in proportion to his body, than an eagle, and makes a much quicker motion, and is not able to support his weight as long. By determining the proportions and motions of these, some data could be got for ascertaining how many motions would be required, of wings of different lengths, to support a man, of a certain weight a minute.

The body might be covered with regular rows of quills, or umbrella work, so adjusted as to spread out at an angle of forty-five degrees; and thus, form a parachute, at the moment a retrograde movement should commence.

Were the body sustained by a balloon, direction might be given to the balloon by a long light shaft, forming the centre of several umbrellas, which the æronaut, grasping at its centre, could thrust forward and pull back, or he could row with oars formed, on the same principle, to open as he pulled, and shut when thrown ahead. This might be done with steam, without the exertion of any very extraordinary mechanical ingenuity. Tempests could only waft, not rend the aerial navigator, save when in counter currents of air, which seldom occur.

ON PUNISHMENTS.

THE object of punishment is to prevent crime. How is this object best attained ? To be just, it must be apportioned to the offence. If it is unnecessarily severe, it does wrong to the criminal; if insufficient, it is unjust to society; for to refuse to prevent an injury, is almost as wrong as to commit one. It is assisting the criminal; because it shields him from the consequences of crime; and to all who are disposed to commit crime, the consequences are the main preventives; for no one, whose acts are controlled by reason and conscience, commits crime. It is only those who are under the control of base passions, who perpetrate crime: reason is yoked to their car, acting the part of a slave to the controlling passion; the law, therefore, acts wisely to appeal to the master, the passion, and not to the slave, or the reason of the criminal, and in so doing afflict the organ that urges to the crime: for stealing ten, impose a fine of twenty dollars; the acquisitiveness that impelled the thief, would then restrain, and the strength of the passion be made a barrier against theft. If punishments of retaliation be proper, by what criterion shall we determine their amount? The natural? What is the natural? Open your eyes and see. The Almighty has made a world, governed by laws termed natural. These laws framed in harmony with each other, preserve order throughout nature. To prevent their violation a penalty necessarily follows their infringement, proportioned to the offence ; the extent of the violation being the standard governing the penalty ; and so perfectly is the offence balanced by the punishment, that the one announces the extent of the other : hence, extensive violations are less frequent than minor ones ; which would not be the case, if there was no discrimination of punishment. If, therefore, we take the natural criterion, we will apportion the punishment, for crimes, to the extent of the violation of the law. If the law is a right one, the greatest violation it can suffer, is the greatest violation of human rights ; the object of law being the support of those rights. The greatest right, is that of life ; for without it we can enjoy no other : It is therefore, the dearest : It is the strongest; because all the passions, moral, and intellectual, feeling delight in their own gratification, join in the pursuit of that gratification : all being thus interested in the continuance of life, rise in the strength of unanimity to repel any aggression on their common interest. Hence, the fondness for life, or the strength of the passion called love of life. Though passion wars with passion, for the ascendency, yet the same selfishness which separates, unites them when they have a common cause

To protect man's greatest right all his passions should be addressed by the nature of the punishment inflicted for its violation.

The extreme offence and irreparable injury of murder admits only the exaction of life, for life, and the charging of the offender's estate with the bringing up of the victim's children, or family, dependant on him for support.

THE BRAIN AN UNIT.

THE brain is but one organ, and performs but one function: that is, *feeling*. Thought, sentiment, memory, are but different modes of that feeling. There is no perceptible division in the brain, save the cerrebellum. The best microscopic instruments have not shown any division. From the writings of Combe, and others, it appears, that when any organ is excited the whole brain is in motion, pulsating violently against a particular part of the skull.

This pulsation causing, in process of time, a perceptible bump, the phrenologists consider strong evidence of the existence of a corresponding organ underneath, and by comparing heads, carefully, have ascertained, that these protuberances are always accompanied by certain mental qualities, and as these qualities, dispositions, or powers, are different, therefore they conclude there must be different organs ; because, say they, all the other portions of the body perform some function peculiarly their own, as the heart, liver, lungs &c.

I consider the Phrenologists right in concluding that the bumps are caused by pulsations of the brain against the skull, and that those bumps are evidence of a proportionate strength or weakness of certain mental qualities ; but wrong in supposing the existence of different mental organs—mistaking mode for substance.

1st. There is no perceptible division of organs.

2nd. The apparent force of the movement of the brain in particular states of feeling is such, that if restricted to a particular organ, or group of organs, they would have necessarily to be confined by a strong partition of some sort : An organ has greater strength in proportion to its distance from the Medula Oblongata, than from its proportional thickness ; a rule whose reverse is applicable to all other parts of the system : Showing, that in those directions and distances where the whole brain may have the most complete action the feeling is the strongest.

ON CLIQUES.

A CLIQUE is a combination of a few to control the many, for good or for evil. Cliques abound in American society, probably on account of the prevalence of acquisitiveness. The leaders of a Clique, for their own interest, use its members to rule the multitude. These leaders appropriate the present spoils, and feed their subordinates with hopes : if the latter are never blest with an office, they are always expecting to get one : Meantime, with apparent disinterestedness, they elevate their associates in the opinion of the world, by separately, and seemingly without concert of action, speaking in their praise on all occasions ; in this manner gaining an influence over the unsuspecting masses, by concealed arts, like those who originally instituted governments over mankind. The subordinates allude to each other with much respect, and to their leaders with a holy reverence, as unequalled in talents and purity ; thus teaching the public to regard them with awe and wonder. So, the law-givers brought the mysteries of religion to support their views, causing the popular belief that their institutions were sanctioned by the gods. After a simple citizen has heard the same thing approved or condemned, six different times by six different members of a Clique, apparently without intended unity of action, he concludes that the voice of the public, with great unanimity, has approved or condemned that thing, and considers it is useless for him to do otherwise than go with the current of opinion. In public meetings of the people a Clique, unless counteracted by another Clique, generally, if not uniformly, gets its own resolutions passed as the resolutions of the meeting, and as the expression of public opinion. The resolutions are perhaps first drawn up in secret conclave of the Clique, and handed to a person, not of the Clique, to offer to the meeting, the members not even seconding them without need, and apparently taking no more interest in their passage than the most indifferent spectator.

Private, rather than public interest, being the object of Cliques in our republic, they must be generally injurious to the people. All associations whose consultations are in secret, though not necessarily concealing their doings for shame, yet may be suspected of objects of which they are not proud ; because man is prone to divulge what he deems laudable, and to hide only what he deems shameful. Still, there may be a necessity for Cliques in the nature of things—to counteract evil combinations, bring governments into efficient action, and hold them to certain principles. They have existed in all nations. There is scarce a ruler, be he king, emperor, or president, but acts more or less through, and is acted upon, and is ruled in some degree by Cliques. In Russia the emperor has been displaced by such an influence, and in most countries the successive ministries are the creations of Cliques.

We find an amusing exposition of the action of a Clique, of which Agamemnon is the head, and Ulysses is the chief operator. in the trial of the army in the second book of the Iliad. The king tells the Clique he will propose to the troops to go back to Greece ; but the Clique must prevent their embarkation. He then publicly informs the troops, that though once great in arms, they have become the common scorn, and shameful flight, alone, can now enable ten Greeks to escape from one Trojan : Still, the troops desire to embark ; but are prevented by the efforts of Ulysses and his coadjutors. Cliques create fashions ; give form to public opinion ; give popular discontent an inoffensive direction ; create a rage for a steeple hat, or south sea speculation, or the study of dead languages ; in short, their efficacy, in managing poor human nature, and moulding the action of masses for the advantage of one, or a few, or many, is unquestionable. To rail against Cliques seems useless. A Clique of thieves could effect the passage of laws for robbing one man for the benefit of another, on the finest pretences ; such as, advancing religion, learning, or improving the channels of commerce ; and the only efficient counteraction of such a combination, would be found in the union of men of honest purposes ; for Cliques are most successfully combatted by Cliques.

OBSERVATIONS.

LOITERING in a town I got into conversation with some of the people : A merchant informed me his neighbor's goods were low, because they were inferior in quality ; but that his were lower in proportion to their real value than those of his neighbor ; while the latter claimed that his goods were equal in quality to the higher priced articles of his rival. I heard a man addressing, in an emphatic tone, a small group, on avarice ; denouncing parsimony, and assuming to be among the liberal. On enquiry, I found that his generosity was more conspicuous and wordy, than expensive ; that he never gave in the night ; but at noonday. Another, who sat beside him, was equally loud ; yet I was informed, that he never gave, except from experiment, already tried by others, he was certain of profiting by the gift, or rather the investment ; resembling, in this, some politicians, who affect generosity, when they are advancing but a low price for the loaves and fishes of office. Thus effecting a double object ; making a good bargain for place, and setting an example of liberality to the disinterested and unsuspecting observer. A benevolent looking gentleman, that was said to excel in acts of charity, who listened indifferently to these worthies, remarked, that without economy and industry one might be generous, but he would soon have nothing to bestow, and then, his generosity would be useless to society ; that, as for himself, he owed to industry and economy his capacity to aid his fellowmen ; and the aid he had given was so small it was not worth mentioning, except as a reproach, because of its insignificance ; that, probably, what entitled him to most credit, was, his having maintained himself and family, by his own exertions, so as not to be a burden to his fellow men, whom he was so little able to assist : that he should consider himself amply repaid for raising his children, when he found they could support themselves, relieving both him and the township from apprehensions on that score, which he believed they would effect; for he had succeeded in instilling into them a contempt for the superfluous and the vain, and a respect for the needful and the useful. My sons, said he, are their own barbers; they have no taste for artificial stimulants in segars, or otherwise : hence, I may hope they will not become drunkards, or gluttons. I have been careful to keep them employed at something ; for idleness tempts to mischief ; and taught them, that the observance of law and order was indispensable, and all departure therefrom, without justification or excuse : hence, I have not been disgraced by their acting with a mob of any description. My girls regard the useful, more than the ornamental ; they do their own washing, and dressmaking, and are industrious and frugal : hence, I may reasonably hope they will attract the attention of sensible men ; and such men, if poor, will become rich, and if already rich, not only are likely to remain so, but to make a rational use of their wealth. As he thus spoke, searching glances were cast by certain by-standers at others, and all seemed to pardon the egotism of the speaker, from a conviction of his sincerity.

In another group, a couple of ladies, in pursuit of contributions for some good object, solicited the aid of a respectable citizen, in the presence of several persons. He objected to give them anything, because there was scriptural admonition against doing it in public.

I noticed some dandies exhibiting phrenological certificates of their respective mental capacities, ascertained by the extent, and shape of the box, that held their brains. One showed a diploma from a college, with an air of triumph and satisfaction, without evincing much other evidence of erudition : another seemed to expect to silence opposition by stating the great length of time he had studied a subject : another railed at economy, while he indulged all his appetites, and contracted debts he never expected to endeavor to pay : thus stealing under another name ; the crime consisting in depriving others of their property, without compensation : in the one case, the thief takes advantage of the owner's absence, in the other, of his confidence.

I concluded that self-interest was the principle of action in most men, and took many forms, as modified by vice or virtue, wisdom or folly, acuteness or dullness, and that enlightened, and sagacious selfishness, greatly aided the cause of charity and all good works.

SHOULD A ROMAN CATHOLIC BE ELIGIBLE TO OFFICE IN THE UNITED STATES.

Lyceum Oct. 1838.

To exclude the Catholics from office in the United States we should not do unto them, as we would wish them to do unto us : thus, both a precept of religion and *virtue*, the principle of republican government, would be violated. Even monarchical England, whose principle of government according to Montesquieu is honor, has found it expedient to admit Catholics to office. How much more expedient to admit them here, where virtue *must* be the ruling principle, and perfect equality maintained among all the citizens. If the majority refuse equality of privileges to the minority, they thereby subvert republican government, and erect a despotism, the more odious, for the number of its tyrants; who, in turn, may be enslaved on their own principle, by such as have the power to do it. They recall the days of barbarism, when the strong enslaved the weak. They do, in light and knowledge, what barbarians did in darkness and ignorance; not stimulated to virtue by the Christian religion; nor guided by the lights of history; nor checked by the immediate presence and observation of an enlightened world. The Protestants, by thus acting, would show, that they rather profess than practice the Christian religion. Nor can they excuse themselves, by pointing to the tyranny of which the Catholic religion has been the instrument, in Spain; in which that form of religion has been more offended, than offending; for, on account of its very goodness, it was assumed as a cloak, by bad men; who, under it, perpetrated crimes, and tyrannized over the people. It being the religion of the whole people, it was the strongest lever which ambition could wield to effect its purposes, good or bad. Religion always has been, and ever will be, converted from its use into an abuse, because of its strong hold on the people. No matter what religion, or what mode of worship in the same religion has the majority, that religion, or that mode, will be used by the ambitious to effect their designs. Alexander the Great received from the Priestess of the temple of Apollo, at Delphos, the response, that he was invincible; of course, his soldiers could never see any need to retreat, while animated with such assurance.

The hatred of the vicious to Socrates, found means to destroy him, in accusing him of disbelief in the Gods. Thus religion in proportion to its power, is in danger of abuse : suppose the inhabitants of these United States were as unenlightened as the mass of the people in Europe, and as bigotted as the people of that country were formerly : suppose, too, a Cataline were a candidate for the presidency ; every person knowing his bad character ; and suppose, that the Presbyterian mode of worship were the most popular ; would he not join the church which had the greatest popularity ? And suppose a Washington, but a Catholic, were a candidate : imagine the success of the Cataline ! And what would be the argument in his favor ? Would it be, that he is a moral man, that he possesses greater virtues than the Washington ? No ; but that he is a Presbyterian ; This name would awaken passions that would overpower all others.

The proposition to exclude Catholics from equality of privileges, or to tyrannize over them, is a proposition for Protestants to do the very thing, which they condemn in Catholics ; to pervert Protestantism to the same purposes to which Catholicism is perverted in Spain. It is a proposition for one class to exercise tyrannical power over another class, and not the only class; other classes would also be victimized: power is seldom satisfied with one encroachment. The ambitious would assume the Protestant cloak for the same reason, that, in Spain, the Catholic one is assumed. There would be but few Catholics in a short time, if Catholics had no privileges. The Protestant would be the prevailing religion in this country, as the Catholic is, in Spain, and would be used for like purposes. Not that the Protestant religion sanctions such proceedings ; nor does the Catholic : It is the goodness of both that gives them influence. It is not religion ; but wolves clothed in the garments of righteousness, that do the mischief.

It follows that diversity of modes of worship constitute a nation's safety against any one mode being made an effective instrument of tyranny ; and that every sect is deeply interested against permitting any sect to assume power over another. The common safety of all requires, that all shall have equal privileges, and that the rights of no one shall be infringed.

POETRY.

INVOCATION OF THE SPARTANS AT THERMOPYLÆ.

The Greeks for fatal war prepare;
Stout hearts and arms, firm souls are there;
Leonidas, of god-like strain,
Proud, rules the death-devoted train.
Each knee is bent to Jove, on high;
Each hand is rais'd, upturned each eye:
 Oh! let us, Heaven, as Spartans, die:
Accept the sacrifice we give,
And let, oh let, our country live!
Thermopylæ, that drinks our gore,
Shall boast, our mothers heroes bore:
Our parents have no cause to grieve:
We, with our lives, a wreath will weave;
That through all future time shall wave
In fadeless verdure o'er our grave;
Our noble deeds, in deathless light,
As time advances, grow more bright,
If thou wilt let us grace the field,
With wounds in front, and hands on shield.
 That wreath the *human race* shall *crown*,
And *ours* shall be *mankind's* renown:

What *they* may greatly dare, or do,
'Twill give th' admiring world to view;
While we in deathless glory rest,
On Nature's fadeless, fruitful breast;
Or gliding with the spectral host,
Along the shadowy Stygian coast,
Delighted, hear all nations claim,
As *man*, to share our mighty fame.

We thus appreciate what we ask;
The boon, to well perform our task.
Now grant, O, Heaven, the favoring sign!
'Tis done: We hear the voice divine:
Our *country* calls, and on the *right!*
That thunder stirs the soul to fight.

WHY POETS ARE HONORED.

'Tis hard to get bays on the mount of Parnassus:
A poorly-fed nag is the horse call'd Pegassus.
'Tis selfishness weaves the poor crown, that is given
The name of the Poet, when he is in Heaven:
A wonder-work, sure! and the worker, you see,
Was related to Adam, and therefore to me!
I point to the pile, as a trophy of mine;
Because 'twas accomplished by one of the line!

MAN IS GOVERNED AS HE DESERVES TO BE.

Far, in the East, a spacious kingdom lies,
Where bounteous Nature every want supplies;
A dark-haired sultan, there, holds iron sway
And God's crush'd images, with fear, obey.
There cities, gilded bright, conspicuous shine;
Within whose walls imprison'd beauties pine.
There groves, luxuriant, wave before the gale;

O'er silvery waters floats the silken sail;
Through flowery meads, are crystal rivers roll'd,
And orange orchards seem to bend with gold:
Through spicy groves, a tuneful murmur flies
From sweet toned songsters, of unnumbered dyes,
Whose spangled feathers glitter in the air,
And all the colors of the rainbow wear:
From giant trunks, stupendous branches rise,
Form rural domes, high towering in the skies:
Th' extended limbs, at length, down bending low,
Infix in earth, take root, and upward throw
Vast rival trees, with verdant arches fair,
That aid their sires the storms of life to bear.
From these green halls, the tuneful nations greet
The gold-eyed morn, with music, wild and sweet.
But here, despotic power dominion holds:
No liberty this lovely clime beholds:
Degenerate man obeys his passions fell;
Blots reason's sun, and makes his home a hell:
For him how vain the brilliant landscape glows!
And Nature's breast spontaneous harvests throws!
An inward darkness dims his mental eye;
Vice clouds his life with scenes of misery.

It is by Heaven's immutable decree,
Man ever is, as he deserves to be,
Enslav'd, if vicious, and if virtuous, free.
If some the rights of others would invade,
The menaced portion seeks the bayonet's aid;
O'erwhelming force usurps the place of laws,
And tight the rein o'er vicious masses draws.
The lesser evil of monarchial sway
Is sought, the Anarch's pirate-course to stay:
His acts, unjust, create the need, that brings
Severe constraint, and builds the thrones of kings,
Whose sway is tempered, as the people feel
Disposed to justice, or to rob and steal.

JUDGES.

What most deserves unmingled scorn;
The vilest things of woman born;
The meanest tools of spirits fell;
The foulest instruments of hell;
The shame of man, the curs'd of Heaven,
Who ne'er can hope to be forgiven,
Are Judges, partial and unjust,
Who nothing do, but what they must;
Lest error's court, approaching near,
Should put their faults in light too clear:
Who purity, with prudery, keep;
So sure its guard must never sleep;
So conscious of its tender kind,
'Tis nurtured, till 'tis hard to find.

How sad, to see, a felon's brow,
One mov'd by instincts mean and low,
On past decisions cast his eye,
As daring not to pass them by;
And like estray, enclos'd in pound,
At length, yield, forc'd on legal ground.
Where angel purity should tread,
To see of vice the hateful head:
A rabble judging Socrates!
A Sydney judg'd by vile Jeffries!
Can hell give more disgusting sight?
On filthier scene can fall the light?
Ah, trust not those of base desires:
Let lofty aims, let science' fires,
With signal fondness to be just,
Rule such, as men with judgment trust.

THE SKY-EXCURSION,

In a moon-like boat, how, in thought, full of glee,
I loftily sail Heaven's star-spangled sea.
The oar, that I use, is a silvery ray
I caught, as it dropped from the king of the day.
I spread the bright canvas of light, for a sail,
And onward I move, in immensity's vale;
Regardless of all the vain labors of earth;
The triumphs of wrong, and the sorrows of worth.
The wicked have ceased from all troubleing here.
In peace and in splendor, o'er clouds I career:
And now, through a comet's bright trail, as I pass,
I find it is truly of spectres a mass:
The dim, twinkling stars, through their forms may be seen;
By signs, they make known, that like me they have been;
They beckon me, quickly, to join their long train,
And cast off mortality's burden of pain.
Their forms of sweet beauty round gracefully glide;
Briseis and Sappho I find at my side;
Great heroes, and artists, and poets, of yore,
Whose works and whose names are now heard of no more:
On asking for Homer, they point far away,
As if, " He dwells higher than we," they would say.
The play of affinities moral, no doubt,
Make similar natures each other find out.
Though none but the well-meaning spirits are here,
The loftier shine in a loftier sphere.
What music! transcendantly sweet; but, alas!
Can it come from these spirits, translucent as glass?
'Tis a tone, beyond mortal conception or power,
From angel harps falling, in love-lighted bower.
It never will sound in the valley of tears:
That strain is intended for heavenly ears.

Ulysses and Nestor glide into my boat,
As through the dim, shadowy spectres I float:
I see their names glimmer in light on each brow,
As graceful they stand on my sky-roving prow.
Bright drops from fair Poesy's life-giving pen!
'Tis long since they wandered with flesh-covered men
I spoke to them quick of their earth-filling fame,
But gleams of contempt on their vizages came;
Their eyes, turning upward, to me seemed to say,
The point of perfection is still far away;
And scarce to be reached in eternity's day:
How small is our merit, embalmed in the lays
Of loftiest bards of mortality's days!
Our wisdom was hinder'd in managing men:
As folly was lopp'd, it oft sprouted agen.
A labor unthankful how often it prov'd!
How loath is mankind to have error remov'd!
But here, for protecting the thoughtless from wrong,
We reach what to mortals may never belong;
A happiness destin'd forever to last;
The consciousness certain of good actions past;
Whose record, in day everlasting, will shine
Above all commotions, unchanging, divine!
It shows of meek virtue each act that endears,
By angel hands writ, as they wipe off her tears.
Although unrecorded in pages of earth,
No deed is here lost of the doings of worth:
The humble slave's merits, deep in the dark mine,
Beside the great monarch's refulgently shine:
Protectors of Virtue, forever on wing,
Her smallest acts gather, and heavenward bring.
The woes of her children, in sublunar sphere,
Make often to trickle the angelic tear.
Man's trial, while mortal, is only begun;
'Tis long ere the crown of perfection is won!

THE SPOUSE.

Ah! who can tell, what are the charms,
That draw me to Aldura's arms!
Is it the rose and lily cheek;
The tuneful voice; the eyes that speak;
The form Love's goddess might bestow,
Whose limbs with rival beauty glow;
Th' enchanting graces of her mien;
The looks, befitting Nature's queen;
Or thoughts of pure and upright mind;
Or spirit, gentle, meek, and kind;
Or wish to do her mother's will,
Evincing industry and skill?
In virtue, beauty, usefulness,
Aldura has the power to bless.
Entangled in the triple chain,
Kind Hymen hears my heart complain;
But now, disease's withering blast
My day of life is darkening fast.
Who me would wed, thus graveward prone,
I scarce could for a lover own;
For Nature, strength with beauty blends:
To perfect forms creation tends:
On those who most her law regard,
Perfection waits; a rich reward!
But those who, heedless of it, stray,
Disease and ruin gloom their way:
Death's pruning hand th' offending race
Discards, and casts from Nature's face.
Enough then, if to Virtue wed,
What transient time life's paths I tread.
As low declines my fleeting day,
And into darkness fades away,
My Spouse, in graceful kindness, waits:

Assists me through the shadowy gates,
And up the star-walks of the skies:
Sweet tones from steps of angels rise
Along the sounding pathway bright:
What beauty, splendor, and delight!
By her attended, heavenly born,
How joyful breaks th' immortal morn!

THE USES OF THE PAST.

The things that flourished in the past,
    Are in th' oblivious tomb:
Existing things are tending fast
    Into the eternal gloom.
In swift, unintermittent flight,
    Earth's kingdoms pass away:
Like bubbles, nations rise to sight,
    And flourish and decay.
Their monuments, not long to last,
    But dimly strike the eye,
And, on the present, sadly cast
    Their doubtful history.
Their life's short tale alone remains,
    Th' experience of gone days;
Instructive lessons it contains,
    To light the statesman's ways.
Since useful to themselves no more,
    Their lives may serve to give,
To those who run their race-ground o'er,
    Instruction how to live:
Show what to seek and what to shun.
    Upon the face of earth;
How vice has lost and virtue won:
    And light the road of worth.

What teaches and exalts our kind
  Will not be let to die:
In man 'twill that protection find
  Self-interest may supply;
Save when rude hordes, from polar shades,
  O'erwhelm the polished states;
Then mental darkness, too, invades,
  And death on science waits;
Which transient swells, like wave of light
  Along a sea of gloom,
On Time's bleak stream, and sinks in night,
  As savage conquerors doom:
And save when thoughtless ignorance rules,
  Unknowing what is good,
Conferring trusts on knaves and fools,
  Who know not what they should;
Who see not in the warning past,
  Strewn with republics' graves,
That States by wisdom, only, last;
  That Virtue, only, saves.

THE SLAVE-POWER INVOKED.

In truth, I must arraign the good;
Because they do not what they should.
How can they thus inactive be,
While vice enacts our destiny!

The nation ruled by knaves or fools,
The tyrant's scorn'd compliant tools,
Already reels beneath a shame,
That grieves the patriot heart to name:
Though heaven its choicest blessings brings,
Regardless whence our glory springs,
The virtues of the good and great,
In wrong's dark gulf is plunged the State,

To Mars and Mammon bow'd the knee,
On weakness warring cowardly!
The strong, who robs the weak in arms,
His fame, more than his victim, harms.

What fiends! to ope the gates of wo,
That Slavery's poisonous plant may grow!
For this, the bomb-torn city burns;
In blood and tears a nation mourns;
The iron hail on houses falls;
Destroyed, beneath home's injured walls,
The frenzied mother, with her child,
And husband, lie, in ruins pil'd!

Dread Moloch, thron'd on votes of fools;
Since these may long remain thy tools;
Since names of high repute are thine;
Time-servers on the middle line;
To thee, I humbly make my prayer,
The dough-faced progeny to spare.
Permit us of degenerate blood,
T' enjoy as much of worldly good,
As Slavery's interests will allow:
Ah! more than this we ask not now!
Perhaps, howe'er, thou soon may'st see,
Our interests quite with thine agree;
When States, acquir'd by murderous war,
Make you outweigh in Senate far;
Then, grown less jealous of our power,
Thou may'st not seek to starve us more.
O, be to us indulgent, then;
Let snags nor tariffs ruin men:
But let thy kind, paternal sway,
Our past enormous loss repay.
O, that it might to life restore
The thousands, dead, we vain deplore!

DAYS OF CHILDHOOD.

How alive is the heart of a poor dying creature
To all the sweet aspects and music of nature!
The life-giving Sun; the green meadows and flowers;
The smiles of dear friends, and the loves of gone hours;
The joys and the sorrows of childhood and age,
That shine, as mild stars, upon memory's page!
E'en woes that are past, without pain we recall;
The joys that surrounded, have softened them all.
How pleasant the time of our childhood appears,
In light, scarcely clouded, of life's vernal years!
The spots on the sun of its fresh blooming day,
Its tear-starting griefs have all vanished away!
Hope gilded its future with happiest beams:
The state of the blest was enjoyed in its dreams;
As yet uninformed of life's troubles and cares,
And blind to its dangers, temptations, and snares.

A BACHELOR'S MUSINGS.

Though roseate dyes
   The cheeks o'er spread,
Bright glancing eyes
   Their splendors shed,
As health would dwell
   In every vein;
Yet, who can tell
   The *seat* of latent pain !

The form may wear
   A winning grace;
And seem to bear

Of woe no trace;
Yet, misery lurk
　Within the heart,
And secret work
　Of *death* the fatal part!

Though angel smiles,
　The face adorn,
The heart hath wiles,
　As rose its thorn:
The false assumes
　The garb of truth;
And age presumes
　In paint, to shine as youth.

In vain the eye
　And Heaven's pure light
Combine to pry
　Into the plight
Of forms, that grow
　A bustle under,
Perplexing so
　It makes the judgment blunder.

From guile may gentle manners grow;
Sweet looks hide bitterness below;
Health's blush conceal diseases fell,
Whose presence, soon, the wasted form shall tell.

Though Nature mould with matchless grace,
In wavy lines, the soul-lit face,
Not distant is the barren day,
That sees it wrinkled under tresses grey.

PITY.

Man-helping power;
In sorrow's hour,
Thy soothing balm,
His soul may calm,
Oppress'd with cureless grief,
That waits winged Time's relief.
A charming lay
Thou seem'st to play,
Whose music sweet
Makes pain retreat,
Or join in tuneful glee,
The witching harmony.
Of virtues mild
The blooming child,
Thou lov'st to be
With Charity,
And, e'en in fancy, feel
The smarting wounds you heal;
Enduring mine,
As woes of thine;
Kind echoing dole
Of troubled soul;
Like that Samaritan
You mov'd to aid the man,
Near by the road
The selfish trod
In ancient time:
Deed ever prime.
O, Could all statesmen feel,
Like thee, man's wo or weal,
Would they unbar
The gates of war,
And glut with food

Hell's ravenous brood;
Yet dare, with tyrant's plea
Of its necessity,
    To justify
    To God on high
    The bloody deed?
    Will he see need
For streams of blood to flow,
That States may larger grow?
    See need to break,
    Or e'en mistake
    His tenth command?
    Th' avenging hand
Of Justice soon will show
Their deeds have brought them wo.
    Where wert thou, when
    Napoleon's men,
    To gratify
    His lady's eye,
Were ordered into fight?
That she might see the sight!
    Some lives were lost;
    Some loves were crost;
    Hearts, anguish-torn,
    Were doomed to mourn.
The Chief, in life's late hour,
Term'd it—the abuse of power!
    Nor call'd it crime,
    Which chance, nor time,
    Nor pomp, nor pride,
    From Heaven can hide:
Which Justice must avenge,
Or God's fixed order change.
    Be always near
    Man's wants to hear;
    Incessant wield
    O'er him thy shield;
Lest tardy reason's hour
Find him abusing power!

BATTLE.

Now rolling more near,
War's thunders I hear;
Loud music of death;
   The dirge of the brave,
   Who sink on the heath,
   In fame-honored grave:
   Their proud spirits ride
   On war's fiery surge;
   The wild raging tide
   They eagerly urge,
Midst shrieks of the wounded, the groans of the dying,
The shouts of the victor, the screams of the flying,
Wild terror before, and confusion around,
The harvest of ruin bestrewing the ground.

THE MARCH OF ANGELS.

AND now the heavenly hosts together throng;
An ocean of bright beauty pours along,
Glittering with gems, unnam'd in human lore:
A blaze of splendor gilds that ocean o'er.
A flood of sweetness from its countenance flows:
Each face, in bloom divine, with love immortal glows.
What graceful motion under nodding plumes
Of beaming amaranth, that forever blooms,
And sun-topp'd standards, casting fiery blaze,
And flags, high-floating, streaming moony rays!
Amidst them strides the reverence-winning forms,
Realm-shouldering souls, defying evil's storms:
Their lofty nature all their looks declare,
And marks of high resolves forever bear.

Advancing o'er the sounding pathway clear,
Unearthly melodies delight the ear:
The sounds of angels' tuneful feet arise;
The frequent step successive tones supplies;
The swelling melody pervades the skies,
And music wide on joyful pinions flies!

DAY—AND APOSTROPHE TO THE WINDS.

Gay morning rises fresh and fair,
    Bedeck'd with robes of rosy light;
And through the music-breathing air,
    Casts cheerful looks of beauty bright.
Upon the dewy glistening clime,
    What pearls and rubies pours the day,
As up the vault of heaven sublime,
    The burning orb pursues his way!
Bright glancing sunbeams splendors rain
Upon the foam-wreathed glimmering main,
In radiance toss'd by breezes fair:
How sweet their soothing voices are!
Their silvery misty garments fly,
Soft streaming, in the sunny sky:
Though hearing oft their melody,
Their happy forms we never see.
Gay wanderers on the vast of air,
Angelic travellers, sure, ye are,
Careering o'er the changeful scene,
Of seasons pallid, brown, and green.
The flowery fields, in colors gay,
To you their fragrant tribute pay.
The blossoms, waving, as you kiss
Their lovely faces, shine in bliss.
And, while they feel your gentle blows,
The leaves, upturn'd, more tints disclose.

Earth spreads her verdant arms, and hails
Your coming o'er her hills and vales.
O, could one, with your pinions, soar,
To fan sweet beauty evermore;
To lull on evening's dewy breast;
Or pant on clouds that gild the west;
Or ride the brilliant air of noon;
Beneath hot sun, or chilly moon;
Or roll the mists in cloudy forms,
And move in grandeur, with the storms,
The conscious spirit blest and free,
Unshackled by mortality!

THE LANDING OF CÆSAR IN BRITAIN.

On Britain's coast, majestic Rome looks down;
But meets of barbarous foes the angry frown.
With grace of Cicero's rival, Cæsar pours
The sea-borne armies on the bristling shores.
From the beak'd galleys, grounded on the sand,
The naked Gauls, in barks, assist to land.
The standard bearer, leaping in the waves,
Breaks danger's spell, its fearful aspect braves,
And bids his legion follow, or betray
The glorious banner, pride of many a day;
While sinewy slingers showers of missiles throw,
And clouds of arrows leave the twanging bow.
The Britons, gall'd in flank, in front o'erpower'd,
The Roman Eagle, soon, in triumph tower'd.

THE YEAR.

In Spring's moist growing season born,
Fair nature's robe gay flowers adorn,
As bright she blooms in fragrant breeze,
Soft kissing dew-drops from the trees,
The swelling buds ope smiling eyes,
Like beauty, wak'd in sweet surprise.

Fruit-bearing Summer's banners stream,
'Till brown'd by Autumn's ripening beam;
While mingled tints, of various dye,
The landscape mellow to the eye:
Then charming prospects spring to view,
Of Nature, dressed in every hue:
While each spry wind, with saucy blows,
Makes foliage secret tints disclose;
And all the hues that Nature bears,
In union twine their lustrous hairs:
A beauteous scenery, thus, is made,
Of every pleasing tint and shade;
But, oh, not long the prospect bland,
For admiration's eye will stand!
The north wind, shortly, moaning loud,
Will o'er it cast a snowy shroud:
E'en like the glowing rainbow gay,
'Twill shine awhile, then, fade away.

DECLINING DAY.

And now the red-eyed Sun looked from the West;
A silvery cloud, with border ting'd with gold,
Hugged the tir'd winds against her downy breast,
And through the mellow heaven, in grandeur, roll'd:
Nature, enamored of the radiant day,
Blush'd deeper hues, and spread her flowery arms:
The gilded seas gleam'd back the shining ray,
And softer light the glowing landscape warms.

MORNING—NOON—EVENING—AND NIGHT.

Thrice came refulgent morning, glorious rob'd;
Grey eve, the golden-haired, came thrice, and o'er
The zenith Sol thrice poured his fiery beams;
Night, sable-plum'd, thrice rear'd her starry shield,
Beneath whose ample verge lay dusky Earth,
With all her mountains tall, and oceans huge,
Loud murmuring through the vast and sullen gloom.

INTELLIGENCE AND VIRTUE NECESSARY TO LIBERTY.

When vice and error's baleful breath
A nation threat with moral death
Let wisdom, virtue, seize the Press:
'Tis theirs the menac'd land to bless;
As sentries on the important tower,
Keep watchful guard, in danger's hour;
Nor labor on less useful arts,
Till truth and virtue, minds and hearts,

Have snatch'd from error's downward way,
And plac'd beneath their blissful sway.
   'Tis not reading;
      'Tis not writing;
      'Tis not bleeding;
         'Tis not fighting;
   That liberty will save:
   But Virtue, wise and brave.
Man knowledge needs; (besides its tools;
Which oft o'erload the hands of fools:)
   Incline him this to crave:
   Such as gives power to save!
How many Greek and Latin words;
How many names of stones and birds;
How many sciences, will fit
Him to avoid the dismal pit,
Down which republics old,
Through vice and ignorance roll'd!
  Be then his rights and duties taught;
Let light be on his interests brought;
(Such light as Washington would give,
And others, who for man could live;
Not those who help themselves, alone,
And, for reform, have ruin sown;
Old rules forsaking, with such zeal,
They fain would God's own law repeal:)
That, spite of error's mists, he see
The needful props of liberty.

   The day that sees our virtue die,
     Prolific teems with woes;
   Fell tyranny and hateful crime,
     From that disaster flows:
   The hydra-headed despot, then,
     The excellence-loathing mob,

Will, lawless, hold their brutal sway,
  And desecrate and rob;
Till crush'd beneath the giant blow
A sceptred chieftain may bestow.
The friends of order, gathering strength,
From those abuses teach, at length,
Are pleas'd to lesser ills endure,
From force responsible and sure,
And sadly rest beneath the shade
By its *protecting* ægis made.

  Would man from deeds unjust, abstain,
He long might liberty retain:
But if he breaks the tenth command,
He feels the tyrant's iron hand.
Mere virtue's unassisted light,
Will guide a people's steps aright.
What more can knowledge do, than show
What leads to bliss and what to wo?
The virtuous, then, reach learning's end
At once, nor by slow steps ascend
To that blest height: The heart attains
Results, without the toil of brains;
Instinctive, takes the happy road;
Spurns thieves and knaves, and clings to God.
Were learning sought at Virtue's cost,
Less happiness were gained than lost.

PEACE WITH MEXICO PRACTICABLE.

  THIS land, to feeble Mexico,
Should kindness, not injustice, show;
When Britain's threats our ears assail,
Peace, still, can o'er the sword prevail:

Mournful, midst Niagara's roar,
   Hear our murdered bretheren cry:
Restless, still, they stalk the shore,
   Where their injur'd corses lie.
What disdainful, sullen smile,
   Lights their ghastly eyes of death,
While the murderers's steps defile
   That lov'd land which gave them breath!
While beneath Canadian sky,
Swing their friends, on gallows high;
Or, on far Van Dieman's land,
Groan beneath oppression's hand;
Or, on ocean's distant waves,
Sink into dishonored graves.
Valor, wisely rul'd, is ours,
That, in peace, this evil cures:
Why, then, martial vengeance glow
For less faults of Mexico?

STOOPING TO CONQUER UNDIGNIFIED, BUT PERHAPS EXCUSABLE.

Who can but despise
  One's meanness of heart,
That never can rise
  To act a free part!
    Though learning he have
    And intellect good,
    Enacting the slave
    Degrades his manhood.
Mean, pliant, and low,
  In courting the rabble,
How far can he bow
  To trash miserable!

In stooping for favor,
He plunges his head
In places, whose savor
His feet might well dread.
But since the poor sinner
An office may seek,
And might not be winner
If candid he speak,
 Permit him to ramble
 Awhile in the mean;
 If bless'd in the scramble,
 He then may wash clean.
Perhaps he intends,
If favor'd with power,
Magnanimous ends;
Then blame him no more.
 Perhaps 'tis the king,
 Not courtier, in wrong:
 Who likes a vile thing
 Will get it ere long.
If sources of power
Lie deep in the mud,
One cannot high tower,
If reach them he would.

THE EVENING SAIL.

On ocean launch'd the bellying sails
Are spread aloft to catch the gales;
 While shadows dun
 Succeed the light
 Of setting sun,
 And murky gloom
 Of sullen night

The colors gay
 Of rosy day
 Entomb.

Soon, rising slow, in queenly state,
Shines Luna, in her golden veil:
The courtier stars her coming wait,
Till in her rival glow they pale.
Unclouded, with majestic gaze,
She lavish pours her silvery rays.
The breast of Ocean heaves in light,
And gleams in glimmering twinklings bright.

 Far off, a mist from craggy steep,
 On hazy wings, floats o'er the deep.
 In fleecy gilded clouds it breaks,
 And forms of various objects takes.
 In spots, with sunny whiteness fair,
 It spreads, till lost in silvery air,
 And in the mirror waters seems to play,
With dancing moon and stars, along the rolling way

THE RETURN.

To native land return'd, with joy, I strode
The well known path to Florian's plain abode:
St. Clairsville leaving, I approached a wood,
Which tall, before, in verdant grandeur, stood;
Rough Sugar trees, in darkest green array'd,
With smoother Beeches, cast a grateful shade.
The rough bark'd Walnut rears his stately head;
Gigantic Oaks their lofty arms out spread.
The Pignut, bright of bark, ascending high,
Displays his gold-tinged tresses in the sky:
High o'er the neighboring trees his branches spread,
A frowning Forest King, with storm-defying head !

Earth's fertile surface here, takes every form
Of billows, petrified amidst a storm.
Coal, lime, and living springs enrich the vales:
The blooming Locusts scent the vernal gales.
The bright eyed children, lovely form'd, that play
Among the hills, outbloom the flowers of May.

Next, kiss'd by winds, a fragrant meadow rose:
Its downy verdure undulating flows
In wavy curves; wide spreading as they roll,
In shadowy billowy motion moves the whole;
While here and there, amidst disparted green,
The modest clover's crimson cheek is seen.

The Peach trees, near, with blushing branches bend,
And grateful fragrance to the zephyrs lend.
Wide spreading limbs delicious apples hold,
Of various hues, of purple, green, and gold.
The damson, grape, the nectarine and pear,
On their hale arms a precious burden bear:
And seem the cherries, apricots and plumbs,
To say, we late have borne, again our season comes.

A humble cottage, through the fragrant shade,
Flower-circled, and tree-clouded, I surveyed:
A farmer, there, I saw, and only one;
Who seemed, in rural state, to reign alone:
Contentment on his ruddy features shone,
And simple nature claimed him as her own:
He opes his door, and, with heart-cheering smile,
Bids me come in, and share his home awhile.
Then states, that from unnumbered seeds of pears
He rais'd a luscious kind, his name that bears:
And asks, "If artists please the taste as well
As those who in Pomona's works excel."
And claims, "most seem more blest who taste his pear
Than those who on a pictur'd story stare."

ON THE PROSPECT OF GOING TO ITALY.

Soon, in Italian dust I lay my head;
I go to sleep among the Roman dead:
In the mild radiance of Italia's sky,
Life's drama closes on my longing eye.

Death's misty pall now on my vision lies;
Now, lovely Nature greets again my eyes:
Th' unyielding spirit, still, persists to breathe,
Reluctant, still, the vanquish'd frame to leave.
For life alone I would not seek to live:
It was bestowed, aud I can freely give;
But kindred hearts a strong affection binds;
And dearest ties unite congenial minds.

VIRGIL—BOOK VI.

Here Teucer's ancient beauteous race appears,
High minded heroes, born in better years;
Assaracus, and Ilus, bright of mien,
With Dardanus, who founded Troy, are seen;
Their arms and empty chariots o'er the land,
Admired from far, with spears, earth-rooted, stand.
The coursers, from their glittering cars unbound,
Roam, unrestricted, o'er the verdant ground.
The care of these from former habits came;
In life and death their pleasures are the same.
Midst odorous laurel groves, with joyful song,
In chorus, feasting, some the strains prolong
And rove where Eridanus rolls along.
Who, patriotic, for their country bled;
Who, the blest lives of pious prophets led;

Who, worthy of Apollo, sung their lays;
Who, by discovered arts, adorn'd their days;
And thus, by merit, had become renown'd,
With snow-white fillets all their brows were crown'd.
By these encompass'd, as we came in view,
Museus, taller than the rest, I knew:
Thrice happy souls, my guide, the Sybil, spoke,
And to Museus thus the silence broke:
Blest poet, say, where does Anchises dwell?
For him we cross'd the mighty streams of hell!

To whom the hero quickly made reply:
From hill to vale, from grove to grove, we fly:
In no fix'd place we make a steady home;
But, at our pleasure, through Elysium roam.
At times, we wander in the shady grove;
Or on the mountain's airy summit rove.
But, from yon hight, an easy path I'll show
To where Anchises dwells on plains below.
He spoke, the steep ascent he quickly gains;
And, from its brow, points out the shining plains.

Just then, Anchises, on the future cast
His eye, by chance, as one may view the past.
The souls secluded in a valley green,
About to go to upper light, were seen.
With care, he counted his descendants dear;
Their manners, fortunes, fates, and deeds appear.

And when he saw Eneas, coming near,
He joyful stretched his hands, and many a tear
Pour'd down his cheeks; And have you come at last!
He thus exclaims, the arduous journey past,
Effected by your worth, well known to me!
O son, 'tis given again your face to see;
To hear and answer well known words again:
This was my hope, nor has the hope been vain.
Say, through what lands, and what wide seas you come;

What dangers gloomed your passage to my home?
How have I fear'd the Lybian realms might harm,
The means unknown, which caus'd the vain alarm!

O father, your, your own sad ghost, he cries,
Oft met, has forc'd me to these nether skies.
The ships remain upon the Tyrrhene brine.
O sire, let your right hand be grasped by mine;
And O, withdraw not from my fond embrace:
Thus speaking, while the tears bedew'd his face,
Thrice round his neck, he tried his arms to throw;
Thrice, from his grasp, the form, like empty wind did go

Meantime, Eneas notes secluded groves,
Through whose still shades the stream Lethean roves,
Unnumber'd tribes, and people, round it fly,
Like bees, mid flowers, beneath fair summer's sky.

Eneas, startled at the sudden view,
Unconscious, asks, what cause such numbers drew?
And what, besides, may this calm river prove?
And what the men, that throng its banks above?

Anchises then: The souls, designed by fate
For bodies new, forget their former state
On drinking Lethe's care-expelling wave,
Which straight of memories past becomes the grave.
These things to you I long have wish'd to show,
And what descendants from my sons shall flow,
That, Italy found, we may the more rejoice.

O sire, can wretches make so dire a choice!
From love of life can lofty souls descend
To sluggish bodies—for what useful end?

Anchises then: In doubt I will not hold
My son; but all things to his view unfold:
And first; an innate spirit feeds the whole;
Of Earth, Moon, Stars and Space th' inspiring soul.

The liquid plains; the shining hosts of heaven;
To all, intelligence has motion given.
Thence, lives of birds, and beasts, and human kind,
And monsters, to the watery world confin'd.
These germs have fiery strength, and heavenly birth;
Nor suffer harm from dying frames of Earth.
Hence, they rejoice and grieve, desire and fear;
Nor, flesh-imprison'd, see the heavenly sphere.
When life's last light departs, some filth remains;
Th' unhappy still possess corporeal stains,
And penalties, for past transgressions pay:
Some, high suspended, are to winds a prey.
Of some, the sins are burn'd or wash'd away.
They suffer while they bear the body's stains;
(Then, left to rove, few hold these joyful plains),
Till long extended time effects a cure,
And frees the soul from everything impure.
When these have roll'd the wheel a thousand years,
To drink oblivion's wave each soul appears,
Summon'd by God—absolv'd from every stain,
To seek the convex world, and robe of flesh, again.

MENTAL INFLUENCE.

Good sense, in poetry array'd,
The cause of truth and man may aid.
All things, in dress of verse or prose,
If vital, sweeter charms disclose:
Lov'd Beauty, rob'd in living light,
Affords the soul increas'd delight.
But few, of all the world below,
Give thoughts, in fadeless life to glow;
These animate each future age;

The virtues rouse to noble rage:
'Twas Ossian's heart-exciting song
That fir'd the Highland nation long;
To resolution added force,
And nerv'd it, in its perilous course;
Impell'd the wavering to the fight;
Illum'd the way, by glory's light;
Made freedom's spirit loftier burn;
The foreign yoke indignant spurn.
And while to England, strong and proud,
More numerous nations humbly bow'd,
This brav'd assaults, in every form;
For Ossian's spirit rul'd the storm.
When crush'd by arms, th' unconquer'd will
Her sons retain'd, and triumph'd still.
When Britain's king would Wales subdue,
Her mind-exalting bards he slew;
For matter yields to man's control,
As mov'd by more or less of soul.
To Sparta, with Tyrtæus' strains,
Came victory on Messene's plains.
Dominion most inclines to stay
Where dwells the high heroic lay.
Greece, leagued against a barbarous world,
To mighty States defiance hurl'd:
By Homer and Eschuylus fir'd,
Before her frown mankind retir'd.
The casket-copy's lofty charms,
No less than Macedonian arms,
Subjected Persia's ample realm,
And gave to Greece, of Earth, the helm.
Rome, mov'd by energy the same,
The mistress of the world became.
No peerless poet Persia boasts:
She falls before the Grecian hosts.
No muse to keep her soul from rust,
Rich Carthage soon is laid in dust.

Each modern State's Augustan age
Preceded its mechanic stage.
Whate'er exalts, increases mind,
In countless ways, to bless mankind;
Demosthenes, with loud alarms,
Awhile, averted Philip's arms.
Awhile, persuasive Cicero,
Delay'd his country's overthrow.
Of all the forces, man, that move,
The power of soul will strongest prove:
It brings the starry deeps to view,
And gives great countries aspects new.
Not half a century yet is past,
Since Mississippi's affluents vast,
With all the wide interior wild,
Untam'd, in savage grandeur smil'd;
And scarce could be approach'd; so stror
Her seaward rivers pour'd along;
Then Fitch and Fulton steam applied,
To breast the swift descending tide:
The great West bow'd to greater mind,
And Clinton, Fitch, and Fulton bind;
That, by Canals, and these by Steam,
And Morse, by quick, electric beam,
The States in firmer union all,
And these to man, throughout the ball!
What millions, now, explore her floods,
And reap, where frown'd her stately woods!
America may well be proud,
That Heaven such palms her mind allow'd.
O'er all the world, its pregnant power
Affects, with change, each fleeting hour
For good; not unalloy'd; disease
May live to cross art-narrow'd seas;
But mind, though gloom'd by sordid trade,
This evil, will, at length, evade,
For of the forces, man, that move,
The power of soul will strongest prove.

NAPOLEON.—BOOK IV.—PAGE 74.

ADVANCE OF THE GUARD AT WAGRAM—TRANSLATED FROM THE FRENCH.

What troops are these, of lofty port, declare,
To honor's field, that now their banners bear?
To see their quiet look, and faces bright,
You deem they seek amusement more than fight:
These are the sons of Mars; th' immortal guard:
They go the palm of victory to award.
What silence deep! the tube of deadly harms,
Unmov'd and silent, rests upon their arms.
Towards the fray, with measur'd step, and slow,
A thick wall forming, they compacted go.
Behold them under fire; their looks serene:
Death opes their ranks, which straight to close are seen;
And all the valor of a powerful host,
Each, in his single heart, may proudly boast!
Mars stops his chariot, and his dusty steeds:
His curious eyes are fixed upon their deeds.
Nor murderous lead, nor cannon, sweeping wide,
Th' intrepid line is able to divide:
Unshaken, it pursues its first intent;
And midst the foe is consternation sent.
Of courage how majestic the repose!
But tis the calm before the tempest blows.
The scene attain'd, where dire Erynnis roars,
And rage, in breasts of either army, pours,
They stop; each points his thunder, with sure aim;
And each, an adversary's fall may claim.
Death, spectral, swelling, horrid, hisses round;
His hideous bones, together clattering, sound,
As, in his heat, his fatal scythe he swings,
That keen and loud through quivering ether rings.

The Germans, o'er them, see his pinions spread,
And on his greedy aspect look with dread.
A smile infernal on his mouth appears,
Redoubling, still, their horror and their fears.
To lightnings, fatal thunder-bolts succeed.
At each explosion wretched thousands bleed.
Broke, by the fearful shock, the Germans yield;
Their shattered masses, scattered, fly the field.

IDLENESS AND MISCHIEF.

Who ever falls to idleness a prey,
Scarce knows to pass the irksome hours away:
As, on the clock, a careless look, he casts,
He deems the day, beyond endurance, lasts.
He sleep invokes, his vacant eyes to close,
And give inglorious life a short repose.
Small ease, to him, the power of slumber brings;
Drear listlessness its influence round him flings:
In restless plight, from side to side, he turns,
Unlike the man who rest, with labor, earns;
Nor this the worst: If aught to ill inclin'd,
With idleness, comes mischief, close behind:
Let all, then, keep their children well employ'd,
Who, by their conduct would not be annoy'd,
Nor see their usefulness in life destroy'd.

CŒLEBS CONSOLED.

On looking, late, at Cupid's wares,
I would not deal in love's affairs.
The market e'er will have supply
Of lasses, charming to the eye.
'Tis difficult, to make selection,
Among the very great collection.
If one regard the talking past,
More turns on luck, than choice, at last.
Perhaps, some day, not giv'n to see
A fault in Jill, I'll double be!
Each, doubtless, must his fate fulfil;
But who can love against his will?
'Tis said, if will be love-inclined,
The wisest scarce a flaw can find:
The little foibles of the fair,
Then, need not Cœlebs' hopes impair.
He yet may be so much inclin'd,
As, with affection to be blind;
Incapable defects to see,
Which shock all sane humanity.

THE NOBLE OF NATURE.

Sol, midst darkling worlds, is he;
Glorious work of Deity!
Ornament of human kind;
Ardent, fearless, wise, refin'd,
Nature's noble; fit to grace,
In the world, the highest place.
Thus, she bids the oak to rise,
With broad arms, amidst the skies.
Towering high, its monarch brow
Looks on forests, far below:

So, he stands, among his race,
In his heaven-appointed place.

Man, can him no loftier make;
Nothing from his greatness take.
Puny mortals ill refine,
On the work of hand divine.
If his foes his thoughts engage,
Pity glows; but not his rage.
Hate, or Envy's venomed dart,
Vainly seeks his lofty heart;
Wastes its force, in empty sound,
Or falls blunted to the ground.
Storms thus strike a mountain's brow
Break, and roll, in tears, below.
Mild and firm the giant mass
Rests, while blustering tempests pass.
But his world-embracing soul,
Ocean-like, from pole to pole,
Wings would spread of kindly care,
Human joys and woes to share.
To no sect, or place, confin'd,
Vast his range of heart and mind:
Evil from his presence flies;
Virtue on his strength relies.
Men, in danger's fearful hour,
Trust his heaven-descended power:
If a conflagration breaks;
If a tempest overtakes;
Whatsoe'er th' occasion be,
Him, above the rest, you see;
Be it on the waves, or land,
All, to him, yield chief command.
Such, it is my bliss to know:
Much, how much, to him I owe!

THE COMMON SOLDIER.

His kinsmen have heard, that in death he fell low,
By wasting disease, or the arms of the foe.
They heard of his fall; but of fame the loud breath
Swells not through the nation, proclaiming his death.
O'er the unburied corse the fierce fowls of the air
Exultingly scream, as his carcass they tear,
Or scanty heap'd sods scarce conceal him from sight,
Till hungry wolves, growling, exhume him by night.
In national halls, no one thinks of the blow.
That struck down the brave, as he rush'd on the foe.
Of blood-purchas'd triumphs the state has the boon;
Holds fast the advantage, forgetting too soon
The price, not the prize; for this ever in view,
Exulting she sees; nor omits to pursue.
His blood is a unit, that little appears;
When fame, to his leader pays off her arrears.
Though such be his portion, what numbers now roam
From bliss-giving peace, and endearments of home;
Face death amidst pestilence, famine, and war,
And wild winds, and waters, all for the lone star!
The spoils few will share, who the dangers have brav'd
What rapine secures, for an end will be sav'd;
To add to the class; (each possessing, in fee,
A county or state,) call'd the Oligarchy.

All may not command, I, at once will agree:
But if, for low objects, such forces may be,
We n'er should lack soldiers, in high righteous cause,
Protection of country, its freedom and laws.

THE POET.

He pours the soul of battles in his lay:
With him, you rush amidst the bloody fray;
Through shatter'd ranks, behold the thundering car,
Infuriate whirl'd, and all the rage of war.
And when he sings of love, the conquering flame,
What spirits move through all the glowing frame!
Uncommon beauties clothe the smiling fair;
Superior graces all her motions wear.
What glowing scenes are by his fancy wrought!
What new creations to the mind are brought!
Instinct with life, the varied prospect glows:
Fields lovlier bloom, and water brighter flows;
The sun with greater radiance, fills the sky:
More mild effulgence flows from Luna's eye.
Familiar truth in greater strength appears:
Man, wisdom's counsels, with more reverence hears;
In soul-exalting numbers, genius bounds,
And things of earth, transports to heavenly grounds.

OF REMEDIES WORSE THAN THE DISEASE.

In medicine, a science dark,
Some, without compass, launch their bark,
On some Catholicon rely,
That dooms, by chance, to live, or die.
They boldly sail, with life for freight,
Through shoals of drugs, and mercury's strait;
Obstructing more health's current clear,
Than all distempers mortals fear.

Oft if one takes but little cold,
As curatives, great poisons, hold
Him long in trouble; a small matter,
Is made the health and strength to shatter:
And, many a year, the patient groans,
As change of weather pains his bones.
'Tis better trifles to endure,
Than swallow poisons for a cure.
But small assistance Nature needs,
To kill disease's sprouting seeds.

In Paris, a physician, dying,
His brethren, on his skill relying,
Spoke of his loss to human kind:
Grieve not, said he, I leave behind
Three excellent physicians, still,
With far more power to heal, than kill:
All, eager, wish'd the names made known:
Not doubting, each, to hear his own:
He straight pronounc'd, to their surprise:
Pure Water—Diet—Exercise.

Of water, quick the system feels
The active force, on all its wheels.
Full many a herb, in fame that blows,
To water, all its glory owes.
Large draughts dilute the morbid mass,
And make secretions swifter pass.

Not interested appetite,
But judgment, gages diet right:
Let reason place upon the plate,
At once, th' amount that should be ate.
A meal's omission may delay
A fever, or reduce its sway.
In exercise, let every part,
Exerted, answer to the heart;
When all have equal strength, and tone,

None bears a morbid weight alone;
Condemn'd, as others on it throw
Secretions foul, to weaker grow:
Disease (repell'd by all the strings,)
The body from its members flings.
For health, exertion nothing makes,
If urg'd until fatigue o'ertakes.
But those who, prudent, labor most,
May health's superior favors boast:
The central organ, least at rest,
Diseases least of all infest.

THE STORM.

Scowling, in the troubled west,
See the gloomy-mantled storm.
Lightnings glimmer on his breast,
Murmuring soars his giant form.

Wide his robe floats o'er the sky;
Like an ocean, dark and vast;
Or a continent thrown on high,
And around his shoulders cast.

Lightnings, prancing bright before,
Fierce he mounts his cloudy car;
Swift 'tis whirl'd, with stormy roar:
Earth's foundations feel the jar.

On Heaven's thunder-shaken field,
Giant horror, frowning dread,
Titan force he seems to wield,
'Gainst Earth's forest-crested head.

As she nods, with crashing sounds,
Shuddering in the ponderous blast,
Billowy-mantled Ocean bounds,
Smites, in foam, his margin vast.

Rocks and trees are rumbling borne
Down the lofty mountain's side;
By the raving tempest torn
From the peaks they crown'd with pride.

In the valleys, wide and deep,
On their peopled borders long,
Flood and wind tremendous sweep,
Bearing tumbling groves along.

Rocks and buildings, fences, trees,
Cattle, struggling with their fate,
Helpless man, in terror, sees,
And deplores the ruin great.

Sailors to the clouds are tost,
By the rushing waves and wind;
Then, replunging, seem as lost,
Till, again, the light they find.

Reckless mortals heavenward turn;
Feel their greatest power in prayer:
Beg, while Nature's furies burn,
He, who rules the world, may spare.

ATLAS.

Atlas lifts his giant head,
Pil'd with frosts of ages fled.
Highest point of Afric ground.
Erst of Heaven the prop renowned.
Icy helm and snowy crest,
Shine above his flinty breast.
Calm his lofty brow appears,
As in old Carthago's years;
When, of storms, he saw the tides
Rend his forest-cinctur'd sides.
As the trees that round him wave,
Rise, and sink into the grave,
Many a nation has his day
Seen, to rise and pass away.
Round his Heaven-invading brow,
Throng their ancient patriots now;
Scipio, Fabius, Hannibal:
Who perform'd their part so well,
With each other, love to dwell;
Of their earthly trials, tell;
Talk of fleeting glories, past,
And of States that could not last.
Party spirit's minions fly,
When they see a patriot nigh:
Guilty Hanno shrieks with fear,
When great Hannibal is near:
From his mild, accusing eyes,
Faction's State-destroyer flies.
Zama's terrors, Scipio's sword,
And his wretched country, gor'd
Ever haunt the Barcan's mind;
Doom'd but little rest to find,
Trooping with the sullen train,

Souls, malignant, vile, and vain:
Ever prone to hellward fly,
At the look of honest eye;
From its glance they troubled start,
Like the thunder's fiery dart,
That o'er Heaven, with quivering leap,
Bursts from stormy dungeon deep.

WHAT *IS*, MAY BE BEST.

Were hell so near,
That all could hear
The damned groan,
'Twould less be known,
If love, or fear, mankind
To righteous deeds inclin'd;
For knaves would, more
Alarm'd, daub o'er
Their whited tomb;
In deeper gloom,
Pursue confiding prey:
More trusted, more betray.
Uncertainty
Leaves will more free
The path to find
Whereto inclin'd,
Less forc'd by terror's yoke,
To wear ill fitting cloak.
Who knows but Heaven
Enough has given
Of needed light,
To guide aright,
And save the well inclin'd,
From snares of evil mind!

TRANSLATION FROM THE BEGINNING OF THE HENRIADE.

I SING the hero, that o'er Gallia reign'd,
Whose throne the right of birth and conquest gain'd.
By great misfortunes taught, to rule, he knew,
To calm the factions, pardon and subdue.
He made Mayenne, the League, and Spain, retire,
And prov'd his people's conqueror, and their sire.

Truth, power august, from lofty Heaven descend,
And to my song thy force and radiance lend;
Let ears of kings be used to know thy voice;
Of what they ought to learn, make thou the choice.
'Tis thine, before the eyes of States, to show
What ill effects from their divisions flow;
How discord curs'd our provinces reveal,
Nor people's woes, nor princes' faults conceal.
Come, speak; if fiction knew, in former days,
To blend her dulcet with thy lofty lays;
If her fair hand adorn'd thy stately head,
And if her shades made bright the beams you shed,
Permit her, on thy steps, to march with me,
To grace, not hide thy charms, that all may see.

WHO IS THIS?

His eyes are projected; his manner is green;
His reason is whirl'd in a torrent of spleen;
His nose is acute; his cheeks pallid and flat;
His voice much resembles the mew of a cat;
His gait is uneasy, uneven, and shy;
Head, body, face, members, are always awry;

And, e'en when in slumber, is drooping his head,
He wanders, in dreams, through the glooms of the dead:
And evil conceits keep the sleeper in scowl,
As nestling with serpents, or vermin most foul.
The mind on the vizage leaves tracks very queer,
And certifies sadly of some mortals here.

ON CHANGES.

Morn glows, noon flames, and the dim, shadowy eve
Of the ripe day, turns into sullen night.
Change is the child of Time, and Change marks all.
Each hour, a varying feature shows of day:
Each moment gives to coming moments place,
Unlike in semblance, each, and varying all.
The day from day, the year from year, and age from age.
Now Nature glories, jubilant with life,
Her green hair waving under smiling skies;
Fair summer teems with fruits, in colors gay;
Life's music, and life's beauty, fill the world;
The sighing zephyrs kiss the blushing flowers,
Whispering their loves along the fragrant meads;
Now screams the tempest wild, and scowls the storm,
With dark-brow'd rage, with rumbling thunder charg'd:
Wide-flaming lightnings strike heaven's startled void;
The sluicy torrents fall from melting clouds,
Gladdening the thirsty breast of foodful Earth:
Now winter's icy pall life's march restrains,
With heart-pervading chill, and aspect cold,
To rocky ice transforming murmuring streams.
Earth's talking strata, the lost pleiad, shells,
And bones of races, now extinct, proclaim
The constancy of Change: and seem to say,
Existence is but motion to successive ends.

TRANSLATION FROM ILIAD—VIII.—130.

DEFEATED, now, the Trojan host had fled
To sheltering Troy; but Heaven the battle led;
Jove, thundering downward, quivering lightnings hurl'd;
Loud, near Tydides' steeds, he smites the world;
Their breasts on earth, the car against them roll'd.
By blazing sulphur stunn'd, they rent the wold:
No longer Nestor's hands the reins could hold:
Alarm'd, he warns the Chief: Can'st thou not see
Great Jove, this day, no victory sends to thee?
Swift seek the fleet; such seems the God's command:
And luckless they, who dare his will withstand;
This moment, Hector's glory, Jove ordains;
Hope, then, his future aid, and fly these dreadful plains.

BEAUTY OF NATURE.

RUDDY morning soon will break;
Lordly Sol ascend the sky;
Birds, with cheerful songs, awake;
Night, with all her shadows, fly:

Nature, then, with robe of light,
Will her sweetest charms display,
Crimson rose and lily white,
Blooming on her face of day.

Dazzling sunbeams, odorous air,
Kissing, steal her dewy tears,
As, in joyful beauty, fair,
Nature, crown'd with day, appears.

In her brilliant pomp of stars,
Mountains high, and oceans wide;
In her elemental wars,
Grandeur dwells with her, in pride.

Space, her Temple; God, her Sire;
Lights eternal gild her dome;
Boundless were the soul's desire,
Boundless were her joys of home.

THE SOUL.

Restless, in her prison dark
Glad the soul would pinions find,
Far to rove, in freedom stark,
To no bounds of earth confin'd.

Tost on waves of hope and fear,
'Tis not yet for man to know
States in many a higher sphere,
States in many a sphere below.

If the soul material be,
But of lightning's nimble gleam,
Happy hosts the freed may see,
Round the earth, in brightness stream.

Others cast a lurid ray;
For, in time, their deeds were bad:
Still, whom evil instincts sway,
Must endure the hard and sad.

THE BALANCE.

ADDRESSED TO THURSTON H. GENIN, SEPT., 1845.

WHY spend we life in search of gold?
Can one, in death, the treasure hold?
In time, how small th' allotted share!
The food we eat, the clothes we wear!
Of Providence, we hold at will.
Each only can his measure fill.
All wealth is but a vexing toy,
Beyond the bounds we may enjoy.
The tinsell'd trappings, shining gay,
Can chase no pain or grief away.
The savory meats, so much that please,
Oft aggravate, or bring disease:
And he who seeks far more to gain,
Than what suffices to maintain,
O'erclouds his days with needless care,
Nor gets of bliss a common share.
Seek, then, a competence, nor be
The slave of wealth or poverty.
Like true utilitarian, try
All things to usefully apply.
Nor deem corporeal wants alone,
To man, of deathless soul, are known.
The wants of body and of mind,
Should, equally, indulgence find.

Sweet pleasures dwell in mental fields;
Delightful harvests wisdom yields:
Thrice happy they, of noble aims,
Whose souls are warm'd by generous flames,
Who by no sect or passion bound,
To all mankind are friendly found:
Who on the earth not stay, but live;
To every sense enjoyment give;
Nor pain the ear to gratify
The taste, the smell, or curious eye:
Nor let one passion bear away,
What should the others' wants allay:
For all have equal rights from Heaven;
To none exclusive sway is given.
Gay Fancy, in her frolic mood,
Delights to feast on flowery food;
While judgment, sober-vizag'd, brings
In fit relation, things to things.
Imagination likes to soar
Through starry fields, and worlds explore:
Invention glories by her side,
And god-like reason, glorious guide!
They win, for wisdom, useful spoils;
Oft found and grac'd by Fancy's toils.
All aid each other, and should be
Maintain'd in sacred unity.
I, *Reason*, and you, *Fancy*, now,
You teach me *well* to make a bow;
Which adds a trifle to my grace;
And hence more welcome makes my face:
Thus, Fancy's uses are most plain:
To argue from abuse, is vain.

With us, thrift's claims are not allow'd
The arts, or poetry, to crowd:
We, now, in epic grandeur soar;
Now, over legal learning pore;
Now, gratify th' artistic mind;

Now, do the task, by gain enjoin'd.
No cause neglected at the bar,
One sings, at large, Napoleon's war;
One makes the canvas brilliant glow,
With scenes of human joy, or wo.
One thing at once! and we may see,
Our practice bring prosperity.

CINCINNATI, Oct. 10, 1845.

DEAR BROTHER :—Your ode, on governing the desires, and treating them with reasonable indulgence, is received—You know I have not the patience to rhyme, or to paint—The reason I gave satisfaction to a dozen, or more, sitters, when abroad for my health, was, that I felt over supplied with leisure. I am now much disposed to "do the task by gain enjoined," or amplify in the law on those elementary principles we have discussed so often, in our walks, in the fair groves of Belmont.

I have thrown together some ideas in prose, in answer to your ode, as follows :

We should not waste time at any thing. If gratified, by accumulating riches, some happiness is gained ; which, once enjoyed, death itself cannot take away. This gain, then, is sure, and without waste of time. If one can scarce hold six feet of ground at last, he still may hold more when he *can*, and when it is of *use* for him to do so. The millionaire can enjoy no more than the beggar; yet, his competence is more certain ; and the cares of wealth are not more troublesome than the anxieties of poverty. Bright trappings cannot banish pain ; but the possession of comforts need not increase it. The abuse of luxuries affords no argument against their use. No wealth is so great, but it may be employed to add to one's enjoyment, and no fortune is so small, but it may prove, with unwise or unlucky management, a source of discomfort. What constitutes a competence, is a difficult question. The middle line is disputable. In seeking the happy medium some get on one side. Fortune often puts the bridle on the owner of riches ; and instead of making them serve *him*, he becomes *their* slave. This is his own fault. Because some permit themselves to become asses, others should not be deterred from laying up, even a large store, against accidents, infirmities, old age, poetry and painting, the wants of children, grand children, and other relatives, whose obliging attentions are desirable, aud who can scarce be expected to accord them, with pleasing alacrity, without hope. The mind is pleased with the gratifications of the body ; it might be more pleased with its own. Who neglects mental wants, neglects the best opportunities of enjoyment. The mind should be kept in balance : The equal cultivation of each faculty imparts greater energy to the faculties collectively. The lessons of reason, would often not be read, without the embellishments of fancy. In the schools, memory is too much cultivated at the expense of judgment, and imagination. Thus, the active scholar becomes a dull lawyer, or preacher : and the world marvel, that he looses the ascendency, when thrown upon his judgement, that he maintained, when at school, by the strength of his memory. Hence Milton, Goldsmith, and even Daniel Webster, had less repute at school than others of less note. The intellectual wings, legs, or faculties, should not outgrow each other, causing a hobbling gait ; but be able to give reciprocal support, by possessing equal capabilities. One should not be educated to be like a fiddle without a bow. It needs several notes to make harmony. With some, Fancy plays the Siren. Those who control their impulses, who have great concentrativeness, and decision of character, may be civil to enchantresses, without being captivated and led astray. Those who can discharge from their minds other matters, and concentrate the mental force on one thing, may do it well ; still the safer opinion is, that one business, only, will fit one genius. On the whole, we cannot do better, than to employ what God has given us, to the best advantage ; Avoid ex-

tremes, and, in all things act very reasonable ; not forgetting that improvement of mind is treasure laid up in heaven.
So you have my ode, still farther removed from verse, than Dr. Donne's satires, and the wit, perhaps, less harmonious.
Affectionately yours, &c.,
THURSTON H. GENIN.

JUDGES XV.

SAMSON.

They brought him fetter'd, feet and hands,
Before the arm'd Philistine bands;
Whose numbers, lances, banners gay,
Bright glittering, fearful odds display.
The hostile host around him drew,
Intent the wonderous man to view;
While Israel's sons, in sadness, slow,
And pensive, from their hero go:
By force oppressive, forc'd to yield,
To hated foes, their country's shield.

While some great Samson's form admire,
Or, from his startling glance, retire,
Awe-struck, before his speaking eye,
Accustom'd to behold them fly,
The vile, not deeming danger near,
Speak ribald jests he scorns to hear:
But, at th' insulting shout of foes,
A force divine, within him rose:
Like bow-string, snapt, he sudden sprung;
Beneath his feet, Earth hollow rung:
For shield, a well-arm'd chief he took:
His dexter hand a jaw-bone shook;

On high, the fatal weapon bore,
With teeth, athirst for human gore.
His sinewy arm spread ruin wide;
Beneath his fury, hundreds died.
As some strong swain the sickle wields,
And fells the grain of fruitful fields;
So the fierce chief, with angry might,
Sweeps down proud ranks to endless night.

SAMSON'S DEATH.

His arms the pillars grasp; his feet below
Against them press, and, with exerted strength,
His muscles swell, and from their places rend
The blocks of marble, which sustain'd the dome:
Dread crash, and wail, and terror-vizag'd men
Amidst the tumbling edifice are seen.

A DREAM.

Me thought I stood in hell, and past me troop'd
Grim shadowy forms and strange; while through the gloom
Shot fitful gleams, and plumes, and fiery helms.
A voice, like stifled growl of lions, swallowing blood,
Rose from infernal throats; and hateful looks
Were cast, as march'd they o'er the smouldering ground,
With hollow-sounding tread, o'er cast, by fits,
With zig-zag lightnings, and wrath-flashing forms.
Discord, revenge, and every plague was there,

With evil zeal, exerting powers malign.
Their march died on my ear, like ocean's roar,
When the tired winds scarce fan his weary waves.
Then, thinking of the just, the good, and kind,
Through hell's dark shroud I pass'd to upper light,
Near Heaven's eternal splendors. Floating round,
With easy grace, in sparkling locks, with air
Of beauty, that celestial sweetness beam'd,
I saw th' angelic host, in joy supreme,
And felt the balmy, music-breathing wind,
Charg'd with the fragrance of etherial groves.
  A lofty-streaming pennon's glossy folds,
Reflecting quivering blaze of restless light,
Wide undulating o'er the starry deep,
For leagues, from o'er an arch of flaming suns
Of every dye, that mingled splendors shower'd,
My sight arrested. While I tried to read
"Here none but those of upright heart and pure
May come," upon the billowy flag, I woke,
And found myself a subject still of Earth.

MY PEGASSUS.

  SEE how my old Pegassus with a slight thwack,
Upbears me aloft on his sharp bony back!
His tail stands erect, though it has not a hair;
His paunch rumbles loud, as we rush through the air.
High kicking the clouds, in a frolicsome flirt,
He sends up a mist, just as others do dirt.
He wore out his tail by outrunning the wind;
It scarce could keep hold on the spinal behind.
Both nag and the rider are lean as church mice:
In flight, their bones rattle, like hail on the ice:

No matter, provided he keeps up his spirits;
And after long journeys, in proof of his merits,
He pricks up his ears, and his tail, with a squeal,
And high in the air throws his spindle-shank'd heel.

DAY GRASPS NOT NIGHT, NOR MAN PURE HAPPINESS:

STILL, sad, and lone, night broods o'er half the world,
Cold dew-drops trickling down her twilight veil,
Spread over brows star-gemm'd. With aspect east
Grave, from her realm of gloom, she views the day,
Fringing with gold her ample robe of shade,
And sullen, moves majestic from his gaze
Westward, o'er continents huge, and oceans vast.
His ardour wakes the thunder; but in vain
He chases round the Earth the dusky queen,
Giving glad interchange of light and shade,
And rest and motion to organic forms:
Thus mortals seek, but never overtake
Pure happiness; yet in the long pursuit
Diffuse great blessings, as, with glorious toil,
They work the general good to effect their own.
One tempting bubble breaks, as soon as gain'd;
Another, in bright prospect, straight excites
Assiduous labor, and as empty proves:
Still, hope untir'd, the barren chase resumes;
The priceless prize must be beyond the grave.

TO DEATH.

O death, all conquering, when will cease thy reign!
Wilt thou be vanquish'd, or shall all things die,
And thou, in triumph, hold the blighted Earth!
The world quakes in thy presence : nations quail
At thy dread march; more swift, than eagle wing'd,
More strong, than lion of the desert wild,
In vain, fell hunter, flies thy shrieking prey:
It falls amidst its flight, pierc'd by thy shafts.
From thy sure aim poor man no refuge finds;
No safe retreat; the castled citadel;
The tangled woods; the warriors arms and shield;
The pharmacy of science' sons, ward not
Thy arrows keen. The soft-arm'd infant mild,
The maiden, rosy-cheek'd, are prostrate laid,
With mighty men. Nor vigor iron-nerv'd;
Nor tender innocence; nor sunny eyes
Of winning beauty, thy remorseless heart
Can move. Where art thou not, O dreaded power!
In ocean's dark recesses thou art thron'd:
The mariner meets thee on the roaring surge,
Toss'd in the angry whirlwind's foamy path:
Thou rid'st the black wings of the stormy blast,
Shattering tall-masted navies; and thou mov'st
In pleasure's flowery ways; in sorrow's shades;
In power and splendor's stately palaces;
In poverty's obscure and sad abodes;
On crimson battle fields; in peaceful homes;
Rending, with grief, the amiable and kind,
And steeping earth with sacred friendship's tears.
Pale vizag'd terror, and loud wails, attend
Thy desolating steps. O, kindly bear
Me to thy shades, by sudden lightning stroke;

Nor let me hear the voice of anguish'd hearts
Around my bed, burdening my soul with grief;
Nor, pining, see thy ghastly slow approach
Through lengthen'd years of life-consuming pain.
But come not, with thy heart-o'erclouding gloom,
Until the frost of age shall blanch my locks;
My parents be repaid their tender cares;
My manly strength support their tottering age;
My deeds the annals of my race adorn;
And virtuous life establish claim to Heaven.
But if unfurnish'd with the needful wings
To scale the glorious heights; still stay thy dart;
For well endeavoring wins Heaven's kind regard.

RESOLUTION TO ATTACK THE PERSIANS AT THE GRANICUS.

To where the imperial standard wav'd, above
The stately tent, in glittering folds, each eye
Was turn'd, as trumpet's voice call'd every chief
To meet in council, with Olympia's son;
Who strode his tent, impatient to discern
In every face, if confidence prevail'd,
Ere he the meditated battle join'd.
Obedient came the gray hair'd, and the young;
Those, who made Philip hope to rule the world;
And those, who saw no danger, but in rest:
A manly throng, from noblest nature hewn;
By exercise, and temperance, improv'd.
Hope, prudence, firmness, valor, glorious scars,
Sat on their brows, recalling battles past,
And triumphs over Greek and barbarous foes.
O'er Granicus, they eyed the Persian force:
Indignant viewed the foe-protecting stream;
The bristling, steep acclivity beyond,

And look'd as if, in thought, engag'd in fight,
Impressing on their minds the country's shape,
And true position of the Persian host,
Resolving just opinions to advance.
  Before the youthful king, all reverent stood:
Youth's ardor, age's wisdom from him blaz'd:
He eyes the veteran council; in them sees
Firm self-reliance, dissipating doubt
Of sage Parmenio: he, in their past,
Beholds their future triumphs, and for fight declares;
At which, each vizage sudden glows with joy:
Enough, he cries; each from his heart assents;
Although the Sun is on his downward march,
Bucephalus shall soon his monarch bear
Up yonder steep; who would with him keep pace,
By strength and valor need be greatly serv'd:
Haste, plunge the phalanx in the rushing waves,
Ourself will, forthwith, lead the bounding horse.

MANY-VOICED COMMOTION.

  CLOUDS pil'd on clouds, in tempest, darkening roll,
In ocean masses; loud, the rushing wind,
Resistless, sweeps along the groaning earth,
That reels beneath its forest-crashing power.
The huge trunk'd woods, in stormy chaos whirl'd,
With roots and limbs commingled, ride the air,
Tangled and shiver'd in their gnarled hearts;
Snatch'd from their realm of shade, by giant hands,
And thrown, like chaff, upon the troubled sky.
Black night, and fiery day, alternate reign;
Condensing clouds land-flooding torrents pour :
The broad Earth trembles at the thunder's march,
And many-voic'd commotion stirs the soul.
Hoarse raves the wind-torn main; convulsive heaves

His mighty breast; he madden'd strikes his shores,
In foamy rage, and flings his billowy arms
Against cloud-shielded heaven. Mankind, with awe,
Behold the storm, and hear its various voice :
Its frenzied rage; the rush of floods; the wild
World-startling roar; shaking wide continents,
With all their sky-crown'd mountains, lakes and seas.

ODE TO THE WIND.

O, GENTLE ,furious, various-toned wind;when first didst thou blow, and, with refreshing breath, fan the rolling Earth ? When first rise in thy rage, to break the tree, among whose branches thou hadst often played ? Didst thou first breathe, when gentle Eve, in goddess-like beauty, made lovelier by innocence and primæval manners, fresh from her Creator's hand, in Eden placed, on flowers ever fair, of brightest tint, first felt thy balmy breath upon her cheek of graceful curve, where the bright rose, harmonious mingling with the fair lily, formed the rich carnation ? She raised her ivory hand to feel what touched so softly, her fair face, and moved her curling hair ; but thou hadst fled : She felt in vain, then raised her pleasing eyes, bright in lovely innocence, and turned her graceful head. Her raven tresses floated on her neck, in waving curls, and down her snowy back, and over her heaving breast. With wonder moved, again she feels, again she tries to see the reed, that late stood still, now waved before her view ; holds it with her hand until it ceases to move, then, released, beholds it wave again. The forbidden tree whose lofty height she had beheld with wonder, as, calm it reared its lofty head, met next her gaze. She backward shrunk, astonished : It seemed to move ! O wind, then didst thou blow in Paradise, the wonder of the primæval race : Then first they felt thy soft wing ; and afterwards thou wast their joy, when they heard thee coursing through the rustling trees :

and when, by Satan's power, and moved by sin, they disobeyed God's law, and mournful wept, condemned to leave their natal home, and wander in a lower world of wo, thou camest to sooth their toilsome march, and cheer their barren home, their fainting spirits to revive, their feverish heat to cool, and sweep from their abode pestilential exhalations, with thy health-preserving wings

How they loved thy greeting, O wind, in the vernal mornings, when laden with the fragrance of fresh-born flowers ; or when thou fann'd the sultry noon of leaf-crown'd Summer, panting in verdant pomp, and listening with increased delight to the music of the gurgling stream ; or made the lofty groves, and the meadows and fields of bearded grain, to wave in graceful undulation, casting varying shade as they bowed to thy airy power ; nor did they hear without emotion thy autumnal voice in the faded woods, as the many color'd foliage was borne along on thy pinions ; nor view unmoved the various forms wrought by thy fluency on the snowy breast of cold winter as the white banks rose in fantastic shapes unnumber'd, under the lee of the leafless hedge, or bleak hill, moulded by thy whistling breath.

The year, from thy kisses, glows with beauty, and nature attains more varied charms, as thou givest graceful motion to the leafy branches of the verdant groves, dimpling the smooth surface of the lake, stirring the deep seas, the giant-limbed forests, the flowery meads, wafting the fragrance of blossoms, rejoicing in youthful freshness, rolling the clouds through the sun-illumed sky, or along the face of the silvery moon, when the voice of the bird of night is heard, and urging the roving mariner over the heaving breast of ocean, and making sail-winged navies crowd the dark waters into banks of snowy foam, before their rushing prows.

In thy slumber, when the waves subside in a level plain, the impatient sailor, mourning his listless plight, in æolian tones, invokes thee to rise. With joy he sees, afar, thy light feet dimple in spots, the lazy flood. At length thou comest, in thy power, and the monotony of the watery wild departs : over its broad bosom roll foam-crested billows; the canvass swells ; the strained cordage owns thy power ; and the reanimated tar, flushed with high hopes, is borne on, in foam, towards the home of his youth.

The breath of nature, thou addest to the vivacity of the fair sunny day, and to the grandeur of the storm, as thou bearest his throne of clouds through the frowning heaven. Mild, yet dreadful; gentle, yet terrible; who can describe thy rage, when rocks are swept from the mountain's brow, and forests borne aloft by thy frantic arms!

LABOR.

Useful labor, fit employ,
Source of health, and every joy,
Warms the cheek with rosy dye;
Lights, with gladsome smiles, the eye;
Swells the form with buoyant grace;
Moulds, with beauty's curve, the face;
Makes thick tresses, shining, float;
Gives the voice its joyful note;
Every nerve sensations sweet;
Soft the steady pulse to beat:
To the harp " of thousand strings,"
Harmony and vigor brings:
Makes the chords of life to chime,
Uttering dulcet tune to time,
As, with constant hand, he flings
Days and years across the strings.
Woes of idleness unknown,
Comes no self-accusing tone;
Outward ills afflict alone,
Sprung from causes not our own.
Sleepless nights and tedious days,
Haunt not peaceful labor's ways;

By whose energy advanc'd,
Every blessing is enhanc'd;
Water, more the taste delights;
With more strength the feast invites;
Each repast, with gust, is blest;
Slumber brings refreshing rest:
With reflection, comes content
For the past, with profit spent;
And in works, forever good,
Finds the soul immortal food.

DAY OF JUDGMENT.

I SLEPT, while centuries roll'd, and state on state
Rose on the tide of time, and pass'd away,
As exhalations from the marshy wastes,
Oceans, and rivers, that o'erload the air
With wind-tost storm clouds, and from troubled sky,
In rain drops fall, and mix with lands and waves.
As raging tempests, blasting conquerors swept
The green earth's face, with desolating force ;
Then ceas'd, like spent winds, and earth smiled again,
As clear'd of storm. In alternation, thus,
Like causes like effects producing, mov'd
The good and evil fortunes of mankind,
Through the long period of my deep repose.
And now, the time prescribed by fate, had come ;
Nature's last pulse had beat ; life's wheels were still ;
The waning sun grew cold, and pale ; the moon,
Darkening, was scarce discern'd ; a mournful gloom
O'er spread the earth ; her barren breast no more
Was fann'd by gales ; no silvery rivulets flow'd,
Watering the meads ; but stagnant, still, and cold,

They slept on blasted lands ; the rivers roll'd
Their glassy waves no more to Ocean's bed
Of brine ; his mighty deep itself was still ;
Nor moan'd in sounding caves, nor lash'd the murmuring shores:
A deathful silence reign'd, and gloom profound ;
When, lo, the archangel, in mid-heaven, on wing,
Before Jehovah's throne, mouth'd the dread trump,
With throat ordain'd to rouse the sleeping dead :
So high its voice, that all the thunders loud,
And all the furious storms, that ever swept
A planetary world, in one conjoin'd,
Compar'd to this, were but a bee's faint hum,
Contrasted with the angry lion's roar.
Blast after blast, in quick succession, sends
Intense vibrations through creation's bounds ;
While the vast circle with the unnumbered worlds,
Trembling, like aspen leaves, disgorged their dead :
Then mortal substance vanish'd ; nought remain'd,
But the immortal spirit freed from dust,
And indestructible. The countless host,
From countless places, in the land and waves,
Ascended, summon'd by the trump of doom.

The good and wicked, mingled stand before
God's throne, in humble plight, for sentence just,
Mild, or severe, as they, in righteousness,
Or wickedness, had pass'd their lives on earth.

On dazzling throne, that living radiance shed,
On sapphire pillars rais'd, the Almighty sat,
In dread effulgence veil'd : awe-struck, had shrunk
Unnumber'd millions ; but no hiding place
Immensity could give. Some faces beam'd
Distressful apprehension, and some beat
Their visionary breasts : For each retain'd
The semblance still of his terrestrial form.

Before, with reverent air, two seraphs stood,
Their pearly brows grac'd with ambrosial curls,
Which down their waists, in graceful ringlets flow'd,
Cast rays of mild effulgence, as they bore,

On high, the book of fate : each filmy leaf
Once the sensorium of each being's frame,
Or transcript of each soul's each act, and thought,
Thereon self-stamp'd and conscience-judg'd, in *time*.
Their hands, like gentle winds, the leaves turn o'er,
Big with the weal or wo of all mankind.
Innumerable angels, now, with speed
Of lightning, move among the assembly vast,
Swift separating the commingled souls,
As final judgment on their thoughts and deeds
Gave them to endless wo, or heavenly joys;
Or for a bounded period, doom'd to pain.
 The omniscient eye, meanwhile, th' existence view'd
Of every being in the numerous host ;
And all their actions, good and bad ; designs
And circumstances ; weigh'd and judg'd the whole.
A momentary gloom of grief o'ercast
His face, and nature droop'd through all her worlds,
To see what numbers had their ruin wrought;
So few, compar'd with all, secure of bliss.
 They knew not why the great division made;
In racking doubt, and buoyant hope they stood,
Uncertain of their everlasting doom.
 With mingled majesty and goodness, smil'd
The Eternal Father; and the gracious look,
Immensity illum'd, as he uprose
To enjoy the bliss of just benificence,
That goodness only feels. He to the blest
Upon the right, while at each motion, flam'd
Etherial splendors, spoke with kindly tone:
 "Ye victors o'er the frailties of your race,
Who ruled your passions; taught my precepts well,
By great examples, and my laws obey'd;
Ye benefactors of the human kind,
Who virtues taught, and virtuous deeds perform'd;
Ye sons of science; legislators wise;
Who pitying man's estate his miseries sooth'd;
His wants reliev'd; who nourished useful arts

And sciences; and thus the groveling mind
Prepar'd to comprehend and take my lore;
And in all things behold the lord of all;
Ye claim my great regard: Henceforth enjoy
Immortal peace, in my eternal realm."

He spoke, and at cherubic signal, to the right,
Elate with joy, the multitude advance;
In brightness swelling, flush'd with light divine,
As heavenly spirit heavenly vigor took:
Sweet strains from instruments and voice, arose,
As o'er the fields of Amaranth, and rills
Of nectar, and ambrosial joyful scenes,
They march'd, with easy graceful steps, away.

The unhappy host, from their position, gaz'd
With longing eyes on that receding mass;
Which vanish'd from their vision soon, in clouds
Of splendor. Darkness now, as when eclips'd,
The central light is shorn of half his beams,
Pervades the presence of the eternal throne;
And to the unblest thus speaks the Lord of worlds:

"Ye, who made show of virtue, till, yourselves
Deceiv'd, imagin'd Heaven itself was blind;
Form-practisers, not substance-doers; bold
Game-makers of my sway; upsending prayers
From tongues, not hearts; vain boasters, proud
Of formal righteousness, of Heaven despis'd;
And ye, more honest knaves, who frankly gave
Your lives to vice, go, all to ceasless wo.

But you, less thoughtful souls, that, well inclin'd,
Were urg'd by circumstances into sin;
Omitting to resist temptation's wiles;
Whom yonder hypocrites with felons yok'd;
Exposed to crime, withholding wages due;
Your youth polluting, punishing your age;
Forgetful of your past existence, soon,
Another mortal trial shall ye have;
Life's cares and toils and hopes and fears again
Upon another planet shall be yours.

He ceas'd; these wept; those wail'd in hopeless grief,
As in dark tempest whirl'd they downward roll'd.
These, pitying angels bore to distant orbs
Through gloom Lethean, there to be reborn.

MERCY.

Sprung from greatness, glorious born,
Rose of beauty on life's thorn,
Meek-eyed Mercy! thou above
Passion's storm, mild-beaming love,
Draw'st the reverence of mankind.
Though to war's harsh rule confin'd,
Valor's votaries own thy sway:
Noble hearts thy voice obey.
Justice draws her sword for thee,
Sheaths it at thy high decree:
All her actions lovlier seem,
Temper'd by thy heavenly beam.
Dweller, kind, in lofty souls!
Statesmen wise, thy lore controls.
Wisdom, Virtue, Justice, twine
Wreaths, to grace thy brows divine.
  When the day of war shall fade,
Sinking in reproachful shade;
When his horrid glories bright,
Fall in never-ending night,
His connexion with thy name,
Still, from death, shall save his fame:
Brilliant, o'er his sad career,

Oft will beam thy starry tear.*
Virtue, with indignant tread,
Walking midst the slaughter'd dead,
Feels of joy a heavenly glow,
As she hears of solac'd wo:
On the hateful scene of blood,
Gathers what thou sow'd of good,
And records each act of thine,
In the book of things divine.
 Man may numerous nations sway:
Genius wonderous powers display;
Still, unblest by Virtue's smile,
Barren proves the mighty toil!
Goodness vital spirit gives,
To the deed that deathless lives.

*VARIATION.

Justice, with a scornful glance,
Where oblivion's shades advance.
O'er the monster's tomb of night,
Shrouding actions, ghastly bright,
Sees, in sadness, beaming clear,
Mercy's many a starry tear.

THE HOME OF BEAUTY.

O, who can look on Nature's face,
Nor feel her sweet attractive grace!
Deep blushing in the bloom of May,
Or bright with fruits of Autumn's day:

Or in the blaze of morning's light;
Or in the star-deck'd veil of night;
Or in her virgin garb of snow;
Or green attire in summer's glow.
　How beautiful the wind-wav'd trees,
The nodding flowers, in grassy seas!
The song of birds, the flow of rills,
The varied forms of vales and hills!
The cloudy shapes, through heaven that sail,
With varying aspect on the gale!
The fleetly-rolling snow-capp'd seas,
Gay dancing to the buoyant breeze!
Earth wrapt in silvery robes of light,
Returning Luna's glances bright,
Back smiling on the Queen of Night!
As through the blue expanse she glides,
And heaves old ocean's mighty tides;
The dewy tears of grey-eyed morn;
The glories, that her face adorn;
The tints of golden-misted eve,
As day, with pensive eye, takes leave,
And twilight's hand, nights gate unbars,
Mild ushering darkness, crown'd with stars;
A shadowy queen, that rules alone,
Mysterious, on her dusky throne;
The gloomy grandeur of the skies,
As vapory masses darkening rise;
The lightning's leap from stormy cloud,
Chas'd by earth-shaking thunder loud;
While rise the winds, down rush the floods;
Dim seen through mist, wild wave the woods;
But soon the clouds, dissolv'd in tears,
The earth in brighter smiles appears;
Sol's rays, with gladness, seem to rest
Upon her life-sustaining breast:
In brief, all things to sight that come,
Proclaim, that here is Beauty's home.

INDIAN GHOSTS AT NIAGARA.

Niagara calls from loud thundering throne,
And throws up the spray of swift torrents more high;
When trooping, in tempest, with storm-trumpet tone,
Come Indian ghosts, glancing along the grim sky.
The vales, where their wigwams and children had been,
The hills, the fair rivers, the glens that they love,
They quit for high revelry in the wild scene:
In th' earth-rending uproar they joyfully rove.
In mist, high ascending, some gracefully rise;
Some glance, as on thunder bolts, o'er the white foam;
Some, with the storm spirits, dart round in the skies;
And some on the breast of the tumbling flood roam.
They join in the crash, in the shout and the wail,
The trembling of nature, as rages the storm,
The cataract's thunder, the wild rushing gale,
And ride the vex'd air on dark clouds of grim form.

CIRCUMSTANCES ALTER APPEARANCES.

O, LOVELIEST, sweetest flower of earth!
From Paradise, an angel straying?
Thou sure art not of mortal birth;
But heaven-born seraph, with us staying.
Around thee, closely clings my soul;
For thee, I live; for thee, would die:
Love's warmest fires my heart control;
Now make me laugh; now bid me sigh!
  So sung the swain; but chang'd his tone,
When he, rejected, stood alone:
  You ugly, speckled, wrinkled frog,

With gutteral tones of bristly hog!
A curse upon your squinting eye!
I bid your crooked shanks, good-bye:
You hump-back'd, hollow-breasted loon!
You slab-fac'd dog, with eyes of moon:
You wry-mouth'd cheat; low, heartless knave,
With soul too small, for aught to save:
Thy ill-form'd scalp, and sneaking face,
Proclaim, thou art mankind's disgrace.

VICE ITS OWN PUNISHMENT.

ALIKE to states and men shall flow,
From sinful deeds, avenging wo.
   Whene'er the hand of reckless power,
Hurls justice from her sacred throne,
   The seeds of plagues, that must devour,
By that unrighteous act are sown:
   Straight springs a hideous monster brood,
With instincts of infernal source;
   Fell rapine, wrong, and hate, their food,
And blood and ruin mark their course.
   Unhappy, who their country see,
Become too vicious to be free;
They need not grieve to childless die,
Or fade beneath a foreign sky,
When wrong, with heaven-defying head,
On laws and oaths, makes dastard rulers tread.
   O, land of Washington and Jay!
Whom virtue blest with freedom's day:
What mighty cause hast thou to weep
Thy sons, in Mexico, that sleep:
To slavery's Moloch bow'd their life;
Their deeds were brave, but vile the strife:

They fell, no native land to shield:
Their triumphs deadly plagues will yield.
They gain'd fell discord's fatal prize;
From which, shock'd Freedom turns her eyes,
And looks on other days, with tears,
On virtuous men, and happier years;
Feels hope within her bosom die:
She heavenward lifts her tearful eye;
Lest Justice, with indignant hand,
Blast, with war's scourge, th' invader's land,
O'erwhelm'd beneath the tide of wo,
That refluent rolls from Mexico.
 O, impious race, can justice sleep ?
From Heaven, impends th' avenging blow:
Repentant tears you soon may weep:
For your proud States, what fearful harvests grow !
 Your lawless rapine's raging flame,
Turn'd on yourselves, will it grow tame,
When discord's hand your Union's knot unties,
And war's red sword divides your pirate prize ?
 You, then, may weep o'er Freedom's tomb,
Oppress'd with shame, and hopeless wo;
No ray to cheer the mournful gloom;
Reproachful degradation know;
Faint, writhing at oppression's heel;
And Slavery's crimes, in bitterest anguish, feel.
 For ravenous Ruin's haggard eye,
Shall ghastly glare on midnight sky;
Fell slaughter rave, in boundless rage;
Nor spare or beauty, sex, or age:
The torch of discord angry glow;
Fraternal blood in battle flow;
Until the wild and madden'd tide,
Shall, at a tyrant's voice, subside,
And in despotic calm remain;
Nought heard, but sighs, and clank of Slavery's chain.

THE STEAMER.

The fire-steed of ocean now springs from the shore;
How lightly he prances the green billows o'er!
He tosses his star-spangled mane to the skies,
And snorting, in thunder, fast seaward he flies:
       The waters below
       Are whirl'd, as in wrath,
       And whiten, as snow,
       His green rolling path:
He spreads his broad pennons, the breezes to hail;
Impatiently stretches his arms to the gale:
The quick-spouting breath of his strong iron lung,
Is far on the winds, like a stormy cloud, flung.
       And laboring more loud,
       As waves on him crowd,
       He rushes along,
       Triumphantly strong!
Out-running the tempest, the sails belly back;
Behind, pant the racers of air, on his track;
High wafting the vapors his nostrils have cast,
O'er heaven's expansion, unbounded, and vast.
       Still trampling, in pride,
       The world-grasping tide,
       Untir'd in the race,
       He urges his pace:
His giant arms faster belabor the flood;
And swifter he bounds on the billowy road:
The big foaming surges he scatters in spray,
And crushes the billows that leap in his way:
       While far in his rear,
       The swept waves appear
       To pause, in surprise,
       As from them he flies:

His silvery wake, on the tempested breast
Of ocean, remains in comparative rest:
The strong rushing currents he dashes behind,
O'erpowering the strength of the billows and wind,
    In swift eddies cast,
    Run smoothly and fast;
    Still feeling the force,
    That gives them their course.

VIRTUE.

O, THAT, secur'd by Virtue's power
No vices could one's fate control,
Or taint th' unguarded youthful soul,
  In sad misfortune's luckless hour;
That every act and thought might be
Kind, just, and wise; high, bold, and free.
  Let wisdom rouse, in timely hour,
The glorious death-defying flame,
That gives the nobly useful aim,
  The lofty structure-rearing power;
    The energy divine,
    That makes the soul incline
    To what is great and good;
    To breast th' opposing flood
Of passions, breathing siren song;
Enticing man, himself, to wrong,
As oft as feeble reason sleeps,
Or carelessly her sentry keeps.
Assisted by its heavenly power,
    And guiding light,
    Intent on right,
In safety, or in peril's stormy hour,

With zeal, th' unyielding soul
  Shall seek the glorious goal,
Uncheck'd by vice, or folly's adverse tide,
Or aught that darkens or illumes the way,
On victory's eagle pinions bent to ride,
Till high success the worthy toil repay.

THE DEAD.

When steer'd across life's stormy wave,
My lone bark harbors in the grave,
O, let not love, or hatred, keep
The place in memory where I sleep;
Nor tears of wo, by friendship shed,
Bedew the cold sod o'er my head;
Nor bursting sighs disturb the gloom
Of silence, round my lonely tomb;
But heedless pass the human race,
And no fond eye e'er seek the place,
In contemplation sad, to see,
Of life's bright hopes, th' inanity.
There, let me sleep, unknown to all,
In endless shade of death's dark pall:
Let no memorial o'er me rise,
To vainly tell, what under lies:
Of greedy death, curtail no claim:
Give him my body, deeds, and name;
Nor memory one sad relic keep;
Let all in dark oblivion sleep.
For fame's loud blast, or friendship's moan,
Pass o'er the grave, unheard, unknown,
To coward vile, and hero brave;
To tyrant master, and his slave;

Ambition's fools, and sons of worth;
The smallest, greatest, of the earth;
To those who tower'd above the crowd;
Or, far beneath it meanly bow'd.

Oh, if one's life example give,
To greatly do, or wisely live,
Or add to virtue's blissful power,
Its fragrance death shall not devour:
Ordain'd forever to endure,
Where virtue's recompense is sure;
Ordain'd, above, to deathless shine,
With things immortal and divine.
  If not o'erlook'd, like floweret fair,
Whose sweets are lost on desert air,
Man's interests will demand its praise,
When for the dead no food 'twill raise;
When truth can work no rival's ill,
And envy's baleful voice is still.

Beyond the reach of mortals fled,
Not man, but Heaven rewards the dead.
For works, they on the world bestow'd,
The debt must be forever owed.
They, through past toils, man's wants relieve,
But nothing, in return, receive:
What seems for them, or done, or said,
Is for the living, not the dead.

THE POWER OF LOVE.

The beams of love, thy bright eyes dart,
Nor brazen shield, nor cuirass, ward;
Love's witching voice will reach the heart;
O, who, from love, secure can guard!
　A tear-drop glisten'd in thine eye;
　My soul was mov'd with sympathy:
　'Twas then you saw the unguarded part,
　And captive, then, you took my heart!
Press'd by thy beauty's conquering arms,
I turn'd, to shun their dazzling ray;
Thy voice, then, uttering tuneful charms,
Subdued me, as I fled away!
　Thy songs of joy, thy tears and smiles,
　Induc'd me to unveil my breast:
　Encompass'd, thus, by Cupid's wiles,
　No wonder, you my heart possess'd!
Now earth deserted seems, and drear;
Unless your sunny eyes are near:
Joyless and slow the moments roll;
Unless your presence lights the soul.

THE SEASONS

Spring advanc'd with joyful pace,
Youthful glow'd her rosy face;
Earth she kiss'd, and blossoms sprung!
Smil'd, and countless songsters sung!
Down the verdant sprouting hills,
Murmuring pour'd the silvery rills.
  Summer next, with graceful mien,
Enters on the thrifty scene:
Moving, a majestic queen,
In her flowing robes of green;
Stretches forth her leafy hand,
Dances with the breezes bland.
On her fondly looks the day;
Wooing, he prolongs his stay:
From gay east to glowing west,
Greets, with smiles, her lovely breast;
Gives it every pleasing shade,
That may fruitful beauty aid.
Fierce, his ardent beams he pours;
Tells his love in thunder showers;
While the winds, in cloudy garbs,
Starting swift, on airy barbs,
Through the lightning-blazon'd hall,
Course o'er seas and mountains tall,
Sweeping through the rustling woods,
And foam-crowning ocean's floods.
  Autumn comes, with robes of gold,
Auburn hair, luxuriant roll'd;

Graceful waves each shining fold;
Joyful hopes her arms uphold;
Crown'd with tints of various dye,
Softly sweet, as blended sky.
Here and there, are faded seen,
What was once a brilliant green;
And the cool mild frosted morn,
Shines on blushing peach and corn.
 Winter comes, with snowy wreathes;
Realms grow paler, as she breathes:
Howling winds disorder'd bear,
In mad whirls, her frosty hair.
O'er the ice-encumber'd flood;
Through the leafless stately wood;
With chill glance, she passes by,
Blanch'd her cheek, and cold her eye.

ON POETRY.

BRIGHT colors shall fade, and the canvas decay;
But the song of the poet shall ne'er pass away:
Through voices of ages, 'twill glorious roll:
The wide earth its kingdom ; its home, the great soul !
Its reign and its realm; coexistent, shall stand ;
The voice of its wisdom affect the wide land ;
Till death, high triumphing o'er creation vast,
Of all things, beholds the destruction at last.
The poet must die, though his song may remain ;
But ere he returns to the dust of the plain,
Fit works are the fruits 'tis his duty to bear ;
Whom genius illumes, deathless structures should rear.

Resume thy vocation, then, master of song ;
Pursue the high end, though the world seem in wrong ;
What if thy conceptions exceed common power :
This only insures immortality's dower :
Who, of the large masses, attracts many eyes,
May doubt if his muse is belov'd by the wise.
This good, from neglect, one may confident reap ;
And thus, be encourag'd to heavenward keep.
Who looks to the woods, or the owls, for renown,
Would nothing effect, that, with pride, he could own :
They seek the esteem of the learn'd and the wise,
Whose glory is destin'd forever to rise.

CÆSAR.

A DAMNING reign succeeds great Cæsar's fall:
By nature moulded nations to command,
High thron'd by godlike virtues, genius-crown'd.
Imperial nature's own appointed king
Falls by assassins: Vile men, faction-sprung,
Cumber his darken'd throne: The sickly State,
To purge herself of these, heaves, anguish-torn.
Cæsar was burden'd with the State—the State with them.

SAME SUBJECT.

THE sculptur'd Pompey views the assassin's knife,
Uprais'd, to end brave Cæsar's glorious life.
The hero's robe, inveterate Casca holds:
The approach of Brutus, treason's depths unfolds.
Then, graceful in extremity, he throws
A mournful glance at one he sadly knows,

"*Et tu Brute!*" exclaims, and o'er his face,
Swift draws his robe, and ends life's fitful race.
Th' astonish'd Senate, shuddering at the deed,
Beheld, in him, their guilty country bleed:
The *Effect* was slain: the pregnant *Cause* surviv'd:
Vice stalk'd gigantic, and corruption thriv'd;
A hellish brood, from these, full soon, was seen,
Of horrid aspect, and of triple mien:
The conqueror and the father, rul'd no more;
But ruthless tyrants, drunk with virtue's gore.
Great Julius bore the State, with kindly cares;
But now the State, with pain, the fell triumvirate bears.

PART OF FINGAL'S SPEECH AFTER OSCAR'S DEATH.

How long on Lena shall we weep!
How long our tears green Erin steep!
The mighty dead will not return;
Oscar ne'er leave his mouldering urn:
The day that sees the great and brave,
Beholds them sink into the grave.
O, tell me where our fathers are;
The chiefs of old: O, warriors, where?
Gone, like bright stars, that once have shone;
Nought, but their fame on earth, is known:
But, in their times, they were renown'd;
And men their power, with terror own'd.
Thus, shall we perish in our day:
Then gather laurels while we may.

ON THE TRANSIENT NATURE OF THINGS.

How mild is the sky, and how brilliant the sun !
But soon, in this clime, will our journey be done:
Ye oderous flowers, how long will ye blow;
How long, dimpling waters, for us, will ye flow:
Ye trees, that so gracefully wave your green hair,
How long will you nod to the sweet-scented air !
   Ah ! short is your day;
   'Tis flitting away:
   The moments, your doom
   Fast weave in time's loom.
The brightness of youth now illumines your sky;
But that will grow dim, and its colors soon die.
Yours is the sweet morning of life's clouded years;
The flower bedecked way to the valley of tears;
A prelude enchanting, that Nature doth play;
A beautiful scene, that is passing away.
   Although, clad in light,
   This clime be so fair;
   Though Sol glitters bright,
   Storm dwells in the air.
Though now, on smooth seas, with mild breezes, we sail,
We know not how soon may be raging the gale:
Fame constantly brings upon every breath,
The tidings of changes, and ruin, and death:
That Jauda, the goddess, who all things foreknew,
Was ne'er known to smile, is not strange, were it true.
   Leave not till to-morrow,
   Thy task; for in sorrow,
   Thy life's setting sun
   May see it undone:

For wan-vizag'd sickness, and accidents, bring
Perpetual tribute to Terror's dread king;
Inflicting alike, on the high and the low,
The good and the evil, the life-killing blow.
Midst jollity's smiles, and the music of mirth,
Throws darkness and sorrows, this tyrant of earth;
  Consigns to the tomb,
  Sweet beauty, in bloom;
  And crushes the just,
  And wise, in the dust.

ON INSTILLING WISDOM AND VIRTUE.

O, THAT the untutor'd mind could know
The exstatic joys, that only blow
In souls illum'd by wisdom's lore !
  What keen desire
  The eager breast would fire,
  To share her precious store !
Upon her lofty heights to mount,
 Regardless of the attendant toil;
To drink from her exalting fount,
And reap unfading glories on her soil.
  Labor is a pleasure true,
  If the heart the toil pursue.
  All will joy in labor find,
  Of the body, or the mind,
  If upon the current strong
  Of incentive borne along;
  Or ambition's active fire,
  Urge the soul to high aspire.
With care, then, train the infant mind,
Till to the good and great inclin'd,
And fill'd with love of noble deeds:
  Rouse young desire,
  For things the *just* admire,

Till nature heavenward leads:
Give right direction to the thought;
Then, under habit's forming sway,
The soul for glorious ends is wrought,*
And moves, with natural grace, up virtue's flowery way.

*VARIATION.

Let wisdom train the infant mind;
Inspire the love of noble deeds;
To lofty aims the spirit bind;
Avert of vice the hateful seeds;
Awake, with art, the young desire
To reach the heights the good admire;
Give just direction to the thought,
Till channels, by its course, are wrought;
Till virtuous habit's constant sway,
As Nature's self, directs the way.

SPRING AND WINTER.

May will soon return again—
Dreary winter cease to reign;
Vanquish'd by the fiery Sun,
To the polar region run,
Chas'd by Spring, in garment green,
O'er the melted snow between,
Youthful, bright, with joyful air,
Gemm'd with living flowerets fair!
Distant from the God of Day,
Scowling Winter holds his sway;
Acts the tyrant of the pole,
Scornful of the Sun's control;
Pours the barren freezing blast,
Chaining bounding billows fast,
As, in glassy fragments high,

Breaking towards the sullen sky,
Pile they up the icy store,
On the gloomy Arctic shore.

WHAT MIGHT BE A STATESMAN'S CONFESSION.

Towards Fame's dome, by steep ascent,
With labor hard, I slowly went;
My speed increas'd, as men could see
Their interests helped, by rise of me.
My party gave me all the praise
Which they, by every mean, could raise.
E'en Hate and Envy, for their weal,
Seem'd lost in fires of friendly zeal.
The sycophantic, proud, and vain,
In short, all power's expectant train,
Assur'd the simpler ones that I
Could save the State—and only I!
 Alas! as near the gates I drew,
The temple faded from my view!
What, in the prospect, seemed so fair,
Was only tinted vapory air.
No form, nor beauty could I find;
There, nought remain'd but empty wind.
The world still saw the temple fair;
Still thought me blest, for reaching there!
Nor knew that distance gave the look,
Which they for thing substantial took!
 I deemed I had but little done,
And only chaff of glory won;

But hoped to yet deserve the praise
That grows more bright with length of days
Enthron'd in hearts of good and wise;
From whom, alone, true fame can rise:
For puffs of knaves and dunces, cast
An evil influence, while they last:
Their soil yields not the fruit that gives
The food on which high glory lives.
What virtue, and man's interests own,
This, this, immortal fame shall crown.

TO THE SUN.

O world-illuming orb, whose ceaseless blaze
Showering through ages from thy lofty throne
A gladdening rain of fruitful glories down,
Fills planetary worlds with life and joy.
Still undiminish'd, still thou seem'st the same,
As when man first beheld thy kindly beams.
What bright-eyed orbs, courting thy rays, move round
Thy throne, rejoicing in thy bounty great.
To thee, great king, their ceaseless offerings rise.
When from the purple orient, rosy bright,
As blushing nature meets thy morning beams,
Fresh from her starry couch, with dewy hair,
All hail thy coming; with desiring eyes
Gaze on thy splendors; and the mountains huge,
Kindling with living radiance, joyful glow,
Each thicket, shady dell, and airy grove
Rings loud with welcome: notes of tuneful birds;
And insect nations gleeful sound thy praise.

Earth, mourns thy absence, in her wintry garb.
At thy return her palsied climes revive,
And beam with youth; new forms of beauty rise;
Extend their hopeful arms to greet thy rays:
The fresh-born leaves of groves on breezy hills;
The opening daisies on the sprouting sward;
The ice-freed rivulets, gleaming, as with joy,
As swift they murmuring flow and kiss their verdant shores;
All nature joys in thy paternal smile.

INDEX

TO SOME PARTS OF THE BIOGRAPHY.

Birth - - - - - - - 3

Compositions - - - - - 67
Curative of Consumption—Perspiration—indicated by
   night-sweats - - - - - 51

Death - - - - - - 61
Development of the Artistic Faculty - - - 17
Dental Operations cause Disease - - - 56

Education - - - - - - 7 to 15

Letters from S. Genin - - - - 23 to 53
   "   John Trumbull - - - - 34
   "   Thos. H. Genin - - - 45
   "   Rev. Isaac Ferris - - - - 62

Obituary, and other Notices - - - 61—64—67

Paintings—Description of - 20 to 22—54 to 56—69 to 73

Some matters, on education, page 8, and phthisis, page 58, meant to be inserted as notes, have entered the text, *a la Plutarch* : And the *Description of Paintings*, is suspended at page 22, and resumed at pages 54 and 69, as above indicated.

SELECTIONS, IN PROSE.

Apophthegms	93, 96, 99, 118
Attribute of Strength	95
Availability	109
Admission of Indians into the Union	127
Advice on Addressing a Jury	14
Belief may be Consistent with Reason	123
Banks of Deposite most Useful, and Safe	129
The Brain an Unit	153
Creole Case	112
Cliques	154
Catholics	108
Deeds Confute Words	108
Flying	156
Greatness	75
Governments are Effects, of which the People are the Cause	141
General Principles—need of their Observance	147
History	79
Injustice Ruins	101
Knowledge of One, aided by that of Many Things	125
Legislation: Possible Causes of	76
Labor—what Depreciates it	111
National Defence	84
Nature the Art of God	92

INDEX. 249

Observations - - - - - - - -   156

Punishments - - - - - - - -   156
Propensity, Have All the same to Good and Evil ? - -   99
Public subject to Private Interests - - - -   102
Phrenology insufficient for determining the comparative
    Mental Power of two or more Persons - - -   143
The *principle* of a Science must be Understood, to Comprehend it   148

Rotation in Office - - - - - - - -   90
Religion - - - - - - - - -   96

Self-interest, false views of, deprives Merit of Reward -   87
Social the Natural State - - - - - -   89
Slavery Aggressive - - - - - - - -   97

Tariff - - - - - - - - -   81

Usury Laws - - - - - - - -   118

Virtue - - - - - - - - - -   96
Vital Energy—its Source and Supply - - - -   106

Why Wealth has Power - - - - - -   99

POETRY.

Atlas - - - - - - -   201
Apostrophe to the Winds - - - -   176
Advance of the Guard at Wagram—from the French - 192

Battle - - - - - - -   175
Beauty of Nature - - - - - -   205
Balance—Addressed to Thurston H. Genin - -   207
Thurston's Reply - - - - - -   209
Bachelor's Musings - - - - -   171

INDEX.

Changes	204
Council at the Granicus	216
Circumstances alter Appearances	228
Cæsar Landing in Britain	177
Cœlebs Consoled	194
Common Soldier	196
Cæsar's Death	238
Dream	212
Day's Chase of Night	214
Death—Address to	215
Day of Judgment	221
Days of Childhood	171
Death of Samson	212
Fingal on Oscar's Death, versified	239
Henriade—Translation	203
Home of Beauty	226
Idleness and Mischief	193
Iliad—Translation	205
Indian Ghosts at Niagara	228
Intelligence and Virtue necessary to Liberty	179
Intention as to Italy	186
Judges XV. paraphrased	211
Judges should love Justice	164
Labor	220
Love—Power of	235
Many-voiced Commotion	217
Mercy	225
Man is governed, as he deserves to be	162
March of Angels	175
Morning—Noon—Evening—Night	179
Mental Influence	189

Nature's Noble - - - - - 194

Pegassus - - - - - - - 213
Poetry - - - - - - - 237
Pity - - - - - - - 173
Peace with Mexico practicable - - - - 181
Poet - - - - - - - 197
Poets—Why honored - - - - - 162

Remedies worse than the Disease - - - - 197

Soul - - - - - - - 206
Sun—Address to - - - - - - 244
Stooping to Conquer perhaps excusable - - - 182
Statesman's Confession - - - - - 243
Sky-Excursion - - - - - - 165
Slave-Power Invoked - - - - - 169
Storm - - - - - - - 199
The Spouse—Tendency of Nature to Perfection - - 167
Steamship - - - - - - 231
Seasons - - - - - - - 236
Spring and Winter - - - - - 242
Spartans—Invocation of, at Thermopylæ - - - 161

The Dead - - - - - - 233
The Transient Nature of Things - - - - 240
The Uses of the Past - - - - - 168
The Year - - - - - - - 178
The Evening Sail - - - - - 183
The Return - - - - - - 184

Vice its own Punishment - - - - 229
Virtue - - - - - - - 232
Virgil—Translation of - - - - - 186

What is, may be Best - - - - - 202
Who is This ? - - - - - - 203
Wind—Ode to - - - - - - 218
Wisdom and Virtue—On instilling them - 241

ENGRAVINGS.

Portrait of S. Genin, Esq., - - -	Frontispiece
Samson with the Jaw-bone, (on type metal)	255
Napoleon entering Russia, [page 69] (on copper)	1
The Rescue by Jasper and Newton, [page 55]	2
Hell, [page 71] - - "	3
Render unto Cæsar the things which are Cæsar's, [page 71] - "	4
The Death of Cæsar, [see page 55 and 238]	5
The Woman of Monterey, [page 69] "	6
The Landing of Cæsar in Britain, [see page 54 and 177]	7
The Battle of Arbela [page 21] "	8
Death of Samson, [see page 212] "	9
Napoleon and Gen. Gorgaud, at Brienne [page 70]	10
Jephthah's Daughter [page 69] "	11
Nestor and Tydides in the Storm, [see page 21 and 205] - - "	12
The Genins [see page 54] "	13
The Battle of the Granicus [page 20] "	14

Maigne & Hall, Steam Printers, No. 11 Spruce Street, New-York.

SAMSON WITH THE JAW-BONE.

NAPOLEON ENTERING RUSSIA.

THE RESCUE BY JASPER AND NEWTON, OF THE PRISONERS.

Close by the brink, within the jaws of hell.

Render unto Cæsar the things that are Cæsars.

THE DEATH OF CÆSAR.

THE LANDING OF CÆSAR IN BRITTAIN.

THE BATTLE OF ARBELA.

10

Sketched by S. Genin, Esq.

GEN.^L GORGAUD INTERCEPTING THE BLOW AIMED BY A COSSAC AT NAPOLEON, — AT BRIENNE.

JEPTHAH'S DAUGHTER.

THE BATTLE OF THE GRANICUS.

Printed in Dunstable, United Kingdom